Reaching the Urban Poor

About the Book and Editor

As urban populations in developing countries continue
to grow rapidly, one of the most critical issues in the
Third World has become providing shelter and other basic
services such as clean water, health clinics, and sewage
disposal to the urban poor. This book of nine case studies
of urban programs and projects in Indonesia, Kenya, Malaysia, Nigeria, Pakistan, South Korea, India, and Sri
Lanka focuses on impediments to slum upgrading. The
authors discuss each project's evolution, the capabilities
and resources of implementing agencies, the problems of
interagency relationships and coordination, costs and
funding, the difficulties of developing effective linkages
with poor communities, and the accessibility of the new
services to the urban poor.

G. Shabbir Cheema is development administration planner and project coordinator at the United Nations Centre
for Regional Development in Nagoya, Japan, and is coeditor
of Decentralization and Development: Policy Implementation in Developing Countries (1983).

Reaching the Urban Poor

Project Implementation in Developing Countries

edited by G. Shabbir Cheema

Published in cooperation with
the United Nations Centre
for Regional Development
and the Lincoln Institute
of Land Policy

Westview Press / Boulder and London

Westview Special Studies in Social, Political, and Economic Development

----

This Westview softcover edition was manufactured on our own premises using
equipment and methods that allow us to keep even specialized books in stock.
It is printed on acid-free paper and bound in softcovers that carry the
highest rating of the National Association of State Textbook Administrators,
in consultation with the Association of American Publishers and the Book
Manufacturers' Institute.

Published in 1986 in the United States of America by Westview Press, Inc.;
Frederick A. Praeger, Publisher; 5500 Central Avenue, Boulder, Colorado 80301

Library of Congress Cataloging in Publication Data

Reaching the urban poor.
     (Westview special studies in social, political, and
economic development)
     Includes index.
     1. Urban, Poor--Developing countries--Addresses,
essays, lectures. 2. Social services--Developing
countries--Addresses, essays, lectures. 3. Community
development, Urban--Developing countries--Addresses,
essays, lectures. I. Cheema, G. Shabbir. II. Series.
HV4173.R43 1985   362.5'8'091724   85-20342
ISBN 0-8133-7129-5

Printed and bound in the United States of America

The paper used in this publication meets the minimum requirements
of the American National Standard for Permanence of Paper for
Printed Library Materials Z39.48--1984

6 5 4 3 2 1

Contents

Tables and Figures

Figures

Foreword

The rapid pace of urbanization in developing countries has increased the demands for urban services. In particular, the urban poor lack adequate access to services such as water supply, sewage systems, low-cost housing, education, and public health. Effective management of urban services for the poor is being increasingly emphasized by planners and practitioners in developing countries, international organizations, and donor countries.

In June 1983, the United Nations Centre for Regional Development (UNCRD) initiated a cross-national research project on managing urban development, which focused on services for the poor. In January 1984, UNCRD organized an expert group meeting, which was held in Nagoya, Japan, to (1) review country experiences in managing urban services, and (2) prepare a research format for undertaking comparable case studies of projects designed to upgrade slums and squatter settlements. First drafts of some of the case studies were discussed in the workshop on urban services for the poor held in Cambridge, Massachusetts, from 27-29 June 1984 under the sponsorship of the Lincoln Institute of Land Policy and the Kennedy School of Government, Harvard University.

In this book, the authors describe the evolution and rationale of selected urban projects, the capabilities and resources of implementing agencies, the extent and modes of community participation, and the performance of the projects in achieving stated objectives. They also discuss the policy implications of providing basic urban services to the poor in developing countries.

Many experts from developing countries, international organizations, and developed countries collaborated with

UNCRD on this project. Case studies were prepared in
cooperation with the Pakistan Administrative Staff College, the University of Sri Jayawardenepura in Sri
Lanka, the Kenya Institute of Administration, the University of Science in Malaysia, the University of Benin in
Nigeria, the Directorate of Urban Development in Indonesia, and the Korea Development Institute. The UNICEF
East Asia and Pakistan Regional Office facilitated the
collection of data for the case studies and provided part
of the financial support for the project. We are grate-
ful to the case study writers and UNICEF for their cooperation.

The Lincoln Institute of Land Policy provided financial support for reviewing the first draft of the case
studies and for making this joint publication possible. I
would like to record my deep appreciation to Sein Lin,
director of the Institute of Land Policy, and Professor
John D. Montgomery, Kennedy School of Government at Harvard University, for their valuable contributions to the
UNCRD research project on managing urban development,
which led to this book.

I am confident that the book will be of great interest to planners, scholars, and development practitioners
concerned with providing basic urban services in low-
income settlements and that it will lead to a better
understanding of the process of managing poverty-oriented
urban projects in developing countries.

Hidehiko Sazanami
Director, UNCRD

1

Reaching the Urban Poor:
An Introduction

G. Shabbir Cheema

URBAN GROWTH AND POVERTY

Urban population is increasing rapidly in most developing countries. Between 1950 and 1975, the urban population of all developing countries grew at an average annual
rate of 4.2 percent, and projections in UN studies show
that it will continue to grow at more than 4 percent a
year until the 1990s.[1] From 1950 to 1975, the urban
population in Africa increased by more than 4.7 percent a
year, and it is likely to grow at more than 4.5 percent
annually until the year 2000.

From 1950 to 1980, the percentage of urban inhabitants increased from 16.2 to 30.5 percent of the total
population. It is estimated that by the year 2000, 2.1
billion people in less developed countries (LCDs) will be
living in urban areas.[2] A study of 109 LCDs based on
1980 population estimates predicted that by the end of
this century 58 countries will have more than 50 percent
of their people living in urban areas. This demographic
shift implies that many developing countries will be
transformed from primarily rural to largely urban
societies in less than a quarter of a century.[3]

The projections also show that the larger cities in
developing countries will continue to rapidly expand. The
number of people living in Third World cities of 1 million
or more will nearly triple from about 339 million in 1980
to 931 million by the year 2000. The number of cities
with more than 1 million residents is likely to double
from the 118 in 1980 to about 284.[4] In many LCDs, capital cities already contain a significant proportion of the
country's people. For example, the population of Bangkok

1

and Colombo is 60 percent of the total urban population in
Thailand and Sri Lanka, respectively. Similarly, 35 per-
cent of the urban inhabitants in the Philippines live in
Manila.

This rapid population increase and its concentration
in Third World cities will inevitably bring about a significant shift in the incidence of urban poverty. World
Bank studies indicate that by the 1990s, more than half of
the absolute poor will be concentrated in urban areas.<5>
Urban dwellers will make up 90 percent of the absolute
poor in Latin American and Caribbean countries, 40 percent
in Africa, and 45 percent in Asia.

The incidence of urban poverty in developing countries resulting from rapid urban growth is indicated by
the proportion of squatters and slum dwellers in selected
cities.<6> For example, in Addis Ababa and Casablanca in
Africa, people in slums and squatter settlements make up
79 and 70 percent of the city population, respectively. In
Bogota and Buenos Aires, the percentages are 60 and 40
percent, respectively. In Calcutta, Bombay, Delhi, Dhaka,
and Karachi in South Asia, a large percentage of the urban
inhabitants live in slums and squatter areas.

Urban population below the poverty line is 60 percent
in Calcutta, 50 percent in Madras, 45 percent in Bombay,
45 percent in Karachi, and 35 percent in Manila. World
Bank studies indicate that even if the rural and agricultural development programs currently being implemented are
successful, they will have little immediate impact on
changing the pace and direction of urbanization in the
Third World cities: Mechanization and increased agricultural productivity have so far led to surplus labor from
farms and promoted migration from rural to urban areas.

THE DEMAND FOR URBAN SERVICES

In addition to concentrating the poor in cities,
rapid growth of urban population in developing countries
has led to a corresponding increase in the demand for
basic urban services. To varying degrees, the supply of
urban services has not kept pace with increasing need.
Services that are inadequate include transportation, low-
income housing, water supply, public education, and public
health care.<7>

The quality of urban transport services is poor:
Seating capacity is limited, not enough roads are available, and outlying areas have not been adequately linked

with the city center. There is a shortage of low-cost
housing for the poor, and many urban dwellings lack running water, a sewage system, or toilet facilities. In
most cities, a significant percentage of people do not
have access to piped water. Public education institutions
must struggle with shortages of qualified teachers, inadequate classroom space, and the high cost of transport and
school supplies. In low-income urban settlements, inadequate facilities for sewage, garbage disposal, and flood
control pose major hazards to public health.

The magnitude of urban service deficiencies in Pakistan, for example, is described by Viqar Ahmad. He noted
that about 25 percent of Pakistan's population lives in
slums; clean water is available to only 77 percent of the
urban population; only 38 percent of the people in the
largest city, Karachi, have house-to-house water connections; 48 percent of the total urban population has access
to sewage systems; and enrollment in educational institutions in urban areas is available to only 77 percent of
children aged 5 to 9, 52 percent aged 10 to 12, and 39
percent in the 13 to 14 age group.<8>

The situation in Indonesia is equally serious.<9> By
1980, only 26.4 percent of urban households had access to
piped water. In Indonesia, an estimated 300,000 new housing units need to be constructed annually in urban areas
to meet the demand. This figure does not include backlog
and housing redevelopment demands. According to the 1980
census, only about 45 percent of urban households had
private toilets. Drainage systems are inadequate. Flooding in some of the large cities is a problem. Garbage
collection and disposal are inadequate. For example,
according to a 1971 census, garbage from 24 percent of the
urban households was not collected and properly disposed
of.

Urban services are also acutely deficient in Nigeria.
P. K. Makinwa-Adebusoye reported that in Benin City, Nigeria, about 63 percent of poor households have no independent means of transport. Only 7.8 percent of the poor in
neighborhoods surveyed were owner-occupiers. Poor households lacked adequate facilities such as piped water and
kitchens. Garbage was disposed by burning (37.9 percent),
burying (13.9 percent), moat filling (18.3 percent), roadside dumping (27.6 percent), and collection by refuse
workers (2.3 percent).<10>

In Kenya the rapid pace of urbanization has led to
tremendous pressure on existing urban services.<11>
Despite government policies and programs, concerned gov-

ernment agencies have not been able to cope with the demand for public health services, primary education, urban road networks, water supplies, housing, and other economic and social services.

Many reasons account for the strain on basic urban services in developing countries. The financial resources and administrative capacity of central and municipal governments to provide greater coverage are extremely limited whereas the cost of providing basic services is rising. In several cities, central and municipal governments are unable to recover costs through user charges, constraining greater coverage. Increasing numbers of slum dwellers and other disadvantaged groups do not have the capacity to pay for services, and, because of maintenance problems, even some existing facilities are not fully utilized. Furthermore, the poor continue to concentrate in the largest urban centers, causing more and more pressure on urban services in these centers compared with others in the same country. Finally, because employment opportunities in urban areas are inadequate, a large segment of the population cannot afford some of the basic services.

GOVERNMENT POLICY RESPONSES

To reduce urban service deficiencies several combinations of policy alternatives and organizational arrangements have been identified in developing countries. Dennis A. Rondinelli identified the following alternatives:

1. Expanding the provision of services directly by the government by building up municipal government capacity.
2. Using market surrogates to improve efficiency and responsiveness of the concerned public agencies.
3. Lowering the costs of providing services through changes in regulations and methods of delivery.
4. Supporting self-help and service upgrading by the poor.
5. Promoting public-private sector cooperation.
6. Increasing service demand among the poor by providing more employment opportunities and higher incomes.
7. Encouraging the migration of urban population to small- and intermediate-sized cities.<12>

The governments in developing countries have implemented three types of policies for providing basic services in slums and squatter settlements.<13> By laissez-
faire policies they officially ignored the existence of
such settlements. Their restrictive policies were aimed
at reducing the size of low-income areas by excluding them
from urban services, removing and relocating residents,
and evicting residents from their homes to redevelop the
area. Their supportive policies sought to legalize such
settlements, renovate existing structures, and provide
assistance for self-help housing.

A review of policies and programs in developing countries affecting the growth of slums and squatter settlements shows that demolition and clearance of such settlements by the legal owners have been common practices.<14>
Only after the rapid growth of such settlements have planners and policymakers begun to think seriously about policy alternatives. The first response of most governments
was to demolish such settlements and to resettle occupants.

Planners and policymakers in developing countries are
increasingly recognizing the need to improve the social
and economic conditions in existing slum and squatter
settlements. In Korea, for example, three main programs
have been developed for the urban poor.<15> First, a public works program has been established to increase the
income of the urban poor and to provide them with more
employment opportunities and vocational training. Second,
the public assistance program is aimed at providing services to the aged, disabled, and sick, including subsistence maintenance, medicaid, maternity care, and funeral
services. Third, a squatter housing improvement program
focuses on resettlement and upgrading existing squatter
housing. In Kenya, policies and programs aimed at assisting low-income urban residents have included slum and
squatter improvement programs, sites and services projects, and low-cost housing schemes.<16> The government
has attempted to increase the access of the urban poor to
mass-produced houses and to provide them with employment
opportunities. The Sixth Five-Year Plan (1983-1988) of
Pakistan includes a number of programs to meet increasing
demand for urban services and to provide "a safety net to
the poor."<17> Public transport facilities are to be
doubled. The number of low-income housing units to be
constructed by the government is to be substantially
increased. Slum improvement schemes are to be implemented
during the plan period; these would benefit about 2 mil-

lion people and reduce the number of slum dwellers by
about one-third. The plan also seeks to improve water
supply and sewage systems. The government has already
initiated a number of projects to create new jobs for the
poor: Those include the Federal Programme for Skill
Development, a Training Programme for Skilled and
Unskilled Workers, and the National Vocational Training
Project.

In Malaysia, the government is using several strategies to improve services to the urban poor. These include
implementing resettlement schemes, upgrading squatter
settlements, and providing facilities such as drainage,
lighting, water supply, and access roads.<18> In Kuala
Lumpur, the Sang Kancil project and the Nadi program have
been initiated with the assistance of the United Nations
International Children's Emergency Fund. (UNICEF). The
project aims at setting up development centers in squatter
settlements that will provide preschool education, health
facilities, and income-generating activities for women.

A number of other strategies are being used by governments in developing countries to extend services to the
urban poor on a large scale.<19> For example, the Zonal
Improvement Programme (ZIP) in the Philippines aims at
upgrading squatter settlements in Manila. The program
follows a comprehensive approach in improving the living
conditions of squatters: It attempts to improve environmental conditions and provide social and economic facilities. The program emphasizes site retention, local
employment opportunities, and community participation in
decisionmaking. The Kampung Improvement Programme (KIP)
in Indonesia is designed to provide services such as
access roads, footpaths, piped water, drainage ditches,
communal latrines, laundry facilities, and garbage bins.
The community is not expected to pay for services except
for the use of water. However, residents are asked to
contribute land, if needed for the project, without compensation. KIP is primarily an environmental improvement
program and does not attempt directly to alleviate urban
poverty.

The Slum Improvement Programme of the National Housing Authority in Thailand divides Bangkok's slums into
three categories: those to be improved for permanent
low-income settlements, those to be improved temporarily,
and those not to be improved because they are likely to be
needed by landowners for redevelopment. The slums selected
for permanent improvement are those in which government
agencies own about 60 percent of the land. The slums

selected for temporary improvement are provided with minimal public utilities and social services. In Colombo, the
upgrading program excludes those slums located on land
worth more than a specified amount. Other criteria used
for selecting slums and shanties for potential benefits
are the cost of improvements, the degree of flooding, and
alternative uses of the land.

The Bagong Lipunan Sites and Services (BLISS) Programme in the Philippines is aimed at putting "model communities of 50 families in every municipality."[20] Each
BLISS site is to be provided with the minimum requirements
for a healthy community life. Supporting agencies of the
government are expected to provide basic social services
such as water, power, shelter, health care, sports, and
recreation. The Bagong Lipunan Community Association
serves as a channel through which government services and
facilities are delivered.

The Environmental Health and Community Development
Project in Sri Lanka was launched in 1979 with the assistance of UNICEF. The project facilitated the process of
participatory urban planning. Health wardens were trained
to perform tasks such as community development, primary
health care, nutrition education, and environmental sanitation. The communities were encouraged to form local
development councils to provide a channel of communication
between the urban poor and municipal agencies providing
urban services.

The Dandora Community Development Project in Nairobi
and the Chaani Upgrading and Site and Services Project in
Mombasa were intitiated in 1975 and 1978, respectively, by
the government of Kenya with the assistance of the World
Bank. The projects were aimed at providing shelter and
community facilities to low-income dwellers in the two
areas.

Based on experiences in Asia and Africa, five stages
in the evaluation of explicit and implicit public policies
for providing basic urban services to residents of slums
and squatter settlements can be identified: (1) clearance
and forced migration of the poor to other areas or their
eviction without providing them with alternative facilities; (2) the initiation of housing and other schemes
followed by clearance of slums and squatter settlements;
(3) the provision of minimal services for some of the
existing slums and squatter settlements; (4) the extension
of tenure security and physical upgrading; and (5) the
recognition of the legitimate role of slums and squatter

settlements in urban development and the extension of
social services with appropriate standards.

ACCESS OF THE URBAN POOR

The urban poor in general and residents of slums and
squatter settlements in particular have been affected most
negatively by urban service deficiencies. Experiences in
Asia, Africa, and Latin America show that the quality and
coverage of urban services tend to be worst in the poorest
neighborhoods. Most slums and squatter settlements in
developing countries lack basic urban services such as
water supply, sewage systems, transport, roads, garbage
disposal, and health facilities. Even where adequate
services and facilities are available, the urban poor may
not have access to them.

The access of the urban poor to basic urban services
has been constrained by many economic, social, administrative, and political factors. First, in areas like low-
cost housing, the poor cannot afford to pay for urban
services because of their low incomes. Even when some
services are directly provided by government or semiautonomous agencies, the actual beneficiaries may be middle-
income groups. Second, residents of squatter settlements
do not usually have legal ownership of the land they
occupy; thus they cannot be forced to pay user charges for
services. Therefore, the concerned government agencies
are reluctant to provide services such as water supply,
electricity, and sewage systems to them.

Third, the administrative systems of municipal governments and semiautonomous development authorities are
characterized by inadequate community participation in
identifying priorities and needs, formulating projects,
and implementing development activities. Without adequate
community participation, the urban poor are unable to
safeguard their legitimate interests. Their access to key
decisionmakers within government agencies is usually limited. Furthermore, in most developing countries municipal
councils are not directly elected, thereby denying the
urban poor another channel through which some of their
grievances could be communicated to policymakers.

Fourth, government standards for urban services are usually too high, resulting in high costs for these services. Therefore, predominantly middle-income families often utilize some services meant for the urban poor. Fifth, the urban poor are usually not effectively organized. The heterogeneity of their social backgrounds and their poverty hinder the emergence of viable community-level organizations. Although they may have links with political parties, they are unable to assert collective pressure from below to ensure adequate access to urban basic services.

Finally, in some cases no explicitly stated public policies are aimed at providing basic urban services to the poor in an integrated manner. This lack of policy reflects the inadequate political and administrative will of policymakers and planners to allocate adequate resources for providing basic services to the poor.

IMPLEMENTATION OF URBAN PROJECTS FOR THE POOR

A project is a collection of related activities designed to harmonize and integrate actions by government agencies and other organizations to achieve policy objectives. Implementation has been defined as a "process of interaction between the setting of goals and actions geared to achieving them."[21] The literature on implementation identifies two competing views of the process: the compliance approach and political approach.[22] The first assumes that implementation is a technical and routine process of carrying out predetermined plans and projects. The second approach views administration as an integral part of the policy-and project-planning process in which projects are refined, reformulated, or even abandoned in the process of implementing them.

The factors that influence project implementation have not been given adequate attention in developing countries. It is often assumed that once projects are planned they will be implemented by subordinate administrators and that intended results will be achieved in a nonpolitical and technically competent way. However, the experiences with urban projects discussed in this book indicate that implementation is a dynamic and sometimes unpredictable process of political interaction. Several factors determine the extent to which projects are implemented as they were intended and the degree to which they achieve their formally stated goals.

In Figure 1.1, five sets of factors are shown that
influence the implementation of urban development projects
designed to provide services to the poor: environmental
aspects, government policies for urban development, interorganizational relationships, beneficiary organization and
participation, and capabilities and resources of implementing agencies.

Interorganizational Relationships

Successful implementation of programs and projects
for the urban poor depends upon the complementary interaction among actions taken by local, regional, and national
agencies. A program may be formulated, supervised, and
evaluated by a central agency; it may be funded and monitored by a subnational/state government agency; and it may
actually be implemented by an agency at the municipal or
metropolitan level. Therefore, successfully linking the
implementing agencies with others into supportive structures is a prerequisite to achieving common objectives.

The effectiveness of interorganizational relationships in implementing urban projects seems to depend on
(1) the clarity and consistency of project objectives; (2)
the appropriate allocation of functions among agencies;
(3) the standardization of procedures for planning, budgeting, and implementation; (4) the accuracy, quality, and
consistency of interorganizational communication; and (5)
the delineation of procedures for monitoring and evaluation.

As shown in the case studies of urban projects in
this book, local governments, semiautonomous public enterprises, departments of central and subregional governments, and development authorities often have worked in
isolation from each other. The role of urban local governments has gradually declined to the extent that these
are not in a position to harmonize and integrate development activities in cities. In several instances, functions, responsibilities, and resources have not been allocated to metropolitan entities and urban local governments
on the basis of rational criteria. These units are empow-
ered to perform many development functions; yet their
power to levy taxes is limited. Many controls are imposed
by national and/or provincial governments in the planning
and management of activities by municipal governments.
Municipalities, metropolitan governments, semiautonomous
bodies, and government departments in cities lack the

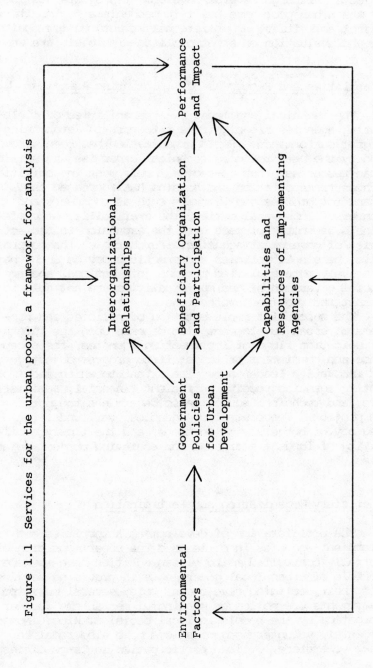

Figure 1.1 Services for the urban poor: a framework for analysis

capacity to monitor and evaluate development programs and projects. Although several development projects designed for the urban poor have built-in mechanisms for monitoring project activities, organizational structures for monitoring and evaluation on a metropolitan-wide basis are weak.

Capabilities and Resources of Implementing Agencies

The technical and managerial capabilities of implementing agencies are significant factors in determining program performance. Rapid urbanization has been accompanied by the need for more technical expertise and skilled human resources. Public-sector involvement in activities such as transportation and housing has increased the demand for professional workers such as engineers and planners. In several cities, the availability of professionals has not kept pace with the expansion in the activities of government agencies. Furthermore, the governments' personnel policies and practices may be such that relatively more qualified persons join national and provincial governments, and municipalities are not able to attract the required professionals.

The successful implementation of policies and programs of urban development also depends upon the internal communication flows of implementing agencies, the acceptance and commitment of the staff to program objectives, and innovative leadership. The extent to which the implementing agencies receive sufficient financial, administrative, and technical support also determines the outcome of the project. The control of agencies over funds, the adequacy of budgetary allocations, and the timely availability of funds are crucial for achieving project objectives.

Beneficiary Organization and Participation

The proliferation of development authorities and government agencies in cities and the superimposition of centrally controlled metropolitan entities have weakened the role of urban local governments in providing services. With their declining development role, several municipal governments are no longer meaningful mechanisms for participation by the people in local decisionmaking. Nongovernmental, voluntary organizations have also remained weak. Therefore, citizen participation in large cities is negatively affected, and the trend is toward a greater degree of control by professional administrators in the process of managing urban projects.

The need for beneficiary organization and participation is particularly significant in poverty-oriented urban development programs and facilities.<23> The organization of beneficiaries will enable them to apply pressure from below to get their demands accepted. Projects and facilities, which are recommended by community-based organizations of the urban poor, are more likely to succeed in eliciting popular response. Local resources can be more easily mobilized for such projects. Furthermore, the organization and active involvement of the urban poor would facilitate program implementation and evaluation and increase their awareness of their own environment. Indeed, management requirements for programs for the urban poor are not necessarily the same as those for conventional urban development projects. Squatter upgrading programs, for example, require active community participation, self-help, and partnership between beneficiaries and program implementors.<24>

Environmental Factors

Projects are planned and carried out within complex socioeconomic and political environments. These circumstances shape not only the substance of projects but also the patterns of interorganizational relationships and the characteristics of implementing agencies, and they determine the amounts and types of resources available for carrying them out. Therefore, an understanding of the social, economic, and political setting is vital for comprehending the constraints on and opportunities for implementing organizations to translate policies and projects into actions. A nation's political structure, the characteristics of the local power structure in urban areas, the social and economic characteristics of groups within urban communities, and the procedures for project planning influence the process of implementation of projects designed to provide services to the urban poor.

Performance and Impact

   The performance and impact of urban development projects for the poor can be measured on the basis of the
achievement of the project's stated goals; the impact of
the project on specific groups within the society; the
effects on the capacity of local units of government; and
the effects on productivity, income, popular participation, and access to government facilities.

FOCUS OF THE CASE STUDIES

   This book presents the findings of a comparative
research project entitled "Managing Urban Development:
Services for the Poor" sponsored by the United Nations
Centre for Regional Development (UNCRD), Nagoya, Japan. It
includes case studies of the following selected urban
development programs and projects: the Nadi Integrated
Social Services Project in Malaysia, the Lahore Walled
City Upgrading Project in Pakistan, the Integrated Social
Project in Korea, the Katchi Abadis Project in Pakistan,
the Environmental Health and Community Development Project
in Sri Lanka, the Block Grants Project in Indonesia, the
Dandora Community Development Project in Kenya, the Chaani
Upgrading and Social Services Project in Kenya, and the
Olaleye-Iponri Slum Upgrading Project in Nigeria. In
Table 1.1, a profile of the projects is presented that
shows the services provided and their time frame, loca-
tion, sources of funding, and implementing agencies.
   The book examines the process of implementation of
programs and projects designed to provide basic urban
services to the poor in slums and squatter settlements.
More specifically, it focuses on

   1. The analysis of support available for providing
      urban basic services to the poor.
   2. The discussion of interorganizational relation-
      ships in project implementation.
   3. The review of the characteristics and capabilities
      of implementing agencies and their environmental
      context.
   4. The discussion of the extent and modes of benefi-
      ciary participation in the process of providing
      urban services to the poor.

Table 1.1 Selected case studies of services for the poor

Country	Project Type	Services Offered	Time Frame	Location	Sources of Funding	Implementing Agencies
Malaysia	Nadi Integrated Social Services Project	Comprehensive health services such as family planning & mother & child health Basic amenities such as water supply, refuse collection, & electricity Community development activities & services	1979 to present	Kuala Lumpur	Government UNICEF	Ministry of Federal Territory Other related agencies
Pakistan	Lahore Walled City Project	Water supply Sewage system Electricity Street lighting Community centers	1982 to present	Lahore	Government World Bank	Lahore Development Authority Lahore Municipal Corporation Water and Sanitation Agency House Building Finance Corporation
Korea	Ingrated Social Services Project	Health care Housing improvement Public utilities Income generation activities	1975 to present	Seoul	Government UNICEF NGOs	Municipal government NGOs
Pakistan	Katchi Abadis Project	Community centers Sanitation Income generation activities	1981 to present	Lahore	Government UNICEF Community	Lahore Development Authority Provincial government Lahore Municipal Corporation Social Welfare Directorate

Table 1.1 continued

Country	Project Type	Services Offered	Time Frame	Location	Sources of Funding	Implementing Agencies
Sri Lanka	Environmental Health & Community Development Project	Water supply Sanitation & health education Preschool education Community organization	1979 to present	Colombo	Government UNICEF	Colombo Municipal Council Urban Development Authority Common Amenities Board Other agencies when necessary
Kenya	Dandora Community Development Project	Plots for houses Access roads Community development facilities, i.e., schools, markets, community centers Sewerage system	1975 to 1980	Nairobi	Government World Bank	Central government agencies Municipality
Kenya	Chaani Upgrading and Services Project	Access roads Water supply Sewage system Plots for houses Community facilities, i.e., markets, schools, community centers	1978 to present	Mombasa	Government World Bank	Central government agencies Municipal council
Nigeria	Olaleye-Iponri Slum Upgrading Project	Improved roads Community clinics Markets Public water supply Sanitary and sewerage facilities	1983 to present	Lagos	Government UNICEF NGOs	Central ministries/boards Community
Indonesia	Block Grants Program	Sanitation Preschool education Income generation activities Other social services	1979 to present	Surabaya	UNICEF Municipality Community	Community Municipality Department of Home Affairs

5. The examination of the performance and impact of selected projects and the critical factors accounting for their success or failure.

Each of the case studies discusses the evolution, rationale, and the process of implementing a particular project within a specific location.

NOTES

1. United Nations, Department of International Economic and Social Affairs, Patterns of Urban and Rural Population Growth, Population Studies no. 68 (New York, United Nations, 1980).

2. John J. Donohue, "Some Facts and Figures on Urbanization in the Developing World," Assignment Children 57/58 (1982), pp. 21-41.

3. Ibid.

4. Paul Bairoch, "Employment and Large Cities: Problems and Outlook" International Labor Review 121 (1982):519-523.

5. World Bank, World Development Report 1980 (Washington, D.C.: World Bank, 1980).

6. John Donohue, "Some Facts and Figures on Urbanization in Developing World," Assignment Children 57/58 (1982), p.36.

7. For discussion of these services in LDCs, see Annemarie H. Walsh, The Urban Challenge to Government: An International Comparison of Thirteen Cities (New York: Praeger, 1969); M. Honjo, ed., Urbanization and Regional Development (Singapore: Maruzen Asia, 1981); International Bank for Reconstruction and Development, Urbanization (Sector working paper, June 1972); United Nations, Department of Economic and Social Affairs, Administrative Aspects of Urbanization (New York: United Nations, ST/TAO/M/51, 1970); and Alan Turner, ed., Cities of the Poor (London: Croom Helm, 1980).

8. Vigar Ahmad, "Management of Urban Services for the Poor in Pakistan" (Nagoya: UNCRD, 1984), mimeo.

9. Mitsuhiko Hosaka, "Urban Services in Indonesia: Focus on Kampung Improvement Programme" (Nagoya: UNCRD, 1984), mimeo.

10. P. K. Makinwa-Adebusoye, "Urban Poverty in Benin City, Nigeria: Interim Report" (Nagoya: UNCRD, 1984), mimeo.

18

11. James O. Kayila, "Urban Management in Kenya" (Nagoya: UNCRD, 1984), mimeo.

12. Dennis A. Rondinelli, "Increasing the Access of the Poor to Urban Services: Problems, Policy Alternatives and Organizational Choices," paper presented to the Expert Group Meeting on Managing Urban Development: Services for the Poor held at Nagoya, Japan, from 10 to 14 January 1984.

13. United Nations Centre for Human Settlements (HABITAT), Survey of Slum and Squatter Settlements (Dublin: Tycooly International, 1982).

14. U.S. Agency for International Development, Rural Service Center Project Paper (Manila: US-AID, 1977).

15. Whang In-Joung, "Managing Public Services for the Urban Poor in Korea" (Nagoya: UNCRD, 1984), mimeo.

16. Kaylia, op. cit.

17. Ahmad, op. cit.

18. Lim Hong Hai, "Managing Programmes for the Urban Poor in a Plural Society: The Case of Malaysia" (Nagoya: UNCRD, 1984), mimeo.

19. For an overview of these approaches and strategies, see UNICEF, Social Planning with the Urban Poor: New Government Strategies (Geneva: UNICEF, 1982); and Madhu Sarin, Slums and Squatter Settlements in the ESCAP Region (Bangkok: Economic and Social Commission for Asia and the Pacific, 1980).

20. Arturo D. Aportadera, "Bagong Lipunan Sites and Services Program: The Philippine Experience in Rural Housing and Development," in Y. M. Yeung, ed., A Place to Live: More Effective Low Cost Housing in Asia (Ottawa: International Development Research Centre, 1983).

21. Jeffrey L. Pressman and Aaron Wildavsky, Implementation (Berkeley: University of California Press, 1973), p. 8.

22. Marcus D. Ingle, "Implementing Development Programs: A State-of-the-Art Review: Final Report" (Washington, D.C.: U.S. Agency for International Development, 1979), mimeo.

23. For the role of community participation in implementing programs for the urban poor, see Mary R. Hollnsteiner, "Government Strategies for Urban Areas and Community Participation," Assignment Children 57/58 (1982), pp. 43-64.

24. David Pasteur, The Management of Squatter Upgrading (Westmead, U.K.: Saxon House, 1979).

2

Nadi Integrated Social Services Program, Kuala Lumpur

Lim Hong Hai

THE MALAYSIAN CONTEXT

Almost all discussions of urban poverty in Malaysia
identify the urban poor by referring to their type and
place of residence, namely, flat dwellers, slum dwellers,
and especially squatters, which probably constitute the
largest and in many ways the most deprived of these
groups. Squatting is most prevalent in the capital city of
Kuala Lumpur<1>, which has attracted more in-migrants than
any other urban center in the country. Available estimates of Kuala Lumpur's squatter population range from
one-fifth to one-third of the city's total population. The
Kuala Lumpur 1982 Draft Structure Plan estimated that the
squatter population consisted of 243,200 persons, making
up 48,709 households that lived in 40,934 dwelling
units.<2> According to the same document, the city's
squatter population has increased at an annual rate of 9.7
percent from 1974 to 1980 (compared to the 3.5 percent
annual increase in total population of the city), and the
177 squatter settlements occupy approximately 7.3 percent
of the city area, with 94.6 percent of the occupied land
belonging to the government. The available figures for
other urban centers in the country show that squatter
population in these is relatively insignificant compared
to that for Kuala Lumpur. Thus, existing studies and
discussions of the problem of urban poverty in Malaysia
are almost invariably confined to Kuala Lumpur.<3>
As regards the racial composition of squatters in
Kuala Lumpur, the Malay share has been increasing although
the Chinese still make up the majority. The breakdown of
squatters by racial or ethnic group in the Kuala Lumpur
1982 Draft Structure Plan is 32.9 percent Malays, 52.2

percent Chinese, and 14.9 percent Indians and others. The majority of the 177 squatter settlements are characterized as mono-ethnic; that is, they have a majority ethnic group. Of these 42.9 percent are predominantly Chinese, 32.8 percent predominantly Malay, and 7.9 percent predominantly Indian; only 19 settlements, or 16.5 percent are mixed or do not have an ethnic group in the majority.

Household incomes for squatters are considerably lower than average for Kuala Lumpur residents, reflecting their concentration in lower-paying, unskilled, and semi-skilled occupations. The Kuala Lumpur Draft Structure Plan states that the majority of working squatters are employed as factory workers, laborers, drivers, guards, construction workers, and petty traders whereas only 11 percent are in the professional, managerial, technical, administrative, or clerical fields. Forty-four percent of the households have a monthly income of 600 Malaysian dollars (M$) or below (US$1 = M$2.3). When squatters are described as poor this term is used only as a comparison with other urban dwellers and not in the sense that they are suffering from starvation, lack of shelter, and other manifestations of extreme poverty. However, the squatters belong to lower-income groups in the city. Compared to other city dwellers, they are most clearly and visibly deprived in the area of public services.

Several studies have shown that in addition to living in low-quality housing, squatters are also poorly supplied with basic amenities such as piped water, electricity, proper roads, drainage systems, garbage collection, and waste disposal. Provision of these services to squatter households appears to vary according to location and to whether they are occupying government or private land; the overall picture, however, is still one of relative deprivation. A study published in 1973 estimated the overall availability of piped water at 25 percent and of electricity at 20 percent for squatter families in Kuala Lumpur.[4] Another study about the same time for Kuala Lumpur and the surrounding region found only 14 percent of squatter households with electricity and 18 percent having access to piped water.[5] A decade later in 1982, the Kuala Lumpur Draft Structure Plan continued to note that squatter settlements were still generally deficient in amenities, facilities, and basic physical infrastructures.

The problems of providing public services to the squatters are linked with the illegal nature of their settlements. As Khairuddin Yusof pointed out, faced with increasing political pressure from the squatters, the

municipal authorities have abided by a policy of providing
"enough but not too much."<6> Near the end of the 1970s,
however, an increase or rather a convergence of interest
toward the problems of the urban poor in Kuala Lumpur
resulted in the setting up of the Sang Kancil project.
Subsequently, increased awareness of the multifaceted
needs of the squatters and of the necessity to meet them
in a more comprehensive and integrated manner led to the
incorporation of the Sang Kancil project into a much more
ambitious and wide-ranging program for the urban poor
called the Nadi program.

FORMATION, STRATEGY, AND ADMINISTRATIVE REQUIREMENTS

The growing number of squatter households in Kuala
Lumpur began to attract the attention and concern of the
city authorities in the late 1960s. The early responses
of the city government consisted of attempts to contain
the squatting problem by demolishing some squatter settlements and resettling the affected families in low-cost
high-rise flats. Soon after, however, it became aware of
the limitations of that solution: Not only was resettlement too expensive and too slow to cope with the increasing number of squatter families, but it also was inappropriate because it "may aggravate urban poverty and sustain
the culture of poverty"<7> by forcing the resettled families to use a greater proportion of their income on rents
and transportation expenses.

Other government agencies as well as individuals were
finding themselves affected by the growing squatter population in the early 1970s. Of considerable importance was
the desire of the National Family Planning Board (NFPB) to
spread family planning information more effectively in the
squatter settlements and the concern of a gynecologist
working in the University Hospital. In 1978, the NFPB
secured the assistance of the Japanese Organization for
International Cooperation in Family Planning (JOICFP) to
carry out a pilot project (mainly in the city) based upon
combining parasite control for children with family planning. This approach has been found to enhance the effectiveness of family planning programs in pilot projects
carried out with JOICFP assistance in a number of Asian
countries. The interest of the gynecologist, on the hand,
sprang from his conviction that in squatter settlements
most illnesses of expectant mothers are preventable, that
living conditions should be improved, and that health

problems should be prevented before they become so serious that their treatment was beyond the means of the poor.

Early in 1978, UNICEF started discussions with the city government on urban poverty and on possible projects for addressing the problem. The city government responded in May 1978 by holding a consultative seminar attended by senior representatives from agencies operating in Kuala Lumpur and by a few representatives from the squatter settlements.

During the seminar, problems faced by squatters were discussed and proposals made with a view of designing an appropriate and feasible intervention strategy. Stressing the urgency of the problem, the seminar representatives recommended that a maternal and child care health clinic be set up within a few selected squatter settlements to "bring health to the people." A committee was appointed to study and identify the needs of the squatters. Subsequent discussions with squatter representatives, however, indicated that the squatters themselves accorded higher priority to the provision of basic amenities such as piped water, electricity, and better roads than to health services. Therefore, project plans had to be modified to secure the acceptance and cooperation of the squatters.

Unable to promptly supply the desired amenities because they involve considerable expenditure and lie within the jurisdiction of other government agencies, the committee finally settled upon the provision of preschool education, which was desired by a number of squatter parents. This provision was followed by maternal and child care services and finally by income-generating projects. All these activities were to be carried on in the same building or vicinity to facilitate participation by women. The entire project was named Sang Kancil after the small but (according to Malay folklore) clever mousedeer that was used to symbolize the children in squatter settlements. The first step in the Sang Kancil project was setting up centers to provide preschool education and housing and maternal and child-care clinics in three settlements in early 1979; the project was gradually extended to cover about thirteen settlements by 1983. Income-generating activities, however, have been set up in only five of the thirteen settlements.

Early experience with the NFPB-JOICFP project showed that it was too narrowly conceived. As described in an official document, "it was realized that deworming alone without the complementary environmental and social mea-

sures will not succeed. Hence, the idea of a more comprehensive approach was proposed to the Ministry of Federal
Territory resulting in the present three pronged approach
to improve the conditions of the urban poor."<8>

In 1979, the Ministry of Federal Territory sought to
expand the NFPB-JOICFP family-planning and deworming project to include nutrition and environmental sanitation.
For this purpose, contributions were sought from other
agencies such as relevant departments of the city government, the general hospital, and the Institute of Medical
Research. The expanded program was directed by a steering
committee composed of the heads of participating agencies.
The ministry also asked UNICEF for the services of an
urban social planner who arrived in August 1979.

The Nadi program is the result of an effort to integrate the Sang Kancil and the expanded NFPB-JOICFP projects into a more comprehensive program and to enlarge
them to include other services needed by poor squatter
communities. As reported by the UNICEF consultant social
planner, the meetings held in late 1979, to which interested agencies were invited, resulted in the following
proposals:

> that the expanded deworming project be further
> expanded to cover all development efforts benefiting
> urban poor families in the Federal Territory and all
> agencies (governmental and non-governmental) con-
> cerned;
>
> that with the participation of an increased number of
> agencies and the addition of new tasks, it was essen-
> tial to clearly define the responsibilities of each
> agency in relation to the others; and
>
> that if this comprehensive anti-poverty approach was
> adopted, it should be changed from a project to a
> program, from activities geared to short-term plan-
> ning to activities planned on a long-term basis (up
> to the year 2000).<9>

Thus the Nadi program came into existence in the
closing months of 1979 with the theme of "My Beloved Family." The word nadi means pulse in Malay: The Nadi program is expected to be a key factor in determining the
pulse of Kuala Lumpur's development. The leadership role
was assumed by the Ministry of Federal Territory, and a

steering committee, chaired by the deputy minister for the Federal Territory and having as its members the heads of participating agencies, was set up to direct the program implementation.

The major innovative aspects of the Nadi strategy were also formulated in the course of the discussions leading to the formation of the program.<10> As the Consultant Social Planner pointed out, the strategic features of the Nadi program were (1) a shift from single-agency to multiagency delivery of services through the Nadi teams; (2) a shift from an office- or clinic-based operation to a community-based one with strong participation of the community action committees (CACs) and other groups; (3) a shift from a general focus on beneficiaries to a specific focus on the urban poor as the beneficiary group; (4) a shift from indirect approaches to activities directly involving the urban poor family as the key unit in development; and (5) a shift from single-agency resource utilization to interagency resource sharing.<11>

Two features of the Nadi strategy can be regarded as the major thrusts of the program: making available or potentially available a wide range of services to squatter communities and families through the mobilization of many relevant agencies and providing for community participation.

The following three types of services could be provided through the Nadi program:

1. Comprehensive health services such as mother and child health, family planning, school health, parasite control, communicable disease control, food and nutrition.
2. Services and basic amenities such as water supply, refuse disposal, latrines, pathways, electricity, and play grounds.
3. Community and family development activities such as community education, preschool education, vocational training, income-generating opportunities, family counseling, special facilities for recreational and educational purposes, and general individual and family welfare services.<12>

By the end of 1980, eighteen agencies, most of which were government groups, had agreed to take part in the Nadi program. Contributions from other agencies were to be enlisted when required. For instance, the Council of

Trust for Indigenous People was later asked to assist with the Sang Kancil income-generating projects.

A key Nadi strategy was to provide a wide range of services to squatter groups without explicitly entrusting any organization with the delivery of the entire range of services or providing it with the resources for the job. It is therefore of the utmost importance to examine the structure for activating agencies with the needed resources, for securing their cooperation and if necessary compliance, and for coordinating their contributions to achieve optimum results for the target communities.

STRUCTURAL RESPONSES AND FINANCING

The steering committee set up in the Ministry of Federal Territory to direct the implementation of the Nadi program was subsequently renamed the Consultative Committee; it is attended by heads of agencies involved in the Nadi program and has the deputy minister of the Federal Territory as its chairman. The Consultative Committee is the highest-level coordinating body for the Nadi program. Its objective is to identify the problems and needs of the people in the project area and to find solutions by drawing upon the resources and capabilities of the agencies represented in it. To monitor the implementation of the committee's decisions, the Ministry of Federal Territory proposed the establishment of a new division, the Social Development Division.

The Social Development Division was set up in 1982 and staffed with five officers. Divisional (subarea) offices were also established in five divisions corresponding to the five parliamentary constituencies within the Federal Territory. All divisions have one divisional office except the largest, which has two. However, these so-called divisional offices are actually the area branches of the city government: They have simply been designated as Nadi divisional offices and their respective chief administrative official as the divisional program manager for Nadi. These officials are employees of the city government and are accountable for the management of Nadi activities within their respective divisions to their superior officer in the city government and not to the Social Development Division in the Ministry of Federal Territory. Thus responsibilities for the Nadi program were simply added onto the other duties of the city government's area officials. The third-level neighborhood

development offices, though approved, have not been set
up. However, local action committees have been set up in
most poor communities. Their members include the headman
of the settlement or village, who serves as chairman,
other village leaders, and field personnel of participating agencies.

Policy and planning are the responsibilities of the
consultative committee; the divisional action committee,
and the local action committee. Implementation is the
responsibility of manager, divisional manager, and the
Nadi group. According to the formal allocation of responsibilities, the planning structures and the implementation
structures are almost entirely separate. In particular,
the Ministry of Federal Territory has only a planning role
by virtue of its part in the consultative committee; it
plays no direct role in implementation, which is controlled by the manager and his divisional officers in the
city government. Such a rigid separation of planning and
implementation probably reflects bureaucratic territorial
behavior, the struggle to control scarce resources, and
interagency compromise more than any considered plan of
administration. This rigid separation is not only difficult to maintain in practice: It is manifestly impossible
once the income-generating activities of the Sang Kancil
project have been transferred from the city government to
the Ministry of Federal Territory.

The Nadi project is not designed to be a self-
contained program of any particular agency but depends
upon contributions and cooperation from a multitude of
agencies. Budgetary requests for financing the Nadi-
related activities of these agencies would be included in
the agencies' annual budget submissions to the treasury.
Supporters of the Nadi project, however, sought to combine
the various agency requests for Nadi-related activities
into a single joint request and allocation. They felt
that it is better "to negotiate with the Treasury from an
interagency standpoint, as isolated presentations by each
group of their component in the Nadi has resulted in dras-
tic cuts."[13] From the ministry's viewpoint, joint budgeting would provide a powerful mechanism for substantive
coordination, particularly if the allocation is placed
under the ministry's control, not to mention that funds so
allocated would be specifically earmarked for Nadi activities.

In any event, joint budgeting failed to materialize.
Agencies continue to prepare their budgets in isolation,
and the Ministry of Federal Territory includes in its

budget requests all moneys needed for financing existing
and planned Nadi activities. The ministry then uses the
allocated funds to purchase services for squatter communities from other agencies capable of providing the desired
services. It reimburses these other agencies for all
their expenditures incurred in providing the requested
services.

UNICEF financing for the Sang Kancil project forms
only a small proportion of total expenditure in the Nadi
project. The bulk of it must be financed by government
budgetary allocations. The initial M$10 million allocated
to the ministry for the Nadi program for the period of the
Fourth Malaysia Plan (1981-1985), though not generous, was
adequate for a meaningful start. But as the country's
economy began to show the effects of the worldwide reces-
sion and as government revenues decreased, the original
M$10 million was reduced in 1982 to M$5.5 million. It was
further reduced in 1983. With these cuts, the ministry
can only maintain existing services. On top of that,
UNICEF assistance in the Sang Kancil project is expected
to stop at the end of 1984. To ensure the availability of
funds to continue existing projects, a nongovernmental
organization called the Sang Kancil Organization for
Social Services (SKOSS) has been formed recently for fund
raising. Its chairman is the deputy minister of the Federal Territory, and its success so far is encouraging.
However, the extent to which it can help the ministry
exceed the budgetary limits imposed on the program remains
to be seen.

MULTIAGENCY ACTIVATION AND COORDINATION

The Consultative Committee in the Ministry of Federal
Territory was intended to serve as a forum for discussing
problems, identifying needs, and considering proposals for
meeting them. Agencies could also be requested to look
into problems and community requests, suggest remedial
actions for committee consideration, as well as evaluate
suggestions made during committee discussion. Although
the Consultative Committee has been formally assigned a
planning role, its mission includes the tasks of activation and coordination. What have been the performance and
achievements of the Consultative committee in these tasks?

No new initiatives or programs have been produced by
the Consultative Committee's efforts. Committee members
have accepted the fact that the participating agencies

have their own responsibilities and programs to which they
naturally attach greater importance than they do to any
contributions they might make to the Nadi program. Indeed,
the real problem seems to lie in the agencies' lack of
incentive to contribute to the Nadi program. Future funding of agency programs and career prospects for agency
representatives in the Consultative Committee are perceived to depend upon agency-specific performance and not
upon contributions to the Nadi or other programs. A close
observer commented on the intersectoral coordination in
the Nadi program:

> The most visible form of intersectoral coordination
> begins at meetings and for most, it will end there. .
> . . Kuala Lumpur's experience has indicated that a
> multiagency approach where 20 agencies are called to
> a meeting and have tasks allocated to them tends to
> be counterproductive. Most agencies resented it, and
> some may be openly hostile to coordination.<14>

As expected, however, the agencies give primacy to
their own programs, do not contribute to other programs or
change established and familiar ways of operation without
reason and do not welcome such requests from outside
parties. These policies were clearly foreseen by the
architects of the program. To help crystallize agency
commitments to the Nadi program, the UNICEF consultant to
the Ministry of Federal Territory suggested the use of an
organizational responsibility chart in the later discussions preceding program formation.

Personnel movements within the agencies proved to be
a problem. Such movements removed from the agencies and
the Consultative Committee key persons who had participated in the discussions leading to the formation of the
program and in bringing their agency to participate in it.
Their replacements generally could not be expected to
possess the same depth of understanding of the program's
rationale or to exhibit the same degree of commitment and
support for the program. It is not so much the difficulty
of securing desired contributions as the absence of any
serious effort by the ministry to do so that requires
explanation.

Interviews with a few members of the Consultative
Committee suggest that the meetings have not been used to
activate the agencies into contributing to the Nadi program. Ministry officials have not used the organizational
responsibility chart and appear to have almost forgotten

it. Of course, success would not be guaranteed merely by
using the chart to remind the agencies of their previous
promises. Success in such endeavors at high governmental
levels is a function of such factors as leadership qualities, interpersonal relations, and the particular circumstances in the agencies at the time of attempted activation. Still, the infrequency and weakness of activation
efforts require explanation.

Several factors may help to explain the softness of
the ministry's approach toward its difficult task. First,
it lacks the resources for the task: It lacks the formal
authority to issue directions to the other agencies about
the contributions that they are supposed to make to the
Nadi program. Authority relationships are left unspeci-
fied. The Ministry has so far treaded very carefully to
avoid actions that may be perceived as impositions by the
other agencies. These agencies are equals, associates, and
perhaps even rivals, not subordinates, and their participation in the program is voluntary. Despite the undoubted
legitimacy of the Ministry of Federal Territory`s position
as the highest body for coordinating the development of
Kuala Lumpur, this status has not been sufficient to overcome its deficiencies.

However, the lack of formal authority need not
cripple the ministry or condemn it to impotence. The
would-be activator and coordinator can use many types of
informal influence, persuasion, and pressure in place of
formal authority. The use of formal authority is usually
insufficient for effective coordination without skillful
use of informal influence. Thus formal authority has been
shown to be neither a necessary nor a sufficient condition
for effective multiagency activation and coordination.
That such efforts have not been forthcoming from the ministry cannot be satisfactorily explained by the lack of
formal authority: The reasons must be sought either in
the lack of interest, energy, time, or even skills of
ministry leaders or in their perceptions of their impotence.

Success in multiagency programs depends a lot on the
support of persons in key positions who possess the inclination, the time, and the skills needed for securing contributions from a number of separate organizations. The
departure of the secretary-general of the ministry, who
was by some accounts very interested in the Nadi program
in 1982, may have damaged the program, although the importance of this factor is difficult to estimate. His suc-
cessor, who is also the mayor or head of the city govern-

ment, is too occupied with his mayoral duties to have time
and inclination for actively leading the Nadi program.

The divisional action committees and the local action
committees are supposed to provide the problems and proposals considered by the Consultative Committee. That the
Consultative Committee has neglected to develop its role
in multiagency activation-coordination may result from the
failure of lower-level planning structures to play their
assigned roles.

The setting up of neighborhood offices in which the
local action committees will meet to discuss problems and
possible solutions was discontinued soon after the program
started. The program designers stressed the importance of
training field officials to overcome their limited agency
perspectives, and a number of field officials of participating agencies were actually sent for training at the
National Institute of Public Administration. These early
measures were not followed up, and personnel transfers
have removed most trained officials from the ground level.
Moreover, the training probably was not sufficient to
overcome the ingrained habits and attitudes of the agency
staff. In any case, joint problem solving in the local
action committee has not materialized in most squatter
villages, and many, if not most, local action committees
are either defunct or dormant.

Interviews with divisional program managers indicate
that Nadi activities are peripheral to their work although
they are aware of their formal responsibilities in Nadi
planning and are well informed about Nadi activities in
their divisions. Divisional action committee meetings are
rarely held, and there is hardly any effort at joint planning and programming.

Ministry officials in the Social Development Division
do not suffer from any illusions about the performance of
the divisional program managers: A senior official estimated that divisional program managers spend no more than
10 percent of their time on Nadi responsibilities. Ministry officials recognize that they lack influence over
divisional program managers, who are regarded as outside
their chain of command and unlikely to heed any suggestions from the ministry about carrying out their Nadi
responsibilities.

The ministry has so far confined itself to facilitating communication and exchange of views among agencies,
funding approved activities carried out by these agencies,
and helping whenever needed or requested by any party
involved in the Nadi program. Reliance upon its own lim-

ited funds and human resources has prevented the ministry
from significantly expanding the range and adequacy of
services and the number of squatter settlements covered.
The Nadi program has experienced virtually no snowballing
effect, which is necessary for it to have a major impact
on the welfare of squatter communities. The Ministry of
Federal Territory or, more specifically, the Social Development Division, was never envisaged and is not likely to
be equipped to play such a dominant role in the Nadi program that dependence on other agencies would be unnecessary.

COMMUNITY ORGANIZATION AND PARTICIPATION

A key factor affecting a community's capacity for
participating in demand making and project implementation
is the strength of its organization. Squatter settlements
in Kuala Lumpur are unanimously regarded by Nadi program
officials as well organized. Their feeling of insecurity
and their relative lack of essential public services provide squatters with both the need and the motivation for
organized and political action. The role of national
political parties in politicizing and organizing the
squatters is very important. The mono-ethnic nature of
most squatter settlements has encouraged a vertical and
ethnically structured political mobilization of the squatters by the major mono-ethnic political parties operating
at the national level. This vertical linkage to the major
political parties has important implications for demand
making by the squatters.

The headman of a squatter settlement or village is
usually also the head or chairman of the local political
party branch. Thus in Malay or predominantly Malay villages, the village headman is also the chairman of the
United Malay National Organization (UMNO) branch in the
village, and in predominantly Chinese villages, the headman is likely to be the village-level chairman of the
Malaysian Chinese Association (MCA). In mixed villages,
each ethnic group usually has its own headman, and all
these headmen become members of the village committee. No
real elections are held for village headman and other
village committee members by all adults or household heads
at regular intervals. In the majority of villages, the
elected chairman of the local party branch from the most
numerous ethnic group in the village is acknowledged as
the village headman. Members of the village committee are

usually local political party notables. This overlap in
village and political party underlines the extent to which
the squatter communities rely upon their connection with
the main political parties to safeguard and further their
interests.

Village leaders are generally aware of conditions,
problems, and needs in their settlements, and the more
prominent ones, especially the headman himself, are known
to most villagers. A recent survey of three almost completely Malay villages found that virtually all household
heads knew the names of at least one village leader.<15>
The presence of large minorities of other races or of
rival political parties may attenuate the cohesiveness of
the community and the support for village's main leaders.
Thus in one village consisting of about 2,500 Malays,
1,500 Chinese, and 500 Indians studied by the writer,
marked differences were seen among the ethnic groups as to
the villagers' personal knowledge of the Malay headman: In
reply to the question, "Can you name the village leaders
whom you know personally?" only 40 percent of Chinese
respondents and 35 percent of Indian respondents named the
village headman compared to 85 percent of the Malay
respondents.<16> Even in such a village, the support
given the village leaders is adequate to sustain a high
level of political activity as well as a high capacity for
demand making and project participation on the part of the
leaders.

Demand making appears to be the main function that
villagers expect their leaders to play, and effectiveness
in this function is an important consideration in leader
selection as well as an important criteria of leadership
evaluation.<17> Demands are usually for basic amenities
and public services such as piped water, electricity,
better drainage, access roads, and garbage collection.
Such demands are usually made through the political party
branch in the village. Letters asking for particular
services are typically sent to the agencies concerned,
with duplicates to the next superior level in the party
organization and to the deputy minister or the minister of
federal territory. Political pressure is then used to
secure attention for requests by meeting with influential
politicians, members of parliament, and the minister,
especially before elections.

The designers of the Nadi planning structures sought
to provide an administrative channel for squatters' demand
making through the local action committees, the divisional
action committees, and the Consultative Committee. The

local action committees envisaged in the Nadi planning
system failed to materialize, and village leaders can only
make contact with the next higher level in the Nadi planning system, namely, the divisional level. Even this
level has not developed any meaningful role in planning.
Leaders of the squatter villages are not even called for
occasional meetings or discussions with divisional officials: Many divisional officials do not regard frequent
contact and communication with squatter leaders as desir-
able.

One view is that squatters, rightly or wrongly, make
numerous demands, many of which are difficult to meet.
Another common view is that the squatters are already
spoiled by the government: They occupy land that does not
belong to them, they do not pay local taxes, and they
already receive many amenities and services provided to
taxpayers. Still, they keep on complaining about their
condition and asking for more and better services, such as
piped water within individual houses instead of community
standpipes, prayer houses, and even title to the land on
which they are squatting. One divisional official has
described the squatters' attitude by using the Malay pro-
verb, "beri betis, hendak paha" (literally, "give calf,
want thigh"). By both these views, communication with
squatters and their leaders is best kept to a minimum.

Not surprisingly, squatter leaders do not regard
administrative channels as the most effective mechanisms
for getting what they want: Only political pressure from
the top can overcome bureaucratic inertia and reluctance.
Even when administrative officials are sympathetic, some
leaders reason, they cannot do anything without first
getting political authorization. Hence they prefer using
political channels and involving politicians in power
right from the start.

The frequency and intensity of squatter demand making, however, should not be exaggerated. Leaders are
aware of the nonlegal nature of their settlements, and
appeals for services are usually made on humanitarian
grounds, although very few having dealings with them doubt
their resolve or their resourcefulness. The use of the
word demand here is not meant to imply that the squatter
leaders are aggressive, uncompromising, or insistent that
all their needs be met. Their quiescence--at least for a
while--can usually be bought by giving them something
quantitatively and qualitatively less than what they have
asked for.

The level of demand making varies among the squatter villages. An interesting difference has been observed between Malay and non-Malay squatter settlements: Malay settlements are significantly more organized and more united behind their leaders and make considerably more demands than non-Malay settlements. The reasons for the difference are complex and probably lie in the interaction among the elements of political culture, political structures, and political experience. The relative weakness of the Malaysian Chinese Association and the Malaysian Indian Congress in the coalition national government dominated by the UMNO and the lower incidence of success in past demand making are probably important factors. They have resulted in dampened expectations and a lower sense of political efficacy and hence a lower level of demand making among non-Malay squatters compared to their Malay counterparts.<18> According to some officials in the Nadi program, non-Malay squatters are generally indifferent to some components of the Nadi program, for instance, the Sang Kancil project.

The data on project participation in the Nadi program suggest that both formal and informal acts of influence should be taken by beneficiaries or their leaders to affect decisions before they are finally made. Squatters and their leaders have hardly participated at all in the formal project decisionmaking in the Nadi program. However, village leaders, particularly the headman, can exercise considerable influence over project details through informal means. Village leaders are seldom involved in the formal process of determining the parameters of a project, such as its content, primary objective, and total expenditure. However, they generally expect that their approval and their views will be obtained before a project is implemented in their communities.

Officials entrusted with the project usually consider it advisable to get the support of village leaders to expedite implementation and avoid any unnecessary and unexpected problems. Project officials seek the cooperation of village leaders not only because they fear negative and unpleasant repercussions but also because such leaders can make positive contributions to the project. They possess the legitimacy and form part of an established communications structure needed for reaching and mobilizing large numbers of villagers within a short time. Their knowledge of social and physical conditions in the settlements is useful for some kinds of project decisions. Their contributions are particularly important for carrying out projects that require the active cooperation and participation of many villagers.

The dependence of project officials upon village leaders for acceptance and other valued contributions to project implementation is a source of influence for the village leaders. Requests, suggestions, and opinions can be made to project officials, and bargaining may even take place over important features or aspects of the project, such as location, scheduling, and the selection of beneficiaries. This sort of participation may not be formally sanctioned, but it is consequential participation nevertheless.

Participation of leaders in project implementation can also produce some undesirable consequences. Leaders have personal and group interests besides the interests of the larger community that they are supposed to serve. The pursuit of these narrower interests may conflict with project objectives and guidelines. For instance, they may locate standpipes close to their own dwellings or those of relatives and friends, select family members, relatives, and friends for benefits intended for poor persons, impose extraneous conditions, or demand concessions or side payments. This situation raises many important but intractable issues relating to the representativeness and accountability of the leaders.

CAPACITY OF IMPLEMENTING AGENCIES

Weaknesses appear to exist in some implementing agencies, which will continue to plague the Nadi program and vitiate it to some extent even if the main horizontal problem of multiagency management and the vertical one of participation are satisfactorily resolved.

The first weakness is that the agencies are physically separated and distant from the poor communities, thus discouraging mutual interaction. Although proposed neighborhood centers were meant to correct this situation, the idea has been abandoned. The second weakness is that the agencies are still agency directed and not people directed and value the good of the agency more than they value the good of the people.<19> This approach not only makes coordination and activation difficult but also causes urban poor communities to be viewed in segments rather than as a whole. This structural problem is inherent in the existing organization of the work of government, and it is a problem that the Nadi program was designed to ameliorate.

The third problem concerns staffing or the personnel entrusted with project implementation. The majority of officials lack the appropriate training, the sense of professionalism, and the strong commitment for the complex and demanding task of working for and with the poor. These deficiencies are especially damaging to the effective implementation of the more socially oriented projects in the program, such as those aimed at imparting new skills and knowledge to the poor and changing their attitudes and behavior. Many kinds of undesirable behavior observed in the program are at least in part manifestations of this lack of professionalism and commitment, including the sense of status superiority and the inability and reluctance to interact with the poor on an equal basis, the refusal to work outside office hours, the unwillingness to work or spend time in the villages, and even various forms of predatory behavior such as abuse of authority and petty corruption.[20] Working for the poor is not only more demanding but also offers more temptations, considering the ignorance and fear of government and the feeling of insecurity and powerlessness among the poor and the difficulty or prohibitive cost of hierarchical control of such officials.

PERFORMANCE

In Table 2.1, the kinds of activities carried out in the Nadi program and the yearly allocations and expenditures are listed for the three years from 1981 to 1983. The descriptions of the projects are self-explanatory except for community center and general development. The community center project involved constructing neighborhood service centers; it was stopped in the early stages of the program. In the general development category are included all activities that do not fit under the other projects. As can be seen in Table 2.1, the most important projects of the Nadi program in terms of expenditure are electricity supply, the Sang Kancil project, parasite control, and the provision of public standpipes.

What do the various projects actually deliver to the squatters? How adequate are the services delivered? Data for answering these output questions systematically and for each individual service are difficult to obtain; however, available evidence suggests that a lot remains to be

Table 2.1 The Nadi Program: Budget allocation and expenditure, 1981-1983 (M$ thousands)

Project	1981-1983 Alloc.		1981		1982		1983		1981-1983 Alloc.	1981-1983 Exp.
	Original	New	Alloc.	Exp.	Alloc.	Exp.	Alloc.	Exp.		
Parasite control	1,500	700	550	147	300	229	250	250	1,100	626
Sang Kancil	1,200	1,200	325	319	450	293	550	550	1,325	1,162
Electricity supply	2,000	2,836	900	476	900	921	837	837	2,637	2,234
General development	1,000	100	25	-	-	-	100	100	125	100
Public standpipes	1,700	320	250	-	200	165	150	150	600	315
Community center	1,000	-	-	-	-	-	-	-	-	-
IEC	1,000	200	100	48	50	38	75	75	225	161
Training	400	50	100	-	50	11	38	38	188	49
Evaluation	200	73	-	-	50	-	-	-	50	-
Total	10,000	5,479	2,250	989	2,000	1,657	2,000	2,000	6,250	4,647

Source: Social Development Division, Ministry of Federal Territory, Malaysia.

done. Output data for the Sang Kancil project are the most complete, thanks to an evaluative study commissioned for the project.<21> The investigator found that the incidence of knowledge of the project is very high in all three villages covered by the study: Almost all respondents are aware of the project and 80 percent know about its three components. Participation in the project varies among project components --it is highest in the clinic and lowest in the income-generating component--but overall it is high: 66.4 percent are participants, 7.4 percent former participants, and 26 percent nonparticipants. Proximity and the relevance of project services to their needs are the most frequently cited reasons for participation. The Sang Kancil project exists in only about fifteen squatter settlements.

Data for one village were collected concerning the squatters' perceptions of their main problems and the kinds of government assistance they desired. This village was selected for study partly because officials described it as one of the better-off villages. This assessment, it is later discovered, was shared by most of the villagers. The villagers' perceptions of service inadequacy apply equally to the majority of squatter settlements within the city. In Table 2.2 the data indicate that virtually all the problems perceived by the villagers relate to the inadequacy of common public amenities and services; so do all kinds of help desired from the government, with the possible exception of better housing, shown in Table 2.3.<22> In fact, all the public services and amenities perceived as problematic, except drainage and flood control, are being provided to the village, but they are perceived to be seriously inadequate: The number of standpipes is too small, garbage collection too infrequent, and so on. Hence, the villagers desire more adequate piped water (preferably inside their houses), better roads, and improved garbage disposal.

More basically, are the services currently provided to squatter settlements relevant or responsive to real needs? The data in Tables 2.2 and 2.3 lend some support to the view that squatters mainly express the need for basic amenities and services. Adequate piped water is regarded as a problem by the greatest number of villagers (about 89 percent). Piped water is also the item for which government assistance is desired by the greatest number (69 percent). The available evidence suggests that services currently provided are undoubtedly useful and relevant to

Table 2.2 Main problems perceived by villagers
in Kampung Sentosa

Problems	Malays	Chinese	Indians	All Races
Piped water	93	57	14	164
	(87.7%)	(91.9%)	(82.4%)	(88.6%)
Flooding	87	43	14	144
	(82.1%)	(69.4%)	(82.4%)	(77.8%)
Drainage	29	20	4	53
	(27.4%)	(32.3%)	(23.5%)	(28.6%)
Cleanliness and	12	3	1	16
garbage disposal	(11.3%)	(4.8%)	(5.9%)	(8.6%)
Roads	8	6	1	15
	(7.5%)	(9.7%)	(5.9%)	(8.1%)
Sanitation	11	0	2	13
	(10.4%)	(0.0%)	(11.8%)	(7.0%)
Sample	106	62	17	185

Table 2.3 Services desired by villagers in Kampung Sentosa

Service	All Races	Malays	Chinese	Indians
Piped water	72	45	11	128
	(67.9%)	(72.6%)	(64.7%)	(69.2%)
Drainage and	35	32	10	77
flood control	(33.0%)	(51.6%)	(58.8%)	(41.6%)
Housing	55	15	4	74
	(51.9%)	(24.2%)	(23.5%)	(40.0%)
Roads	13	7	2	22
	(12.3%)	(11.3%)	(11.8%)	(11.9%)
Garbage disposal	10	3	2	15
	(9.4%)	(4.8%)	(11.8%)	(8.1%)
Sample	106	62	17	185

some needs of squatter families but that they are not necessarily those felt to be of the greatest importance.

MANAGING MULTIAGENCY PROGRAMS FOR THE URBAN POOR

The government of Kuala Lumpur must feel very strongly about helping the urban poor because it established an agency with resources and skills to respond effectively to their needs. This approach is very rare. The more usual action is for the government to try to coordinate existing agencies: Organizational territories and functions remain unchanged; agencies are only brought together and asked to contribute their respective competence and operations to a larger and different purpose, that of providing services for the poor.

The coordinator, whether individual or organization, must be oriented toward helping the urban poor as well as able to bring other agencies together and to get them to contribute when needed. However, the coordination and activation of established agencies, often without formal power, are extremely demanding functions for leadership. Coordinator-activators must not only be responsible for getting results but also given visible support by top political leaders before success can reasonably be expected. The choice of coordinators is therefore critical. They must be persons with a strong commitment to the goals of the larger program, proven administrative achievements, and practice in the political arts of accumulating and exercising influence. In the status-minded administrative cultures characteristic of many developing countries, including Malaysia, they probably also need to be persons of high rank within the civil service. This list of requirements is undoubtedly formidable, but the task is also formidable. The Nadi experience suggests that deputy ministers may not guarantee results if only because their attention, time, and interest are always scarce resources. Their role and responsibilities are too diverse and diffuse to expect the sustained and concentrated efforts required for success.

The Nadi experience also emphasizes the importance of lower-level structures and personnel. In particular, the idea of some kind of neighborhood service center merits serious consideration. Location of different agencies at one place at the grass-roots level, referral arrangements, and more joint activities such as games and discussions can clearly facilitate information exchange and enhance

interservice understanding and thus increase awareness of
how each fits into a larger scheme. With time, the leading agency may be able to initiate and regularize procedures for joint planning and programming and thus achieve
the coordination of operations at the field level.<23>
Multiservice centers can reduce corruption among field
staff "because the work of each personnel is known to all
the team members," and a one-stop service center cuts down
the costs to local residents of seeking access to the
provided services.<24>

The Nadi experience may also be useful as a correc-
tive to overidealized notions of participation as a pan-
acea for overcoming bureaucratic unresponsiveness. The
capacity for direct participation is low among the majority of the poor; only their leaders can be called active.
Most squatters do not have the time, the familiarity with
public organizations and their workings, and perhaps even
the confidence to interact with officials as equals. The
community generally relies heavily upon leaders to handle
external relations, especially with government officials.
Fortunately, misbehavior by leaders is not widespread or
serious in the Nadi program. In fact, given the need for
capable leaders among the poor, it may be argued that the
so-called "leaks" and other concessions to the leaders are
not too high a price to pay for unpaid leadership services, provided that the leadership is reasonably effective and that the leaks and deviations are confined within
reasonable limits and do not significantly negate project
objectives. In fact, this view may be prevalent among the
squatters themselves, many of whom regard the leaders'
ability to produce results as more important than common
virtues like honesty.

This study has focused upon the need to develop the
administrative structure and personnel necessary for
effectively implementing the new strategies for providing
services to the poor. A fundamental premise is that innovative strategies imply certain administrative requirements unlikely to be met satisfactorily by existing structures and the personnel manning them. Thus new structures
are often needed to inject the appropriate kinds of institutional perspectives or biases into the existing organizational network. Efforts are also needed to develop or
strengthen the specific organizational competence on which
the implementation of particular projects must rely. The
investment of time, skill, and other needed resources to
putting in place the new structures and increasing the
competence in old and new organizations appears to be a

sine qua non for the successful introduction of a multi-agency program.

Whether this needed investment in building up administrative capacity will be made or why it has not been adequately made in a given instance are questions of a different nature. Probably less the lack of technical knowledge than the lack of political will accounts for the unwillingness to develop the sort of administrative capacity in question. The same factor is probably also the root of the dwindling budget allocation faced by the Nadi program. The Malaysian government's attitude toward the squatters has undoubtedly become more favorable during the last fifteen years or so. The short-term strategy is to improve those areas not targeted for immediate development whereas the long-term strategy is partly to resettle the squatters in low-cost housing but mainly to develop squatter areas. These pronouncements are generally well received by the squatters; the critical matter now is how they will be implemented.

NOTES

1. Kuala Lumpur became the Federal Territory in 1975. These two names now refer to the same geographical area. The local government of Kuala Lumpur will be referred to as the city government and is separate from the Ministry of Federal Territory set up in 1987 as the highest coordinating body for the area.

2. Kuala Lumpur Draft Structure Plan (Kuala Lumpur: Dewan Bandaraya, 1982), p. 177. Subsequent references to the plan are to Chapter 10, pp. 117-131, which is about squatters.

3. When one researcher attempted in 1973-1974 to obtain figures for squatting in other Malaysian towns, he found that none of the towns for which information was available had a squatter population exceeding 6 percent of total population. See Emiel A. Wegelin, Urban Low Income Housing and Development (The Hague, Netherlands: Nijhoff, 1978), p. 97.

4. M. K. Sen, The Rehabilitation and Resettlement of Squatters: The K. L. Experience (Kuala Lumpur, 1973), mimeo.

5. Wegelin, op. cit., p. 108.

6. Khairuddin Yusof, "Urban Slums and Squatter Settlements: Variations in Needs and Strategies," paper prepared for WHO/ISPCAN Pre-Congress Workshop on Child

Abuse and the Urban Slum Environment, Montreal, Canada, September, 1984, p. 11.

7. Z. Alias, "The Jalan Pekeliling Low Cost Flats: An Attempt At the Provision of Cheap Housing," Geographical 9 (1974):66.

8. Nadi Programme: My Beloved Family (Kuala Lumpur: Ministry of Federal Territory, 1980). 9. Ralph Diaz, "Restructuring services to reach the urban poor in Kuala Lumpur," Assignment Children, no. 57/58, 1982, p. 140.

10. See especially the proceedings of a workshop in Planning With the Urban Poor (Kuala Lumpur: Ministry of Federal Territory, 1979).

11. Ralph Diaz, op. cit., p. 142.

12. Nadi Programme: My Beloved Family (Kuala Lumpur: Ministry of Federal Territory, 1980).

13. Diaz, op. cit., p. 106.

14. Yusof, op. cit., p. 19.

15. Khairuddin Yusof, et al., Socio-Anthropological Evaluation of the Sang Kancil Programme, A Consultant's Report Prepared for the Ministry of Federal Territory, 1984.

16. The Kampung Sentosa Survey, 1984.

17. Yusof et al., op. cit.

18. The availability of a channel for demand-making has also been emphasized in Wayne A. Cornelius, "Urbanization and Political Demand Making Among the Urban Poor in Latin American Cities," American Political Science Review 68 (September 1984).

19. Ralph Diaz, "Malaysia: The Sang Kancil Project," in J.F.X. Paiva and Ledivina V. Carino, eds., Increasing Social Access to Social Services (Kuala Lumpur: UNICEF-APDC, 1983), p. 88.

20. This was mentioned by officials. Residents in Kampung Sentosa are also subject to some forms of control by field officers of the city government, such as the granting of permission before leaks in the house can be repaired.

21. Yusof et al., op. cit.

22. The Kampung Sentosa Survey, 1984.

23. Ibid. Chambers stressed the importance of procedures for achieving joint planning and programming.

24. Diaz, op. cit., p. 80. See also Henry Gomez and Richard A. Myers, "The Service Module as a Social Development Technology," in David C. Korten and Felipe B. Alfonso, eds., Bureaucracy and the Poor: Closing the Gap (West Hartford: Kumarian Press, 1983).

25. Yusof et al., op. cit.

3

Lahore Walled City
Upgrading Project

Viqar Ahmed

INTRODUCTION

The city of Lahore in Pakistan is characterized by
decaying urban cores and growing modern sectors. Many
affluent localities conform to the highest standards of
modern construction, whereas the old part of the city and
many middle- and lower-class sections are becoming
slums.<1>
In Lahore the responsibility for planning, development, delivery, and maintenance of various services is
shared by a number of public agencies. According to one
estimate, more than 100 agencies belonging to the federal
or provincial government or local bodies are involved
directly or indirectly in urban development. However,
major responsibilities are shared by the Lahore Municipal
Corporation (LMC), the Lahore Development Authority (LDA),
the Water and Sanitation Agency (WASA), the Lahore Cantonment Board (LCB), and the Model Town Society (MTS). These
agencies provide such municipal services as land development, water supply, sanitation, drainage, and sewerage.
The LMC is an autonomous body under the Local Government Department of the provincial government headed by a
mayor. Its main responsibilities include construction,
maintenance and repair of roads and streets, control of
encroachment of land, street lighting, primary education,
health and sanitation, recreation, and social welfare.
The LDA--like its predecessor the Lahore Improvement
Trust (LIT) before 1975--is an autonomous body under the
provincial Housing and Physical Planning Department
responsible for comprehensive metropolitan planning, land
development, slum improvement, water supply, drainage and
sewerage, building regulation, and environmental improvements. The provision of electricity is the responsibility
of the Water and Power Development Authority (WAPDA) under

the federal Ministry of Power. Lahore is divided into
three circles for distribution of electricity. The Sui
Northern Gas Pipelines Limited (SNGPL) under the Federal
Ministry of Natural Resources is the agency responsible
for the distribution and sale of gas in Lahore.

The House Building Finance Corporation (HBFC) spe-
cializes in financing construction of houses in the private sector. It essentially serves middle- and high-
income groups, and its outlay in Lahore in the late 1970s
was estimated to be about 70 million rupees (R) per year.
Recently major commercial banks of the country have been
allowed to advance loans for construction of houses, but
their present role is only marginal. Transport is regulated by the Regional Transport Authority, whereas the
Punjab Urban Transport Corporation is responsible for
operating public buses in the city. In addition Lahore
has a large number of functional departments such as
health, education, planning and development, finance, and
labor.

This case study deals with the Lahore Walled City
Project. It focuses on the performance and impact of this
project and interaction between organizations responsible
for identification, implementation, and management of the
project. The project aims at slum improvement, but the
walled city is not a squatter settlement or slum in the
conventional sense. The area belongs to the original city
of Lahore from which the wealthier people have moved,
leaving an increasingly poorer group of inhabitants. Thus
in matters of quality of life and amount and quality of
services, the project area has begun to acquire characteristics of a slum.

GENESIS AND EVOLUTION OF THE PROJECT

Socioeconomic Setting of the Walled City Area

The walled city is extremely overpopulated: About
285,000 people are crammed into a total area of 3.09
square kilometers, giving it a population density of
92,232 persons per square kilometer. This area is characterized by multistoried houses built on small plots
(medium size: 40 square meters) connected by narrow wind-
ing lanes, some not wider than three to four feet. Most of
the houses are old with structures of burnt-clay bricks
and timber floors and balconies, many of which were built

more than 100 years ago. Over 17 percent of the houses are officially classified as dilapidated premises, although 20 percent of the people are residing in them. Another 17 percent of the premises are buildings of cultural/historical value.<2>

The original population was a composite representing all income groups, but gradually the more affluent families have moved to suburbs leaving only poorer parts of their families to look after the ancestral property or renting out their premises. The walled city now is peopled mostly by small traders, craftspeople, and service workers. The average household size is 7.3 persons crowded into one or two rooms. The average monthly income of a household is R 800, which is close to the absolute poverty line. A large number of households have only one earner. In 1975, 43 percent of the households earned less than R 500 per month and 37.8 percent earned between R 501 and R 1,000.<3>

Urban Service Needs and Deficiencies

Housing conditions in the walled city are extremely bad. The total number of housing units is over 22,500. Eighty percent of these were constructed before 1947. One out of every twelve houses is in an advanced state of decay. About 70 percent of the houses are owner occupied. A high percentage of households share bathrooms and/or latrines and, in many cases, even kitchens and drinking water facilities.<4>

The houses are mostly multistoried with small rooms and very little light and fresh air. Average occupancy is more than twelve persons per housing unit. Because of overcrowding and the low-income level of the residents, little attention is paid to repairs and maintenance, and frequently houses collapse during the rainy season. About half of the housing units are inhabited by one household, 25 percent have two families, and the rest three or more. One-third of the people in the walled city live in single-room houses.<5>

The walled city has a drainage system whose channels are also used for sewerage since no separate sewers were planned for this area. The traditional type of open drainage system was adequate for a much smaller population; however, with the rapidly increasing population, the system is now extremely inadequate. Because of overcrowding and narrow lanes, collection of night soil and solid

waste is difficult, and arrangements made for them are
inadequate; as a result, an increasing amount of solid
waste is discharged into open drains causing obstruction
and deterioration of health conditions.

The water distribution system was built in the 1880s.
Because very little renovation and replacement have taken
place, the system is hydraulically inefficient, and most
of the water pipes leak continuously and are subject to
contamination. Per capita availability of daily water
supply is 35 gallons.<6> The area is provided with electricity, but the distribution system is old and generally
neglected. Street lighting is available but extremely
inadequate and erratic. For fuel, residents have to
depend upon kerosene stoves, firewood, or cow dung. Gas,
the cheapest and the most efficient fuel, cannot be used
in this part of the city because of the high risk of fire.

Almost no playgrounds, open spaces, or community
centers are located in the walled city. However, some
patches of an old garden belt are present outside the wall
(which was built 300 to 400 year ago), and some small
parks exist outside the walled city. The numbers of
schools, libraries, and dispensaries are also inadequate
to meet the demands of the increasing population. There
are sixty-five schools, three hospitals, and seven dispensaries located either within this area or within easy
reach. There are 300 mosques, most of which provide some
religious education for children. This area is estimated
to require ninety-two additional schools to raise the
educational level to the standard of the rest of the
city.<7>

Public buses cannot be used in the walled area
because the roads are too narrow. Even cars and minibuses
can operate only in the main bazaars (markets), which are
highly congested with bicycles, auto-rickshaws and slow
moving animal-drawn carts.

Overview of the Project

The project was originally based on the Lahore Urban
Development and Traffic Study (LUDTS), conducted in 1980
in collaboration with the World Bank and the Lahore Development Authority. The findings of this study helped identify urban service needs, such as housing, infrastructure,
sewerage and drainage, solid waste collection, water supply, electricity and gas, transport, health, and education.

To improve municipal services and develop strategies
to cope with continuing urban growth, particularly delivery of services to the urban poor, the project included
(1) integrated physical components to be undertaken as
demonstration schemes in the most critical sectors; and
(2) training and technical assistance to strengthen the
institutions responsible for planning, financing, operating, and managing metropolitan and municipal services to
enable these institutions to replace similar schemes on a
large scale in the future.

The project for Lahore urban development consists of
the following components:

1. Upgrading the walled city area between Delhi Gate
   and the Lohari Gate, in which about 50,000
   people live.
2. Providing sites and services in the Gujjar Pura
   area about 65,000 people. This plan includes
   allocation of 10,000 plots; of these 4,000 would
   be for low-income beneficiaries, 2,000 for commercial use, 4,000 for industry and for education, health, and community facilities.
3. Improving solid waste collection and the citywide
   transport and disposal of solid waste by providing bins, containers, and other equipment.
4. Providing training and technical assistance
   related to project formulation and implementation.

Thus the Walled City Upgrading Project (component 1)
forms part of the Lahore Urban Development Project. This
area needs to be upgraded because 25 to 30 percent of
Lahore's people reside there; it forms the center of trade
and commerce; people living in this area are mostly poor;
it greatly needs environmental improvements; and it is
important historically (many culturally important assets
are located this area). Because it is deficient in urban
services, this sector requires improved sanitation, drainage and sewerage, and other social services.

Implementation of the walled city component of the
project is spread over six years, beginning in 1982 and
ending in 1987. In Phase 1 of the project, improvements
in Lohari Gate, Shahalami Bazaar, Mohalla Mollian, and
Mohalla Kakezaiyan would be completed by the first quarter
of 1985, whereas Phase 2 would be completed by 1987.

Objectives of the Project

The objective of the project is to initiate an
improvement program for the entire walled city; the project will focus on upgrading the basic living conditions
while conserving culturally important sites. Further
emphasis is placed on (1) leak detection and improvement
of water supply and provision of sewerage; (2) improvement
of electricity and street lighting; (3) upgradation of
schools and provision of a community center; (4) development of a solid waste collection and disposal program; (5)
preparation of a conservation plan; (6) establishment of a
community development, training and technical assistance
monitoring, and evaluation program; and (7) provision of
loans for house reconstruction.<8>

Project Services and Activities

The LDA is the main agency responsible for implementation of the project. After it conducted surveys and
studies, the LDA initiated project services and activities. To conserve historically important assets the
agency planned to renovate buildings while conserving the
original architecture.

The proposed improvement of the water supply system
would involve a leak detection and the main renovation
program aimed at providing space for sufficient mobility.
Sewers were to be created by laying pipes along and at the
same level as the existing drains or by improving and
covering the existing channels. Street levels were to be
raised, repaved, and profiled to allow for surface-water
runoff. Individually covered sewer connections were to be
provided for each housing unit so that efficient internal
sanitary plumbing could be installed. The electricity and
street-lighting network was to be reestablished in the
project area, and dispensaries to provide basic health
care would be provided.

Actors Involved in Project Formulation

The formulation of the project involved the participation of various other actors such as local consultants
(BKM and CCH Associates) and sociologists from the University of the Punjab. Although the LDA was the main participant from the government, agencies like WAPDA, WASA,

SNGPL, and the Provincial Housing and Physical Planning
Department also did their share in the general formulation
of the urban development project and in the Lahore Walled
City Project. On behalf of the World Bank, foreign consultants assisted in the formulation of the project; these
included Halcrow Fox and Associates of London and Gilmore
and Allen Penn of the Gilmore Hankey Kirk Partnership.
PC-I (pro forma for project proposal for Pakistan's Planning Commission) was prepared for the upgradation of
walled city based on the information from the physical and
socioeconomic survey conducted and initially prepared by
the LDA with assistance from the LMC.

Coordination Among Implementing Agencies

Apart from various agencies involved in the formulation of the project, the four agencies formally charged
with implementation were the LDA, the WASA, the LMC, and
the HBFC. LDA was expected to undertake the main upgrading
task and also the project monitoring; LMC was to be
responsible for improving solid waste collection; WASA to
look after sewerage, drainage, and water supply; HBFC to
finance improvement and renovation of houses by low-income
beneficiaries of this area; and WAPDA to upgrade electricity supply system. Provision was made for establishing an
Inter-Agency Coordinating Committee to provide necessary
linkages and to coordinate the activities of all implementing agencies involved in the project. Working groups
were also formed to take care of day-to-day problems.

However, in time the actual working pattern has
changed, and the coordination has taken on an altogether
different form. The LDA has emerged as the main implementing agency and now occupies the central position in
undertaking the task. Other agencies are called upon like
clients to provide services within their functional area,
but apart from these specific services, other agencies are
no longer involved in the overall implementation of the
project. The Inter-Agency Coordination Committee does not
seem to exist and working groups for coordination also are
not active.

FINANCING THE PROJECT

The expected cost for the execution of the entire
project is R 312 million (see Table 3.1). Of the total

project cost of R 60 million for the walled city project,
R 7.47 million (US$1.57 million) is the foreign cost com-
ponent, and tax component constitutes R 77 million (US$5.9
million).

A total of R 47.87 million (79.79 percent of the
project costs) is estimated to be recovered over twenty
years whereas the balance of R 12.3 million (20.21 percent) is not recoverable (see Table 3.2). The recoverable
cost includes work related to the water distribution network and sewer installation, which is to be recovered
through connection fees and water and sewerage tariffs.
The cost of improving footpaths, electricity supply,
street lighting, and solid-waste collection would be
recovered through an increase in the property tax resulting from raising the annual rental values of property.

Water and sewerage charges are based on the property
tax, which in turn is based on annual rental values of the
property. Out of the total proceeds from the property
tax, after deducting 15 percent for collection, the
remaining amount is equally divided between the LMC and
the WASA. The property tax is reassessed every five
years; the last reassessment was done in 1980 and the next
is due in 1985. On the average, the property tax is
increased by 10 percent on each reassessment. Accordingly
water and sewerage charges and other municipal taxes based
on the property tax also increase.

The investments on beneficiaries' house reconstruction would be recovered as repayments to House Building
Finance Corporation (HBFC). The solid waste management
cost would be recovered through municipal taxes. The cost
of other project components (upgrading schools and community facilities, community development, and conservation)
will not be recovered. The balance of R 12.13 million
will not be recovered because these funds would be applied
to upgrading schools, providing community facilities and
services, conservation, and studies.

The project for Lahore urban development with an
estimated cost of R 312 million (US$24 million) would be
financed by the government of Pakistan, LDA, LMC, the
International Development Agency (IDA), and the World
Bank. As shown in Table 3.3, of the total cost of the
walled city project, R 42 million (US$3.2 million) is
proposed to be financed by IDA credit and the rest would
be financed by government of Pakistan (see Table 3.4).

Table 3.1 Lahore Urban Development Project:
project cost estimate (in million rupees)

Component	Local Component	Foreign Component	Total
Walled City upgradation	45.35	5.90	51.25
Gujjarpura sites and services	136.01	23.56	159.57
Solid waste management	26.67	22.95	49.62
Studies	1.12	.48	1.60
Total base cost	209.15	52.89	262.04
Physical contingencies	13.78	4.98	18.76
Price contingencies	23.90	7.66	31.56
	37.62	12.64	50.32
Total cost	246.83	65.53	312.36

Table 3.2 Lahore Walled City: cost recovery projections
(in million rupees)

Components	Cost Recovery
Infrastructure components, connection fees, water and sewerage charges, and so on	18.64
Design and supervision	1.62
Price contingency (inclusive of inflation and escalation of prices)	7.61
Subtotal	27.87
Repayments of loans to HBFC	20.00
Cost recovered	47.87
Cost not recovered	12.13

Table 3.3 Lahore Urban Development Project:
financial contributions from agencies (in million rupees)

Component	Government	LDA	LMC	IDA	Total
Walled city	18	-	-	42	60
Gujjarpura expansion	-	54	-	135	189
Solid-waste management	-	-	30	31	61
Studies	-	2	-	-	2
Total	18	56	30	208	312

Table 3.4 Project financing plan: agency contribution
to Lahore Walled City upgrading (in million rupees)

Component	Government	LDA	LMC	IDA	Total
Solid-waste management	1	-	-	1	2
Civil works upgrading	17	-	-	14	31
Loans for house reconstruction	-	-	-	20	20
Design and supervision community development, monitoring, evaluation, and training	-	-	-	5	5
Total	18	-	-	40	58

LINKAGES BETWEEN IMPLEMENTING AGENCIES AND BENEFICIARIES

The beneficiaries of the project area have few formal links with implementing agencies. In the project area, there are eleven voluntary organizations, but these restrict themselves to their own sphere of activities and do not act as a representative body or a link between residents of the locality and government agencies. However, the beneficiaries do manage to convey their feelings and complaints informally to the implementing agencies.

Local municipal councilors are represented on the managing body of the LDA. Residents of the locality approach the local councilors in the project area if they wish to voice a complaint or make a suggestion. Individuals can also directly approach people at various levels of the LDA hierarchy, in which case the results may be mixed. The LMC has an elected body, and the residents can approach the councilors or LMC functionaries whenever shortcomings are noticed in performance of the municipal functions; most of these complaints relate to collection of solid waste, and the councilors can quite effectively deal with them. The WASA has only a marginal role in the project area because the LDA has assumed the direct responsibility for replacing pipelines in the project area, and WASA is only concerned with daily water supplies. WAPDA has its own subdivisional office in the area, which receives and deals with complaints. In addition the residents can always influence implementing agencies through national press coverage in which comments can be made and complaints voiced if they have major problems or if the implementing agencies are not prompt in handling local grievances.

BENEFICIARY PARTICIPATION

Project identification, planning, and implementation in Pakistan are usually treated as technical tasks left to the relevant agencies to be handled with optimal use of funds amid rival claims from various localities. Projects are initiated after taking into account the public's assessment of its priorities and the department's view about the best way to tackle them. Beneficiary participation in its literal sense has very little scope in this environment. The Lahore Walled City Project is thus a typical project. In other forms of participation, beneficiaries can affect these projects; they can use the mass

media or go through traditional channels to influence
public decisions, representations to public agencies,
comments and criticism in various public forums, and so
on.

Phase 1 of the Lahore Walled City Project involves a
total area of 45 hectares; an area of 4.5 hectares of this
was selected as test project. Work has been completed in
the test project area and some of the nearby areas. The
beneficiary participation survey thus refers to this area,
which has a population of 5,644 consisting of 741 households living in 622 housing units. A sample of 100 households was randomly selected for the survey.

Beneficiary Participation in Decisionmaking

Sixty-four percent of the respondents came to know
about the project only when the work actually started and
22 percent learned about the project about two months
before the start. Ninety-four percent received information about the project from various functionaries of LDA
presumably during the project's preparatory phase during
which work teams and various officials of LDA started
visiting and surveying this area. Of those surveyed, 87
percent considered the project necessary for upgradation
of the locality, but their reasons were fairly wide ranging: Thirty-four percent thought the project was necessary to ensure general cleanliness, and 29 percent
regarded better sewerage and drainage as factors underlin-
ing its necessity.

Although most people realized the necessity for
upgrading, they did not show proportionate interest in the
performance of the work. Sixty-four percent of the
respondents did not have any discussions about the project
with their fellow residents, and only 31 percent talked
about the project with other people in the locality during
the implementation phase. The discussions that did take
place were informal, showing the low level of organization
among the people (which is surprising in an area in which
a large majority of the inhabitants have lived for over
twenty-five years), the nonavailability of formal discussion forums, and the detachment from such projects.

Beneficiary Participation in Implementation

When asked if the people of the locality faced any
problems during implementation, 69 percent responded that
they did not. The remaining 31 percent experienced difficulties arising from dislocation or obstacles in mobility
or temporary stoppage of services. Of the thirty-one
households that did face problems, twenty did not convey
these problems to the implementing agency because they
considered them normal occurrences when such work was in
progress; of the remaining eleven, nine contacted LDA
personnel individually, and only two formed parts of the
informal groups that called on LDA officials to convey
complaints relating to damage to their houses from digging
and disruption of water supply.

The respondents were also asked if they would have
liked to participate in the project formulation, planning,
or implementation in any manner. Seventy-four percent did
not show any interest in such participation. Twenty-five
percent of the respondents were willing to provide only
moral support, 10 percent were willing to contribute
money, and 13 percent to contribute labor to the project,
whereas 42 percent would not contribute in any manner.

Beneficiary Participation in Project Evaluation

The people of the locality felt that as a result of
the project a better quality of services was provided in
their area. The degree of satisfaction was highest in
case of ease in mobility (93 percent), sewerage and drainage (72 percent), and water supply (65 percent). When
asked if the project work caused any harm to the area, 14
percent complained about the raising of the street level,
which is now higher than the level of their own houses.
However, 84 percent found no harmful effects. Forty-five
percent thought that the project met their expectations
fully, whereas 50 percent thought that it partly lived up
to their expectations.

Two major services, sewerage and drainage pipelines
and the water supply network, have been fully upgraded in
the area surveyed, and the provision of such facilities as
street lighting, sanitation, garbage collection, and beautification of the area are nearly completed. The impact
of the project, as seen by the residents, resulted in a
decrease in migration from the area (3 percent), greater
incentive for reconstruction of houses (4 percent), better

civic sense among the residents (12 percent), increase in
the value of property (7 percent), and a mix of these four
factors (15 percent); 31 percent of the respondents felt
that the project had little impact on general social conditions.

PERFORMANCE

Only Phase 1 of the project has been completed. The
tasks accomplished so far include replacement/provision of
water mains (9,200 meters), replacement of water communications (2,700), provision of sewerage pipe (11,600
meters), house connection sewer pipes (6,900 meters),
street repaving (20,500 square meters), and street lighting (covering an area of 20 hectares).

Although the results of the project are difficult to
appraise at such an early stage when only the test project
area has been covered, some of the impact can be seen
through repeated visits to the area, assessing people's
reactions to the project, and getting an idea of the
impact of the completed portion on the residents in future
project areas.

Insofar as first hand impressions are concerned,
property values in the test project area have slightly
appreciated. The residents of this area have a more positive attitude toward upgrading work either because they
are less cynical toward projects undertaken by public
agencies or because they approve of the work.

People in adjoining areas in which upgrading work has
not started or is in an early stage have developed greater
appreciation for the implementing agency, and they are
taking considerable interest in the progress of this project in their own localities. Less uninformed criticism
of the project is being voiced than before. However, few
data are available to support these impressions, and it
will take some time for such attitudes to crystallize and
stabilize.

POLICY IMPLICATIONS FOR SERVICES TO THE URBAN POOR

The policy implications at this early stage of project implementation are bound to be tentative and subject
to revision as the project moves toward the final stages
of completion; however, some implications can be mentioned. First, there is little justification for setting

up a formal system of beneficiary participation in situations such as those prevalent in this area. Local people, being old residents and having long-standing family and cast links, have their own informal channels of communication not only within the locality but with political circles and government organizations. These channels ensure a continual two-way flow of ideas, grievances, and acceptable solutions. These channels produce an imperceptible process of project identification, implementation, and management. The system is highly flexible and takes different forms according to the situation. Introduction of a formal beneficiary participation system in the form of local associations or committees may only strain the existing communication network and reduce its credibility without ensuring any corresponding gains. Cost recovery in projects in which benefits cannot be satisfactorily ascribed to individual households is difficult. Any effort to recover these costs by raising existing taxes is bound to produce strong resistance.

Upgrading social facilities must be a continuous process through an effective maintenance procedure that does not allow decline in standards of service. Once maintenance standards are lowered and the service network deteriorates, upgrading becomes very expensive and there is little prospect of cost recovery. There is no substitute to a vigilant system of service maintenance.

Responsibility for the execution of such projects should be given to one agency that may call in other organizations on a contract basis for various tasks of special nature. Joint responsibility is not an effective system of project management.

NOTES

1. The data in this case study are from a beneficiary participation survey of 100 households in the project area; selected documents concerning the project; and field visits and observations of the author. The assistance of Feroza Ahsan, Seemi Waheed, Faroq Shah, Farzana Hassan, and Neheed Iqbal in the preparation of this paper is gratefully acknowledged.

2. A. Sattar Sikandar, Proceedings of the National Seminar on Planning for Urban Development in the Developing Countries with special reference to Pakistan, organized by Department of City and Regional Planning, University of Engineering and Technology, Lahore, 1978, p. 7.

3. Lahore Development Authority, Walled City--Lahore--A Socio-Economic Study, Metropolitan Planning Wing, Lahore, 1979, p.41.

4. World Bank/IDA, Lahore Urban Development and Traffic Study, Final Report, vol. 4, Walled City Upgrading Study, Lahore Development Authority, Metropolitan Planning Wing, Lahore, 1980, p. 34.

5. Ibid., p. 37.

6. World Bank/IDA, Lahore Urban Development and Traffic Study, p. 2.

7. Sikandar, Proceedings of the National Seminar on Planning for Urban Development in the Developing Countries, p. 12.

8. World Bank/IDA, Lahore Urban Development and Traffic Study, p. 12.

4

Management of Integrated
Social Services for the Poor:
The Case of Bongchun-dong, Seoul

Whang In-Joung

INTRODUCTION

Since its designation as the capital of the Choson
dynasty in 1394, Seoul has been the capital city of Korea.
Its population, which was approximately 1.6 million in
1955, had increased to 3.8 million by 1966, 6.9 million by
1975, and to more than 9 million by 1983. The rapid growth
of Seoul's population was primarily caused by two massive
migrations: the influx of wartime refugees, mostly from
North Korea in the early 1950s and the rural-to-urban
population shift that accompanied the rapid industrialization of the 1960s and 1970s. Consequently, the annual rate
of population growth in Seoul was approximately 9 percent
from 1955 to 1966, 7 percent from 1966 to 1975, and 5
percent from 1975-1980. In contrast, the average annual
growth rate of the total population was approximately 3
percent during the 1950s, 2.3 during the 1960s, and 1.7
during the 1970s. The concentration of the population in
Seoul is illustrated by the ratio of Seoul's population to
the total population, which was 22.4 percent in 1980. The
rapid growth of population in Seoul created shortages of
urban services, both physical and social, which tended to
be acute not only because of the increase in the demand
for services but also because of the inability of the poor
to meet their needs with their limited resources.

To attend to the increasing needs of the urban poor,
the Seoul city government has provided a wide range of
services with its own resources as well as the aid of the
central government. The urban services include: labor-
intensive public works projects that provide employment
opportunities for the poor; job placement services; vocational training and financial assistance, including loans;
public assistance programs, such as the Livelihood Protection Programme (LPP), which provides four major services

(subsistence maintenance, medical care, maternity services, and funeral services for the poor); and squatter
improvement programs, including squatter resettlement
projects, the provision of low-cost rental housing, large-
scale resettlement programs involving the development of
new towns removed from the center of the city, and the
upgrading of existing slum housing through the encouragement of self-help efforts or the provision of physical
improvements such as roads, piped water, and sewage systems.<1>

The definition of the urban poor in Korea has been
flexible over the years. As there is no official definition of poverty in the country, the size of the urban poor
population varies widely depending on the estimation
method, although household income is widely used as a
criterion of poverty.<2> According to the income criteria
used to define urban poverty by the Ministry of Health and
Social Affairs, in 1983 the urban poor had monthly family
incomes per person below 35,000 won (W) in large cities
and below W31,000 in small-and medium-sized cities.<3> In
Seoul, the poor tend to be geographically concentrated in
a few slum and squatter settlements such as Bongchun-dong,
Sangkeh-dong, and Shillim-dong.

The purpose of this study is to analyze the management system for the delivery of urban services to the poor
in a particular area, Bongchun-dong. The data for this
study were collected through open-ended interviews with
officials working with the Kwanak District Office (KDO)
and Bongchun-dong Office (BDO), voluntary social workers
of nongovernmental organizations (NGOs), and community
leaders. Structured interviews with members of 493 house-
holds<4> randomly selected were also conducted to gather
information concerning the attitudes and socioeconomic
status of the poor.

BACKGROUND AND FRAMEWORK OF THE PROJECT

The project area under study is Bongchun-dong, a
typical urban squatter area in which the majority of residents are poor. The area is located at the foot of Mt.
Kwanak in the southern part of Seoul. Mostly forest and
farmland until 1965, this area was designated a resettlement site for the victims of the Han River floods in that
year. Since then, more poor families have settled in the
area, turning it into one of the largest slum and squatter
regions in Seoul.

The Bongchun area consists of ten dongs (field administration units) with a total population estimated at 125,000 persons. Within this area, Bongchun 5th-Dong was selected for this study because it seems to be more seriously affected by poverty than any other dong in the area. The area covered by Bongchun 5th-Dong is estimated at 0.37 square kilometers, and at the end of 1983 it contained approximately 5,202 households containing an estimated 24,195 persons. These people live in about 2,580 housing units, of which 85 percent are illegal, tiny, and temporary houses.<5> Almost every housing unit is shared by two or three households. Since the neighborhood was built on a steep ridge, the slopes of which angle from 15-30 degrees, modern transport, water supplies, sewage facilities, and other sanitary systems are neither available nor easy to provide at a reasonable cost. Furthermore, since most housing units are illegal and temporary, the city government is reluctant to provide infrastructure facilities in this area, except for temporary and urgent services.<6> Most dwelling units were built without government approval and proper registration and thus are ineligible for legal protection. The poor housing conditions do not allow sufficient living space. Approximately 60 percent of the households in this area occupy a single room whereas 38 percent live in two rooms.

The government has initiated short-term, relief-oriented public assistance programs that emphasize direct and immediate services such as daily job placement, food stamps, and other piecemeal efforts. However, government resources allocated to this area are inadequate, and nongovernment resources are not fully utilized. The deficiency in social services for the urban poor in the area is primarily the result of (1) an approach that overlooked the necessity for an integrated package of services, (2) limited government resources, and (3) various legal constraints such as the city planning code.<7>

In this context, an integrated social service program was introduced as an experimental project. The idea was conceptualized during a series of workshops organized since 1979 by UNICEF<8> in connection with its Five-Year Programme for Young Human Resource Development in Korea as an integral part of the nation's Fifth Five-Year Development Plan for 1982-1986. The identification and selection of this project were made through frequent consultations among concerned ministries and organizations.<9> These included the Economic Planning Board (EPB), the Ministry of Science and Technology (MOST), the Seoul city government, the Chung-Ang University Social Welfare Center (SWC), the Korea Institute for Research in Behavioral Sciences (KIRBS), the Korea Institute of Population and Health (KIPH), and UNICEF.

The main objective of the integrated social service project is to foster the development potential of the urban poor by providing them a package of services through the collective action of a number of agencies. More specifically, the project aims to (1) provide basic services to meet the immediate needs of the poor in the area, (2) help the urban poor become independent and self-reliant, and (3) encourage community participation through grassroots organizations. This integrated approach to urban services covers the incorporation of nutrition, health, and education services for preschool children and maternal and child health care into the existing urban services and the encouragement of self-help organizations formed by the coordination among government agencies, nongovernmental organizations, and international agencies. It is hoped that this project will be developed into a model for self-help community development projects in other urban areas.<10>

The integrated urban service project now covers various activities and services ranging from the relief service to the promotion of self-help. The project will provide the following services: (1) government donation of rice and food grains and cash grants to the poorest families; (2) daily government employment service to provide simple manual jobs such as neighborhood beautification projects; (3) arrangement of vocational training in simple technical fields; (4) income-generating activities, vocational training, and job placement services for women in fields such as household services; (5) financial assistance and loan arrangements for families transferring to rural areas; (6) operation of a day-care center; (7) child nutrition improvement; (8) primary health care services and environmental sanitation; (9) counseling services for poor families; (10) preschool education; and (11) formation of community organizations. Major funding sources for these activities are the municipal government, UNICEF, Chungang University, and the informal sector.<11>

IMPLEMENTING AGENCIES

The integrated social service project is being implemented in Bongchun-dong on an experimental basis through

the coordinated endeavors of a number of agencies. Therefore, an analysis of the effectiveness of this project
must examine the managerial efficiency of both the individual agencies and the cluster of agencies as a whole.

Government Organizations (GOs)

The Bureau of Health and Social Affairs of the Seoul
city government is responsible for policy planning and the
allocation of budgetary resources. The Social Affairs
Division and the Welfare Division of the bureau, which
together provide a staff of forty-three officials, are in
charge of these tasks. At the district level, the Social
Welfare Division of the Bureau of Citizens Affairs of KDO
is responsible for supervising and monitoring performance
at the community level. The division is composed of eighteen officials, although the supervision of this project
is only part of their duties. The Bongchun 5th-Dong
office is responsible for community-level planning, activation of specific activities, and monitoring of job performance. Twenty-two officials work in the dong office;
all are employees of the Seoul city government.<12> In
addition to the regular administrative services, the dong
office provides various services to the poor in this area.
Three college graduates work in the dong office, including
the chief, and the rest are high school or middle school
graduates. More than half have participated in various
courses offered by the Seoul Municipal Officials' Training
Center. They appear to be competent in managing routine
administrative services at the community level and efficient in communicating with the residents of the area.

Nongovernmental Organizations (NGOs)

The SWC as a university branch is technically competent. The professional norms prevailing in the center are
the source of its quality service to the poor in the area.
Stimulated by UNICEF expertise and collegial links with
other professionals, SWC has played a pivotal role in
introducing innovations in social services to the urban
poor. The SWC staff numbers about sixteen, including one
professorial-level expert and three master's-level workers
in various fields such as social work and psychology.<13>
KIPH, a national research institute, also provides
technical expertise for integrated urban services to the

poor, particularly in the field of primary health care.
Having approximately 141 full-time staff members including
10 PhDs, KIPH is a competent and capable organization for
identifying problems, conceptualizing the project framework, and delivering professional services. However,
because of the short history of its involvement in the
project, its service enjoys little community recognition,
and thus popular response tends to be limited. However,
KIPH has the potential to become more effective through
joint projects with the Korean Red Cross, which has
already established functional links with the clients. The
Korean Red Cross has been operating its own branch office
in the Bongchun-dong area, although its location is beyond
walking distance for the residents of Bongchun 5th-Dong.

KIRBS, a private research organization, is a technically competent institute with approximately thirty-five
staff members including two PhDs. They serve the urban
poor in this area primarily through the preschool in the
day-care center of SWC but only on an experimental basis.
Although five other day-care centers are available in
Bongchun 5th-Dong, KIRBS input is limited to that operated
by SWC.

All these agencies except KIPH and KIRBS are well
known among the residents in the area. Because of its
relatively long history of service in the neighborhood and
the professional image of Chungang University, SWC enjoys
credibility within the community. Similarly, because of
its international reputation and long-established presence, the Korean Red Cross also projects an image of
quality service among the residents.

Interagency Coordination

Government activities related to social services for
the urban poor tend to be coordinated and integrated by
the Kwanak District Office and the Bongchun 5th-Dong
office. However, no formal arrangement exists for coordinating the activities of NGOs because they work in the
area on a voluntary basis with their own program objectives. Therefore, the coordination and integration of
services provided by these agencies are primarily left to
the recipients or clients.

UNICEF organizes a series of workshops and review
meetings in which the concerned agencies discuss work
performance in the area. On these occasions, the representatives include not only UNICEF-assisted agencies such
as KIPH, KIRBS, and SWC, but also officials representing

MOST, EPB, the city government, the district office, and the dong office. Representatives of NGOs, such as the Korean Red Cross, and representatives of local community organizations, namely, the Community Development Committee (CDC), also attend those meetings.

These coordinating links seem to be both efficient and effective as far as Bongchun 5th-Dong is concerned. However, this arrangement is only a temporary measure operating with the financial support of UNICEF. Therefore, a formal arrangement for interagency coordination should be made to ensure the successful long-term implementation of the integrated urban service project. This objective might be realized through government channels until the community organization has become sufficiently strong and influential and has the planning skills needed to implement urban service projects through voluntary community participation.

Since Bongchun 5th-Dong is one of the poorest slum areas in Seoul, the additional services provided within the framework of the integrated service project were welcomed not only by the community but also by politicians such as the congressmen representing the area. Experts were interested in the introduction of an experimental and innovative project that would have a real impact upon the urban poor. The national planning agency, the EPB, also supported the idea, although it made no financial commitment because UNICEF started the project and provided the initial financial assistance. Expenditures on the project were also kept low because it was felt that an innovative approach should be inherently low cost so that in the future it could be reproduced on a wider scale for other poverty-affected areas. The city government was somewhat reluctant to give the experimental project a substantial role within the framework of the urban Saemual Undong, Korea's self-help development program for urban communities.

Because of the level of their staff motivation and the flexibility and adaptability of their services, NGOs tend to induce more positive responses from people than do GOs. On the other hand, GOs are usually regarded by the people as more reliable over time because of their long-term presence, routine service, and financial stability. NGOs' services tend to be viewed as inconsistent because of shortages of funds and resources. Overall, however, the implementing capabilities of GOs and NGOs seem to be complementary: The GOs are oriented to immediate relief, centralized management, and delivery of services, whereas

the NGOs employ a developmental, decentralized and participatory approach.

GOs have neither adequate motivation nor the competence to play a coordinating role in the project. NGOs do
not have sufficient authority or connections to initiate
such coordination. Therefore, in this transitional stage,
UNICEF indirectly exercises coordinating functions through
a series of workshops for planning, review, and consultation by getting the implementing agencies as well as professional research institutes involved.[14]

BENEFICIARY PARTICIPATION

Currently, three types of community groups are working in the study area to meet the needs of the urban poor.
They are a cluster of popular organizations set up through
government intitiatives, the Community Development Committee organized within the framework of the Integrated
Social Service Project, and project-specific organizations.

Government-Supported Popular Organizations

Before the Integrated Urban Service Project was
introduced in 1982, a set of popular organizations had
been in operation within the framework of the urban Saemaul Undong. In Bongchun, about thirty-three Saemaul
leaders and thirty-three women's clubs were active under
the guidance of the government and the nationwide urban
Saemaul Undong. There were thirty-three tongs (subdivi-
sions of a dong), each covering approximately 120-180
households. According to this scheme, the unit of community organization was the tong. Geographical and physical
distinctions among the tongs were not always evident in
this crowded area.

A sense of common interests is lacking among tong
members. The residents are heterogeneous in terms of the
perceptual pattern of their regional origins.[15] Upward
social mobility of individuals is the central concern of
community residents, and they perceive their stay in the
area as temporary. Therefore, they tend to be reluctant
to identify themselves as members of the community. This
interpretation is consistent with survey findings, which
show that only 14 percent of the sample respondents con-
sult their neighbors on personal problems. Only 26 per-

cent believe that there is considerable solidarity among
community people as far as community issues are concerned.

The Community Development Committee

The SWC, in collaboration with UNICEF, organized and
set up a community-based participatory organization--the
Community Development Committee (CDC)--on July 25,
1983.<16> It consists of sixty-one men and thirty-three
women drawn from among existing community leaders, including twenty-nine Saemaul leaders, thirty-three tong chiefs,
and thirty-three mothers' club chairwomen. Approximately
47 percent of them have lived in the area for more than
ten years.<17> The CDC is projected to be a unique organization, which is supposed to discover and express collective community interests. It is now operated, with the
technical guidance of the Kwanak District Office, by an
executive staff that includes a chairman, three vice
chairmen, a secretary-general, and five subcommittee
directors. The five subcommittees are concerned with
increasing income, environmental improvement, health and
sanitation, maternal and child affairs, and public relations.

The chairman of the CDC is elected for a two-year
term by committee members in the CDC general assembly. The
three vice chairmen were elected by Saemaul leaders, tong
chiefs, and women's club heads. The CDC general assembly
is held once a year. The projects are prepared through
the subcommittees of the CDC and approved through the CDC
executive staff meeting in close consultation with outside
agencies, such as the dong office, SWC, and KIPH.

The projects undertaken during 1983 included (1)
construction of one public lavatory costing W2 million, of
which the KIPH provided W1.9 million and community volunteers provided W100,000 worth of labor; (2) a sewage
improvement project that cost W3.5 million, of which KIPH
paid W2 million of the costs and local residents volun-
teered W1.5 million worth of labor; (3) the provision of
home heating equipment for the sixty-seven poorest households in this area, which cost W2.5 million, with UNICEF
paying W800,000 and the beneficiaries providing the
remaining W1.7 million; (4) roof repairs for the twenty-
seven vulnerable shanty houses, with half of the W1 million expense being covered by the dong office and the
other half by the beneficiaries; and (5) stool tests for
approximately 200 preschool children between the ages of

one and six years with the assistance of KIPH. In pursuit
of these CDC projects, approximately W11 million was mobilized out of which W3.7 million was contributed by the
beneficiaries, mostly in the form of labor but also some
in cash. Curbing juvenile delinquency by working in close
collaboration with the local police, public health spray-
ing, sewage improvements, and the training of CDC staff
members will be included in the 1984 activities of the
CDC.<18>

The members of the CDC executive staff are in their
mid-forties, and most are high school graduates. Their
basic skills in organizing meetings, reaching a consensus,
choosing capable leaders, keeping records, and handling
organizational funds are the result partly of previous
experience in the military and partly of more recent experience in the urban Saemaul Undong. <19> The SWC, in collaboration with UNICEF, initiated a training course for
CDC members to motivate them and improve their managerial
skills. However, their organizational skills are still
not sufficient to enable them to make as great a contribution to the integrated urban service project as desired.
Fortunately, however, the secretary general of the CDC is
highly motivated and has a strong background in organizational management thanks to his experience in church activities.

Because of the heterogeneous backgrounds of the residents, CDC members cannot easily generate the peer pressure needed to move individuals toward communal rather
than factional or individual interests. Therefore, the
level of popular participation in CDC activities is rather
low and unsatisfactory. Inadequate participation is evident in the fact that CDC members are reluctant to pay
their W1,000 (equivalent to US$1.50) monthly membership
fees. Although there has been no corruption, some residents fear the possibility that CDC funds are mismanaged
regardless of the amount.

Project Organizations

The level of community participation in project-
specific activities, unlike the others, is rather high.
For example, in 1982 a housemaid self-help club was organized with the technical guidance of the SWC to facilitate
work placement for housemaids who are club members. About
180 housemaids participate in the club activities, and 500
households have offered daily housemaid work. The club is

managed by the coordinator and an assistant. The major
decisions, including service rates and the salaries for
the coordinator, are made by the executive board of the
club, which consists of a chairman, vice chairman, secretary-general, and subgroup directors. The SWC organized a
series of courses offering training in housekeeping. The
club members generally participate actively in the orientation course as well as refresher courses. Approximately
800 housemaids participated in these courses during 1983.
They also attended monthly meetings to review their own
job performance and to improve their work skills.<20> A
credit union was set up for the club members to encourage
them to save. UNICEF contributed W5 million as seed money
to this fund.

Another, albeit temporary, example of a project-
specific community organization is the Bongchun 5th-Dong
Housing Renewal Club. Similar versions of this club exist
elsewhere in Seoul. Approximately 160 households sharing
approximately 80 housing units and some open land in one
compound organized a club to reconstruct their housing
units. The implementation of this project involves the
purchase of the illegally occupied land from the city
government, contracting with a construction firm to design
and build modern apartment houses, and arranging a loan
from banks to fund the project. The club is being operated by the executive committee acting as trustees for the
club members. The club will be active for about two
years. During this period all related legal and financial
matters will be settled.

The critical issue in the implementation of this
renewal project is establishing a consensus among the
beneficiaries. This result obviously requires that the
executive committee assume a proper leadership role. The
chairman of the committee, who served as a sergeant in the
army, is in his late 50s, has been living in the area for
seventeen years, and is presently employed in retailing
construction materials. In spite of the effectiveness of
his leadership, consistent support of the other members
and residents cannot be expected because of their high
mobility. In fact, only 75 percent of the beneficiaries
finally agreed on the housing renewal project, despite a
series of discussions and meetings that lasted for one
year. Despite these difficulties, the level of popular
participation in most of the specific community projects
that offer immediate results and benefits seems to be
relatively high.

Although few obstacles to communication exist among
community residents, group interaction seems rather limited because of the wide perceptual gaps arising from
their heterogeneous geographical backgrounds. The formal
establishment of community organizations at the grass-
roots level could be encouraged through guidance by outsiders such as government agencies, NGOs, or other presti-
gious professional institutions. Both the lack of leadership commitment to community development and the high
mobility of residents in this squatter area seem to be
dysfunctional to community participation. Hence, government mobilization of community people might be effective
at an initial stage: Through such forced participation,
people might come to appreciate the need for and virtue of
community participation.

PERFORMANCE AND IMPACT OF THE PROJECT

The delivery of urban services through the integrated
social service project can be discussed in terms of the
following categories. (See Table 4.1 for a summary of the
performance at the Integrated Social Services Project.)

Relief Services

During 1983 the public assistance program was
extended to cover the twenty-four poorest households in
Bongchun 5th-Dong through subsistence protection funds.
The program provided 6,075 household-months in food stamps
under the LPP. Altogether, 1,308 households were partially protected by the public service delivered through
the dong office under the LPP. The dong office provided
15,457 worker-days of public works employment for cash
wages and another 3,639 worker-days for earnings paid in
food grains. Five day-care centers are operated by private institutions. In close consultation with the dong
office, the CDC undertook significant projects such as the
re-roofing of twenty-seven shanty houses and the improvement of heating for sixty-seven poor households. The
improvement of the sewage system in the area and the construction of a public lavatory afforded immediate relief
from some of the hardships of urban poverty.

Table 4.1 Performance of the Seoul Integrated
Social Services Project, 1983

Relief service
Subsistence allowance, LPP   24 households
Food stamps, LPP   6,075 household-months
Public works project--wage   15,457 household-days
Public works project--food   3,639 worker-days
Re-roofing of temporary house   27 houses
House heating system   67 houses
Improving sewage system   300 meters
Public lavatory   1 place

Fostering of self-reliance
Vocational training   37 persons
Job placement   313 persons
Assistance to migrants
  to rural areas   26 households
Construction of community
  workshop center   1 place (25 phong)
Housemaids' self-help club   180 housemaids
Credit union   100 housemaids
Preschool education   80 children
Family health charts   300 families
Maternal health--prenatal   600 visits
Maternal health--postnatal   180 visits
Free medical checkup   1,750 persons
Supplementary food distribution
  for young children   2,500 packs
Supplementary feeding
  lab session   50 nursing mothers
Stool test   200 preschool children
Health education   300 participants

Training
Training for Saemaul leaders   90 worker-days
Training for women's club
  leaders   60 worker-days
Organization of the CDC
  (94 members)   1 general session
Training of CDC members   180 worker-days
Training in housemaid services   110 households
Refresher course for housemaids   400 worker-days

Fostering Self-Reliance and Upward Mobility

Although it is hard to measure the extent of its
contribution to the self-reliance of the poor, the performance of the project during the last few years may be
illustrated in numerical terms. The dong office arranged
training in civil engineering and other technical jobs for
thirty-seven persons through the municipal vocational
training center. About 300 persons were placed in jobs
during 1983, thus providing them with a more permanent
source of income. Alleviation of urban poverty was also
attempted by arranging for the migration of twenty-six
households to rural villages for agricultural employment.
The dong office has been engaged in the construction of a
community workshop center, which will be used collectively
by unemployed women in the area for simple manufacturing
work such as sewing and knitting jobs subcontracted from
factories outside the area.

The SWC fostered income-generating activities by
helping housemaids organize a self-help club for better
work placement and improvement of their job skills. A
credit union for housemaids and an adult education program
for the mothers of the children in daycare programs
boosted the motivation levels of the urban poor. KIRBS's
professional input in preschool education programs at the
day-care center of SWC as well as KIPH's extensive primary
health care are geared toward formation of better human
resources among the poor, essential for productivity and
income improvement over the long run. KIPH, in collaboration with the KRC, provided family health charts to 500
households to promote consciousness of the importance of
health. In 1983, they also provided maternity services
amounting to approximately 600 prenatal visits and 180
postnatal visits to local residents, as well as free medical check-ups to another 1,750 persons. In addition, KIPH
opened supplementary feeding lab sessions at the Red Cross
branch office for nursing mothers. Over 2,500 packs of
supplementary food for young children were distributed by
KIPH in the neighborhood.

Informal Sector Performance

In addition to the delivery of services to urban poor
through formal channels and community organizations, the
urban poor might have received some services from the
informal sector, which acts mostly through traditional and

cultural ties between relatives and friends. In Bongchun
5th-Dong, an interview survey was specially conducted to
analyze this channel.<21> The survey revealed that 36
percent of 107 respondents moved into the area with the
assistance and on the advice of relatives or friends. This
figure signifies the importance of the informal sector in
this poverty-affected area. Thirty-nine percent perceived
themselves as once having received some assistance from
friends or relatives. Specifically, 34 percent received
special services from their relatives and friends by renting rooms or housing units at concessional rates lower
than market rates; furthermore, 2 percent occupied rooms
free of charge. Approximately 28 percent of the respondents agreed that they received food assistance from their
relatives and friends: About 20 percent of the 107
respondents often received food donations from their relatives and friends when they were in urgent need, whereas
another 7 percent entirely relied on donated food. Some
56 percent never relied on informally donated food, and
the remaining 16 percent did not respond to the question.

The significance of the informal sector is difficult
to assess because it is not easy to measure, especially
when compared with the contributions of GOs and NGOs.
However, as the survey shows, informal sector assistance
may be more critical than any form of formal assistance
because it did meet some urgent needs of the poor. The
bureaucratic procedures involved in any formal setting,
GOs or NGOs, might consist of red tape, inefficiency,
improper services, and timing problems. In this respect,
the extent of the role played by the informal sector in
combating poverty should not be disregarded because the
services thus provided are invisible and intangible.

CONCLUSIONS AND IMPLICATIONS

The Integrated Social Service Project in Bongchun
5th-Dong is a mixed version of the two approaches (1) the
top-down, centralized, service-delivery approach, and (2)
the bottom-up, decentralized, participatory approach. The
project developed out of the government's service-delivery
program for the urban poor by incorporating the NGO's
additional services, combined with a strong emphasis on
community participation and self-help.

From the analysis of the project performance, it is
clear that because of the relatively long tradition of the
centralized, service-delivery approach in this area, it is

difficult to incorporate a new approach into the existing framework. Beneficiary participation has not yet reached the optimum level since the residents are not familiar with the objectives, nature, and modes of operation of the CDC. However, in view of the positive assessment of the CDC by community members experienced in CDC activities, the approach seems to be promising.

Government agencies tend to rely on their functional linkages, which are well established through formal channels of local administration. NGOs rely more on their professional image and local connections, which are useful in mobilizing popular support and evoking a positive response from residents.<22> High level of understanding of community needs, strong commitment, and motivation of individual officials and members of organizations have facilitated implementation. For the time being, the coordinating function is performed through an ad hoc arrangement; meetings of representatives of the concerned agencies are held on the initiative of UNICEF. Because the coordination of urban services is necessary to meet community needs, the coordinating function should eventually be the responsibility of the community organization itself.

The managerial implications of the need to enhance the accessibility of urban services for the poor can be discussed in terms of the capacity to supply urban services, efficiency in the delivery of services, and graduation from poverty.<23> The suppliers of urban services include the central government agencies, the municipal government and its district branch offices, the NGOs, unorganized individual volunteer workers, and the poor themselves. The supply capacity is boosted by allocating resources in favor of the poor, thus depending on bureaucratic as well as political channels, and by improving administrative capacities such as organizational networks, coordination, communication, and management techniques. The informal sector seems efficient in delivering services to meet the urgent needs of the poor. The timely use of cooperative ties between neighborhood and relatives is welcomed. It is especially efficient for developing countries in which the market mechanism and public organizations are not yet efficient. Ensuring that urban services reach the poor is another important aspect. In most cases, the critical pitfall of the top-down service-delivery approach is the limited reach of urban services. The proper delivery of services in terms of the right client, time, and place, at a reasonable cost and of the right quality, is a pivotal issue in managing urban services for the poor.

The prevention of massive migration from the rural areas into urban centers could be a long-term, indirect measure to decrease the demand for social services in urban areas. Toward this end, nonfarm income opportunities in rural areas should be emphasized through planned relocation and development of industrial estates, the establishment of cultural and welfare facilities, and the development of small and medium-sized cities as regional growth centers. Eliminating urban poverty through these and other national level policy measures should be the long-term solution to the deficiency of urban services for the poor.

NOTES

1. Whang In-Joung, "Managing Public Services for the Urban Poor in Korea," in G. S. Cheema, ed., Managing Urban Development: Services for the Poor (Nagoya: UNCRD, 1984), pp. 53-62. Indeed, government intervention in Seoul seems to be much broader and more positive than four approaches: (1) toleration coupled with neglect, (2) eviction with or without a sponsored relocation, (3) low-cost high-density mass housing; and (4) slum upgrading. See Mary R. Hollensteiner, "Government Strategies for Urban Areas and Community Participation," Assignment Children, 57/58 (1982), p. 49.

2. Suh Sang-mok et al., Reality of Poverty and Government Policy (Seoul: KDI, 1981) (in Korean).

3. Ministry of Health and Social Affairs.

4. See appendix. Based on reclassification of data obtained through the sample survey of 987 households in Bongchun 2nd, 5th, and 9th dongs, which was conducted by the Korean Institute of Population and Health in 1983. The sample size for Bongchun 5th-Dong was 592 households. For the complete information on the survey, see KIPH, Baseline Study for Development of Health Service Program for Urban Poor (Seoul, 1983), mimeo. (in Korean).

5. Interview with Kim Key-myung, chief, Bongchun 5th-Dong office, on 16 March 1984.

6. Ibid.

7. Whang In-Joung, "Summary and Recommendation," in Whang In-Joung and Kim Dong Hyun, eds., Child Development Policies in Korea: An Approach to Young Human Resource Development in the 1980s (Seoul: Korea Development Institute (KDI), 1981), pp. 5-11.

8. The initial impact was made through the UNICEF/EPB Seminar on Child Development Policies in Korea, Naejangsan Hotel, 20-22 March, 1981. See Whang and Kim, ibid. A similar impact for Malaysia was discussed by Ralph Diaz, in "Restructuring services to reach the Urban Poor in Kuala Lumpur," Assignment Children, No. 57/58 (1982), pp. 137-138.

9. For information regarding the whole series of seminars, see Whang In-Joung, "Summary Report," Economic Planning Board, Project Management Workshop on Young Human Resource Development in Korea (Seoul: May 1982), p. 8.

10. ROK-UNICEF, Draft Programme Plan of Operations: Draft Project Plans of Action (Seoul, 1982), pp. 85-89.

11. For a description of the role of the informal sector providing urban services for the poor, see John D. Montgomery, "Improving Administrative Capacity to serve the Urban Poor," paper presented at the "Expert Group Meeting on Managing Urban Development: Focus on Services for the Poor," 10-14 January 1984.

12. Bongchun 5th-Dong office, Status of the Bongchun 5th-Dong, 1984 (Seoul, 1984), mimeo.

13. The size of the staff depends on both the availability of funds and the level of activities of the center. See Social Welfare Center, Chungang University, Status and Organization of Social Welfare Center, 1983.

14. Whang In-Joung, "Summary Report," op. cit. (1982) pp. 6-9.

15. According to a structured survey of 107 community leaders, including 94 CDC members, conducted from 15 to 20 September 1984, approximately 57% perceived the residents in this area as highly heterogeneous in terms of their perceptual pattern.

16. Primarily based on interview with Moon Tai-Hoi, secretary-general of the CDC, and Kim Key-myung, chief of the Bongchun 5th-Dong office, on 23 April 1984, and 27 September 1984.

17. See note 15.

18. Some of the CDC activities, such as crime prevention, sewage improvement, environmental sanitation, and roof repair, are viewed as tasks to be undertaken by the informal sector, meaning that the central and municipal

government would not play a decisive role. (See Montgomery, op. cit., pp. 10-11.)

19. Personal interview with Moon Tai-Hoi, secretary-general of the CDC.

20. Interview with Kim Hyung Bang, social worker, SWC, on 27 April 1984.

21. See note 15.

22. Whang In-Joung, "Summary Report," in MOST, KIPH, and UNICEF, Annual Review Workshop on Young Human Resource Development (Seoul: December 1983), pp. 12-13.

23. Instead, Dennis Rondinelli lists seven major alternatives as a policy mix. See Rondinelli, "Increasing the Access of the Poor to Urban Services: Problems, Policy Alternatives and Organizational Choices," paper presented at Expert Group Meeting on Managing Urban Development, Nagoya, Japan, 10-14 January 1984, pp. 10-34.

5

Provision of Services
to the Urban Poor: A Case Study
of Lahore Katchi Abadis

Feroza Ahsan

LAHORE KATCHI ABADIS AND SLUMS: A PROFILE

In Lahore, Pakistan, a slum is a densely settled area
of juggies (shanties made of reed matting, jute sacks, or
tin), katcha dwellings (constructed of mud), or pucca or
semipucca houses (made of bricks and cement), all of which
are in deteriorating condition. Furthermore, such areas
have inadequate municipal services and public utilities.
Sewage and garbage collection are generally inadequate.
Receiving an adequate water supply is a basic problem:
Most slum dwellings are without domestic water connections, and community water supply arrangements, if they
exist, are unsatisfactory. Electricity or gas for domestic use is rarely found. Health services, educational
institutions, and recreational facilities are scarce. The
economic status of the slum dwellers frequently touches
absolute poverty levels. The access of slum inhabitants
to the formal services of the government and the private
sector is limited by legal, economic, and social factors.
For example, some of the urban poor live in close proximity to schools, hospitals, drinking water systems, sewerage, gas, electricity, and mother-and-child health care
centers, but they are not entitled to use them. Often,
they cannot make use of public facilities because they are
occupying land illegally. However, in most cases, simple
poverty keeps them from using the formal-private sector
services and the overburdened central government facilities.

Origin of Katchi Abadis

A large number of homeless refugees, who migrated from India at the time of independence in 1947, moved into the slums that Pakistan inherited. A substantial proportion of the Indian migrants settled in big cities like Karachi, Lahore, Multan, and Peshawar mainly because of the greater income opportunities. With the passage of time the migration from rural areas and smaller cities also gained momentum.

Some of the settlements developed within the municipal or cantonments' boundaries in the proximity of government offices, high-income residential areas, and markets. Other settlements grew up in the peripheral areas because of the lack of space within the city. Still others were formed near industrial sites.

More than 100 recognized katchi abadis are spread out in different locations within the city limits of Lahore. The major concentration is in the central part of the city. According to Lahore Development Authority (LDA) estimates, at least 600,000 people live in these abadis which contain roughly 21 percent of the inhabitants of Lahore.

Status of Katchi Abadis

A fundamental problem in almost all slum areas, which adversely affects their overall condition and the effort to improve them, is that residents do not legally own the land or have the legal right to construct dwellings on it. The lack of legal status creates a feeling of insecurity among inhabitants and deters them from improving these dwellings. The law-enforcement agencies are often particularly strict about the construction of pucca or semipucca houses on unauthorized land, especially in areas within the jurisdiction of cantonments and municipal limits.

In Lahore, the first reaction to the growth of these abadis was that a clearing-up operation should be undertaken. But the government could do nothing about them without building a mass housing project to absorb the displaced inhabitants. On various occasions, the inhabitants demanded regularization of these katchi abadis and took the initiative by forming organizations such as the Peoples Planning Project and Awami Rehaishi Tanzeem (People Housing Organization). Through such organizations residents attempted to exert political pressure to safe-

guard their interests. But the fulfillment of their legal
rights remained an election promise, and regularization
was not achieved until the late 1970s.

In 1978, the LDA took over all such abadis, which
numbered about 150. This act was followed by a president-
ial order stating that those occupying government-owned
lands in katchi abadis before January 1978 would not be
evicted but would be given proprietary rights. However,
these proprietary rights were to be granted after the
government had carried out the necessary development work
by providing a basic infrastructure.

The LDA was responsible for providing the basic
infrastructure, such as drains, street pavements, street
lights, and water. The government also decided that LDA
should ensure that all notified katchi abadis under the
latter's jurisdiction should be provided with essential
civic amenities by the year 1981-1982. The work would be
financed from its internal resources and also from development charges paid by residents. After the development
work, katchi abadis were to be handed over to the corpora-
tion/municipal/town committees, which would take over
their maintenance, as required under sections 80, 81, and
82 of the Punjab Local Government Ordinance Act of 1979.

The LDA decided to shift the residents of fourteen
abadis to new developed sites. These settlements consti-
tuted about 30 percent of the total. The private owners
of forty-six katchi abadis are not willing to surrender
their lands, and hence little development work has started
in these areas.

In 1980, the government decided to transfer the katchi abadis, after the completion of development work, to
the departments/organizations owning the land, thereby
giving the department or private owner the right of dis-
cretion to award proprietary rights to the inhabitants.
The new policy was adopted because the LDA failed to
acquire katchi abadis land from different depart-
ments/organizations and private owners. With this shift
in the policy, the residents of the abadis are at the
mercy of the concerned departments or private owners to
acquire the proprietary status.

Socioeconomic Setting of Katchi Abadis

The katchi abadis in Lahore can be divided into several categories based on their physical location and economic strata. In some slums, the rate of unemployment is

very high, and the people live in abject poverty. In
other slums, most household heads are industrial workers
who have regular jobs and are better off than those in the
first category. A third category includes the slums occupied by people with low salaries: clerks, small busines-
speople, semiskilled technicians, small farmers, traders,
masons, nurses, cobblers, and so on. The people in the
third category were attracted by the free land, lower
rents, proximity to work, and access to other facilities.
A small proportion of these dwellers are also found in the
first and second categories.

These settlements exhibit some unique physical characteristics. Some are situated in low-lying areas that
are subject to frequent flooding and are often badly
damaged during heavy rains. Occasionally, large pools of
water abound in the area. The abadis contain both pucca
houses, which are made of mud or brick walls and clay and
sometimes have galvanized iron roofs, and katcha dwellings
made from assorted salvage material such as scraps of
wood, gunny sacks, cardboard, straw, or sticks, supplemented by mud and stone and roofed with straw and mud.

The living conditions in most slums are deplorable.
The areas are inhabited by about 35,000 households consisting of large families; up to 70 percent of the people
are women and children. No maternity or child care centers are located within these abadis, and the high rate of
infant mortality is attributed to the fact that the expectant mothers seldom go to hospitals or maternity child
health centers (MCHs) outside their abadis. Informal or
religious education is common, but a very small percentage
of children attend schools in the vicinity of the abadis.
The school dropout rate is high for economic and social
reasons.

An average household income in most katchi abadis is
R 1,190 (US$79.3), less than the estimated average house-
hold income for Pakistan.[1] The vast majority of slum
inhabitants are illiterate.[2] Only 12 percent of males
and 4 percent females were educated up to matric. The
average number of grades completed by men was 3.6 compared
to 1.7 completed by women.[3]

Political Support for the Services to the Urban Poor

Deteriorating living conditions in major urban centers have continuously received attention from the government, and considerable efforts have been made to improve

the situation although they have almost always fallen
short of requirements. In the early years of independence, the government was preoccupied with the emergency
resettlements of refugees without much planning or environmental consideration. Even after the refugees were
settled and the urban population began to increase rapidly, the government's ability to tackle the issue effectively was limited by the size of the problem, the growing
scarcity of developed land, rising construction costs, and
sustained migration from rural to urban areas. The worst
sufferers, as the Sixth Plan points out, were the poor and
the deprived section of the population, who found housing
in temporary shelters in squatter settlements and slum
areas.

Political parties also have paid attention to urban
development problems because these parties are traditionally based in urban centers and have little organizational
structure in the rural areas. Urban development, particularly that of katchi abadis figured prominently in election manifestoes of the main political parties in 1970 and
1977 and also in many speeches and declarations by
national political leaders. Even now, although political
parties have been under suspension for seven years, political support for improved urban living conditions is evident in discussions in sessions of (elected) municipal
bodies and (nominated) provincial and the federal councils. The residents of katchi abadis are active lobbyists
for their cause and draw considerable attention from the
authorities. They are organized in local associations and
welfare societies and frequently issue statements in the
national press and meet top officials to air their grievances.

GENESIS AND EVOLUTION OF THE PROJECT

The priority objective of the present government is
to alleviate the miserable living conditions in these
settlements and to transfer ownership rights to the residents of these areas. The overall government policy is
aimed at (1) the provision of developed plots in adequate
numbers; (2) environmental improvement of existing slums;
and (3) strict check on development of new slums.

In 1977, the Lahore Development Authority was
entrusted with the task of improving the physical conditions of these abadis. The LDA tied the provision of
proprietary rights to the residents with the enforcement
of proper layout plans so that appropriate access could be

provided to every household and space could be made available for laying down services. Every affected resident whose house would be demolished for proper layout would be provided with an alternative plot within the same locality. The LDA would provide paved streets, open drains, water supply, and street lights, and develop open spaces into parks whenever possible. The construction of houses would be left to residents.

During the 1981 to 1984 period, the LDA has developed twenty-six katchi abadis at the cost of R 31.2 million (US$2.08 million). The LDA has completed the physical infrastructure in fifteen abadis during the fiscal years 1978-1979 and 1979-1980 with an expenditure of R 5.323 million (US$0.35 million). Work in other slums is in progress. After the physical development was completed, it was proposed to provide social infrastructure to katchi abadis. Thus the project, Community Development in Katchi Abadis/Slums, Lahore, was approved by the Provincial Development Working party on 18 May 1981. The project involved major assistance from UNICEF and from the government social welfare, health, and education departments, the LDA, and nongovernmental agencies. The project was sanctioned as a pilot project for three years from 1981-1982 to 1983-1984 to facilitate socioeconomic development in selected katchi abadis/slums. This model project may be extended to other similar localities.

PROJECT OBJECTIVES AND COMPONENTS

The overall objective of the community development project is to improve the quality of life of about 50,000 disadvantaged people living in eleven katchi abadis in Lahore, particularly the children, pregnant women, and lactating mothers, by providing physical infrastructure facilities and social services based on community self-reliant approaches. The strategic objectives include

1. To facilitate community participation in various activities including those dealing with the improvement of environmental conditions and with income generation.
2. To increase educational opportunities for school-age children and illiterate women.
3. To reduce infant and child mortality/morbidity.
4. To reduce the prevalence of protein-calorie malnutrition in the 0-5 year group.

To achieve these strategic objectives, the implementation of the project was divided into successive phases spread over three years. The program included three components: physical infrastructure, resource mobilization, and social services.

Physical Infrastructure Component. The first objective of the project was to initiate development of physical infrastructure including roads and paved streets, drainage system (open drains), and drinking water, street lights, open space, community center/halls, and sewerage.

Mobilization of Community Resources. This component involved organizing elected representatives to serve on community committees and as councilors. These would mobilize the katchi abadis dwellers to solve their problems through self-sustaining development and maintain improvements with the assistance of government services and departments.

Provision of Social Services. This provision involved an emphasis on health, education, female literacy, out-of-school youth programs, and income-generation activities.

For each katchi abadi, local councils and committees were established to maintain the physical and general environment of the locality. The facilities for training members of the councils/committees were provided to develop their capability in planning, execution, evaluation, and monitoring of the proposed slum improvement plan.

PROJECT ACTIVITIES AND LINKAGES WITH IMPLEMENTING ORGANIZATIONS

The execution of the project is being carried out by Planning and Development Department (P&D) of Lahore through a special cell created for katchi abadis/slums. Other agencies involved are LDA, Lahore Municipal Corporation (LMC), the Social Welfare Directorate (SWD), and UNICEF. The project director, who is from the Punjab P&D Department, is responsible for coordinating, overseeing, monitoring, evaluating, and extending the project. The director has three liaison officers from LMC, LDA, and SWD who report to him. Various projects emanating through community participation organized by the katchi abadis and slum development committees and councils obtain support from the office of the project director.

Under its mandate, the LDA is responsible for physical development in the selected katchi abadis. In addition, it assists in the construction of community halls with the help of UNICEF. The LMC actively participates in the project by providing inputs like educational kits for primary schools, dispensaries, sanitation devices, and reading rooms. The councilors of each area in Lahore also help to strengthen the organizational setup of such agencies in katchi abadis. The Social Welfare Department is responsible for motivation, registration of voluntary agencies like the community development committees/councils, negotiations with social welfare agencies in katchi abadis, training of voluntary leaders, and other related activities. The Social Welfare Department also provides training to community leaders and project staff, arranges salaries for industrial teachers, and provides equipment for such income-generating activities as industrial homes.

Because this project requires community involvement in improving social conditions, the project plan envisaged active community participation in the labor, planning, construction, operation, and maintenance. UNICEF provided such contributions as surveys, workshops, equipment for community halls, soakpit latrines, youth activities, income-generation programs, exploration of markets, sanitation, nutrition surveillance, and rehabilitation.

Nongovernmental organizations (NGOs) are also involved in securing qualified professional staff, obtaining and allocating funds to carry out services, and providing training. At present there are two NGOs, the Family Planning Association and Family Welfare Council, involved in helping the poor dwellers of katchi abadi. Other NGOs that have shown an interest include the Family Welfare Cooperative Society, Lions Club, All Pakistan Women's Association (APWA), Pakistan Girl Guide Association Lahore, Reading Council, the International Women's Club, and the Pakistan Federation of University Women. Some NGOs, like the Family Welfare Cooperative, wished to pick out undeveloped katchi abadis in which they could establish comprehensive projects for the beneficiaries according to their own approach. The International Women's Club is interested in establishing a primary school in a selected abadi and has the funds needed for building construction and recurring costs.

Project Support

The financing of the project was approved by the
Provincial Development Working party. The expected capital cost of the project is R 8.034 million (US$0.5 mil-
lion). Of the total cost, 77 percent is financed by UNI-
CEF, 13 percent by government, and 3 percent by the community itself. No foreign exchange component is involved. A
summary of the cost and project financing is provided in
Table 5.1.

The contribution by government is shared by different
agencies. Of the total government contribution of R 1.016
million, R .552 million is being financed by SWD; R .297
million by LDA; and R .167 million by LMC. The NGO's
contribution of R .585 million is aimed at providing services to mothers and children whereas the community contribution of R .238 million is in the form of labor for
construction, maintenance of community halls, and other
related activities. Of the total UNICEF contribution of R
6.19 million (US$0.412 million), R.70 million (US$0.046
million) was allocated to finance office establishment and
staff salaries. An amount of R .96 million was earmarked
for traveling expenses and recurring and nonrecurring
contingencies. However, the bulk of the financing (R 4.51
million) was allocated for various project components as
described in Table 5.2.

The highest amount (R 2.83 million), making up 62.74
percent, was allocated for the construction of community
centers and operation rooms, the development of basic
services and activities like MCHs, income generation,
youth activities, environmental sanitation, and so on. The
amounts estimated to be spent on training curriculum
development and institution building were R 0.26 million
and 0.29 million, respectively. The lowest priority (1.7
percent) was given to the study of income-generating activities for women. Project financing by other agencies is
outlined in Table 5.3.

Actors Involved in the Project Formulation

The project was initiated in 1978. UNICEF in Pakistan contacted municipal and provincial officials in
Lahore, and indicated its willingness to assist katchi
abadis residents in obtaining basic services. A committee
to develop a project was set up under the Directorate of
Social Welfare. In late 1978, the Planning and Develop-

Table 5.1. Lahore project financing summary
(in million rupees and U.S. dollars)

Agency	R	US$	%
UNICEF	6.195	0.412	77
Government agencies	1.016	0.067	13
NGOs	0.585	0.003	7
Community	0.238	0.015	3
Total	8.3	0.535	100

Table 5.2 Utilization of Lahore project funds provided
by UNICEF (excluding overhead costs)

Project component	Amount (in million rupees)	Percentage
Curricula development for training trainers and members of the community development councils of katchi abadis slums	0.26	5.76
Construction of community centers and operation rooms	2.83	62.74
Study of income-generating activities for women	0.08	1.77
Organization of community development survey in two underdeveloped katchi abadis	0.19	4.21
Development of basic services, such as MCH activities, income-generating activities, youth activities, environmental sanitation, demonstration of home latrines, garbage disposal, establishment of day-care centers, and biogas	0.60	13.30
Institution building for creating capacity and capability among beneficiaries	0.29	6.44
Visit to slum development schemes in other countries and within the country	0.26	5.76
Total	4.51	100.00

92

Table 5.3 Lahore project financing by agencies
other than UNICEF

Agency	Components	Amount (in million rupees)	Percent-age
Directorate of Social Welfare	Training courses for voluntary leaders	0.02	1.9
	Staff for overseeing the execution, running/mainte-nance of community activities	0.34	33.4
	11 industrial teachers	0.08	7.87
	Equipment: 66 sewing machines and 11 knitting machines	0.11	10.82
Lahore Development Authority	11 plots of approxi-mately 1 kanal at the rate of R 27,000 per kanal plus other charges*	0.29	28.54
Lahore Municipal Corporation	Public health educa-tion/sanitation, prenatal, natal, and postnatal ser-vice to mothers	0.17	16.73
	Staff: lady health visitor, midwife, and maid each per center, and furniture		
Total		1.016	100.00

*Four kanal equal 1 acre.

ment Board of the government of Punjab organized a workshop on the subject. After this workshop, a coordinating
committee was formed to formulate the project.

The formulation of the project is primarily an outcome of the work of the coordinating committee consisting
of the director general of LDA, the administrator of LDA,
the secretary of the Pakistan Medical Association, the
director of the Pakistan Family Welfare Association, the
secretary of the Medical Association, the director of
social welfare, the chief metropolitan planner, and
elected councilors from the katchi abadis. This committee
worked in collaboration with UNICEF consultants and the
program officer for Punjab. Based on recommendations from
the coordinating committee and the planning workshop, the
project plan was prepared by the project director of the
katchi abadis of Lahore and was approved by the Planning
and Development Board (P&DB) of the government of the
Punjab in 1981. During its preparation, the P&DB also
collaborated with the Economic Research Institute and the
Finance Department of the provincial government of Punjab.

IMPLEMENTATION STATUS OF THE PROJECT

Work pertaining to the development of committees
appeared to have been completed in nine katchi abadis and
slums. The targets of training 150 development commit-
tee/councilors has already been exceeded. The members of
the subcommittee are also being trained at the proposed
pace. Considerable success has been attained regarding
organization of the survey in the katchi abadis. On the
basis of this survey, the action plan of the community
development has been prepared in other areas. Three abadis have already launched development programs.

Land for constructing community homes/halls in ten
katchi abadis have been handed over by LDA to the project
director. The construction work is being completed in
seven katchi abadis/slums. The improvements for the rest
of the abadis are in the design stage. The provision of
easy-reading package service for out-of-school children is
in progress, but no data is available regarding its present status. The MCH centers in seven abadis are already
being completed, and others are under consideration. More
than seven centers are already operating in sites provided
by the community. In the area of sanitation, some equipment, such as dust bin drums, trollies, and garbage
removal devices, has been provided. Model soakpit lat-

rines have also been constructed. Some industrial homes for housing income-generating activities are also in operation.

To establish katchi abadis/slums development information systems, the community members in seven katchi abadis have been supplied monitoring boards. These are set up in the CDC offices where members record their day-to-day operations. An attempt has also been made to develop a social data bank of slum improvement for these abadis. A mini operation room has been established in which maps and other data related to katchi abadis are displayed. An effort has also been made to develop an evaluation and monitoring system. This work is being done on a regular basis by the project office.

The project was originally sanctioned for three years, from late in 1981 to December 1983. It has been extended for another year ending December 1984 to consolidate and complete the activities. Construction of community halls could not be started at the beginning of the project period because committees were reluctant to provide rooms because they feared that the rooms provided to the MCH centers and community homes would be taken away by the project director and the LDA might cancel their allotment.

The Lahore Development Authority played a very constructive role in the implementation of the project. It provided one kanal (four kanal equal one acre) of land as a site for community centers in katchi abadis. In 1981, the Social Welfare Department started setting up community development councils along with the project office. However, no regular staff for overseeing the activities, as envisaged in the project plan, has been provided by the Social Welfare Department; so far, the department has arranged the salary for only four industrial teachers at the rate of R 0.250 per afternoon for each katchi abadi.

The community is currently providing rent for the rooms for the MCH center and the industrial home, and salaries of the lady health visitor, midwife, and nurse. Furthermore, the community pays the bills for water, electricity, and furniture with their own resources, which is a great drain on the community's resources.

UNICEF's role in providing input at all levels to implement the project is greatly appreciated. The UNICEF resident program officer and the program officers, along with the project director and staff, have been visiting katchi abadis and holding meetings with the community

development councils to implement the project successfully.

When the project was initiated in 1981, it was
thought that voluntary nongovernmental organizations would
actively participate or would be involved, particularly in
the establishment of MCH centers and industrial homes in
the project area. A number of nongovernmental organizations (informal sector), such as the All Pakistan Women's
Association (APWA), Pakistan Family Welfare Cooperative
Society, Women's Volunteer Services, and Pakistan Family
Welfare Council, were invited to participate and contribute the part of their share amounting to R 0.58 million.
Despite the efforts of the project office, only one NGO,
the Pakistan Family Welfare Council, took an active part
in establishing MCH centers in the katchi abadis under the
project. The other NGOs wanted to have complete control
over the building of community centers and to manage them
themselves. They did not want any community involvement
in managing the MCH centers and industrial homes, although
the main purpose of the project was to organize community
members in such a way that after proper training they
could run these centers efficiently. Moreover, the NGOs
have shown interest in only three katchi abadis. All MCH
centers and industrial homes set up in three katchi abadis are already well managed by the community. It would
be a great help if the NGOs could cooperate with community
as suggested by P&D/UNICEF in establishing a marketing
system for the industrial homes.

PROJECT PERFORMANCE

It is difficult to achieve the social objectives and
targets set forth in the project plan in the limited
period of three years; nor is it possible to measure the
impact of the project. A complete survey has to be undertaken in 1986, as proposed in the project plan, to
evaluate the achievements of the project. Based on the
experience during the past three years, however, tentative
statements can be made about the results achieved.

Health facilities for eleven katchi abadis have been
provided through MCH centers. In these centers, daily
attendance at first was approximately five to six people
per abadi; at present, daily attendance has reached
approximately forty-five people. Income of these centers
was at first approximately R 100 to R 130 per month in
each abadi, whereas at present the income of some centers

has surpassed R 1,000 per month. Two community girls have been trained as midwives in each katchi abadi through this project. A nutrition program was also launched in 1983; training was provided to workers from the community, and food demonstration activities were organized. By 30 June 1984, 290 food demonstrations had been conducted and nearly 13,869 children benefited from these activities. As a result of these demonstrations and related services, the percentage of malnourished children dropped from 45.6 percent to 31.9 percent. If these programs continue, the targets envisaged in the project plan would be achieved by 1986.

Soakpit latrines were built in three abadis for demonstration purposes. In other katchi abadis, the program to build soakpit latrines is being prepared. Mohalla school education and adult education programs were started; and articles, such as mats, blackboards, chairs, tables, benches, maps, posters, and books, were supplied. At the time of the establishment of the Mohalla schools, the number of students was forty for Katchi Abadis; at present, the number of students is ninety. Besides, eighty-five children have already been educated up to the Mohalla school level.

The project also envisaged an increase in the income of the people living in katchi abadis. Facilities were provided for women and children to earn money, and industrial homes were established so that the family income could be increased. At the time of the establishment of the industrial homes, the number of students ranged from six to twelve, but at present their number has increased to approximately fifty to sixty in each center. As a result of training by specialists, each student is now able to earn about R 300 to R 600 per month. Because of increases in enrollment, the income of industrial homes managed by the community has increased from R 60 in the beginning to R 550 per month at present.

Besides the industrial homes project, boys up to the age of 12 were selected for technical training in motor mechanics, removing dents, welding, painting, and so on. The students are being paid a stipend of R 200 per month by UNICEF.

BENEFICIARY PARTICIPATION IN KATCHI ABADIS

The proliferation of development authorities and government agencies in cities and the superimposition of

metropolitan entities have weakened the role of urban
local self-government bodies in providing services. Local
governments are no longer viable mechanisms for participation of people in local decisionmaking. Nongovernmental
voluntary organizations have also remained weak, affecting
the citizen participation and thereby increasing the
bureaucratic control.

To examine the extent and mode of beneficiary participation in the project, a sample of 100 households was
randomly selected from two densely populated katchi abadis, Basti Saidan Shah (5,899 people) and Patiala House,
Shah Shamus Qari (4,200 people). A structured questionnaire was used for the interview. The sample consists of
the 100 respondents grouped as follows: twelve CDC members, twenty SCM members, and sixty-eight general residents.

The sample was composed primarily of government servants (51 percent), laborers (12 percent), housewives (16
percent), self-employed workers (13 percent), and unemployed and retired persons (8 percent). The household
size of the sample is quite large. About 76 percent have
six to ten members. Fifty-nine percent of the heads of
the households were in government services (e.g., low-
level workers, clerks, gardeners, and others); 18 percent
laborers; 9 percent were self-employed; and 6 percent were
unemployed.

The respondent's duration of the residence in the
locality indicates that the phenomenon of katchi abadi
formation is fairly old and began with the influx of refugees from India (46 percent) after partition followed by
rural-urban migration (27 percent) and migration from
inside the city (33 percent). About one-third of the
sample had lived in this abadi for thirty years or more;
about 57 percent for more than sixteen years but less than
twenty years; and a small minority (12 percent) had lived
there for five to ten years.

The respondents gave very different reasons for
migrating to the Lahore city. For the majority (48 percent), an economic reason such as job prospects was the
primary cause. The second major reason was the desire to
be closer to relatives or friends (20 percent) who were
already in that city or locality. The move provided them
with an opportunity to live in an extended family. This
trend also indicates that the network of friends and relatives played a significant role in the formation and
expansion of katchi abadis in Lahore. The third reason
was the convenience and economic advantage of proximity to

work (13 percent), and the fourth was the availability of
the land free of cost and other restrictive legal and
social controls that apply to urban areas (16 percent). A
small minority (2 percent) felt that it provided them with
a foothold for social transition by raising their standard
of living.

Seventy-seven percent said that migration to the
abadi had improved their economic status whereas 18 percent reported no change. A small minority (2 percent)
reported deterioration. These data indicate the positive
role of the slum: Despite unsanitary conditions and
inadequate housing and amenities, it provides an opportunity for slum dwellers to improve their general economic
status and satisfy some of their human needs.

As already pointed out, the major strategy for implementing this project was beneficiary participation. The
implementation agency and other sectoral agencies such as
Social Welfare Department played important roles in
achieving such participation. A typical strategy for
beneficiary participation in this project involved the
establishment of elected community development councils.

Of the total sample of thirty-two CDC members from
target katchi abadis, about 78 percent reported that they
took an active part in the planning stage of the project,
66 percent reported to have participated in community
survey, and 56 percent indicated their role in the selection of the project and in decisionmaking about funds and
allocation of duties (see Table 5.4).

Eighty percent of all respondents realized the necessity for such a community development project as indicated
by the interest they showed in the performance of the work
and the discussion between community and leaders. For
example, 70 percent of the respondents discussed the project with CDC and SCM, and 17 percent discussed it with
informal leaders.

The respondents showed keen interest in the project
services, indicated by their frequent discussions with the
concerned agencies (see Table 5.5). The most frequent
contact was made with LDA (28.6 percent) for granting of
proprietary rights. WASA was also approached (15.9 percent) about water supply and sanitation, and LMC was contacted (12.7 percent) for cleanliness and other sanitation
issues. The most frequent contact with UNICEF (10.3 percent) was for MCH services (medicines and doctors). The
Water and Power Development Authority (5.5 percent) and
Social Welfare Department (4 percent) was contacted less
frequently.

Table 5.4 Participation of members of Community Development Council
in implementation of the Lahore project

Type of Participation	Yes	No	No Response	Total	Percent
Active participation with CDC at planning stage	25 (78.1%)	7 (21.9%)	-	32	100
Participation in community survey	21 (65.6%)	11 (34.4%)	-	32	100
Participation for selection of project location	18 (56.2%)	14 (43.8%)	-	32	100
Participation in decision-making (funds allocation, duties allocations, etc.)	18 (56.3%)	13 (40.6%)	1 (3.1%)	32	100
Any other help for project	5 (15.6%)	2 (6.2%)	25 (78.2%)	32	100

Table 5.5   Discussions about Lahore project with
concerned authority/development agency

Agency	Number	Percentage
Social Welfare Department	5	4.0
LDA	36	28.6
LMC	16	12.7
Family Welfare Council	5	4.7
UNICEF	13	10.3
WASA	20	15.9
WAPDA	7	5.5
No response	24	19.0
Total	126	100.0

When asked if they faced any problems during implementation, about 19 percent of the people did not answer, and 25 percent did not face any problems. The remaining 56 percent faced difficulties including the noncooperative attitude of authorities toward unclean and plugged drains, inadequate medical supplies, unequal distribution of civic facilities, and damage to their houses. Of those who faced problems, about 60 percent did not convey their problems to authorities, whereas 30 percent contacted CDC members and 10 percent went directly to the WASA usually in two- to three-member groups. Fifty-two percent of those who faced difficulties felt that project-related problems were not properly redressed. As for community participation, the data indicated that people contributed in terms of money (4 percent), labor (2 percent), and voluntary help (24 percent).

A clear profile of the existing leadership pattern during the implementation phase of the project can be discerned. Seventy-two percent of the respondents favored contact with government agencies through CDC and SCM, whereas 26 percent expressed their desire to contact directly implementing agencies about their individual needs. In addition, 87 percent of the respondents expressed their satisfaction with the present set up of the CDC and SCM, although 84 percent felt the need for a separate women's committee. Respondents were also asked: "Do you think that formation of CDC and SCM facilitated the achievement of development objectives of the project?" The majority of the respondents (75 percent) were wholly satisfied with the arrangements, 23 percent were partly satisfied, and 4 percent were dissatisfied.

The respondents felt that the project had brought about improvements in the social environment. About 95 percent felt that the project had affected them positively. About 5 percent, however, aired their grievance against the project. The main grievances were that they had been ejected from their homes (3 percent) and that their dwelling had been damaged by LDA's work (2 percent). The majority of the respondents (76 percent) felt that benefits were equally distributed, whereas 24 percent expressed their dissatisfaction.

The majority of the respondents felt that the project had improved their social environment through the establishment of MCH centers and industrial homes, paving of streets, and installation of drainage systems. They were satisfied with the provision of drinking water (70 percent), MCH service (65 percent), the drainage system (49

percent), training of midwives (30 percent), and income-
generating activities (36 percent) (see Table 5.6).

Seven percent of the respondents were very dissatisfied and 43 percent were only partly satisfied with drainage primarily because of the defective technical design of
the system, which led to flooding. The educational facilities were ranked very low by 10 percent of the respondents
in terms of the facilities provided by the project. Similarly, 2.9 percent showed only partial satisfaction with
income-generating activities.

CONCLUSION

Implementation of the project activities was delayed
because inadequate funds were provided by UNICEF in 1981
and the release of funds was behind schedule in 1982.
Further, LDA could not provide the land in time because it
was under litigation. In some katchi abadis, sites were
handed over to UNICEF consultants by the end of 1982.
However, actual work in some of these abadis could not be
started until 1983.

The effectiveness of CDC would have been enhanced if
the Social Welfare Department had made an effort to motivate more resourceful persons in the community. Also,
community development council members were preoccupied
with making their livelihood and thus could not devote
sufficient time to project activities. The informal sector and NGOs had little response to the project except for
the Pakistan Family Welfare Council. This nonparticipation
impeded the progress of the project as envisaged in the
original project document. Project implementation was
further hampered by the hesitation of katchi abadi women
to participate in social work programs primarily because
of religious and cultural taboos.

The community showed clear evidence of a lack of
initiative in establishing effective links between the
industrial homes and the market. The industrial homes
have so far been used as teaching schools rather than
economically productive ventures. Although the project
office is providing training in different vocations, there
is no indication of any organized or formalized system of
marketing.

Despite motivational campaigns concerning sanitation
and the distribution of sanitation equipment, heaps of

Table 5.6 Lahore beneficiary satisfaction with services (100 respondents)

Services	Wholly	Partly	Not at All	Undecided	Not Applicable	Total
Drainage	49	43	7	-	1	100
Provision of drinking water	70	28	1	-	1	100
MCH service	65	24	1	3	7	100
Training of midwives	30	27	4	4	35	100
Technical training	18	18	7	8	49	100
Income-generating activities	36	29	5	5	25	100
Educational facilities	23	32	10	5	28	100
Management training for community work	27	12	9	1	51	100

garbage are still evident in most katchi abadis. This situation is the result of a lack of adequate community interest in sanitation; inadequate LMC support; and the temporary nature of the project.

One general conclusion that can be drawn from the study is that the scope of the needs, as indicated in the survey of beneficiary participation, are much wider than the policymakers' perceptions or the available resources. To improve such localities, current government policy focuses primarily on upgrading the physical infrastructure. The launching of the Community Development Project, however, shows a gradual shift in the government policy.

NOTES

1. Lahore Development Authority, "Internal Memorandum" (Lahore: 1983), p.1.

2. Government of Pakistan, Pakistan Economy, 1983-1984 (Islamabad: Economic Advisor's Wing, Finance Division, 1984). 3. Government of Punjab, Planning and Development Department, Evaluation Report on Community Development in Katchi Abadis/Slums Project, (Lahore: Government of Punjab, September 1984), p. 72.

6

Environmental Health and Community Development Project: A Case Study in the Slums and Shanties of Colombo

S. Tilakaratna, S. Hettige, and Wilfred Karunaratna

INTRODUCTION

About half the inhabitants of the city of Colombo in Sri Lanka live in slums and shanties. Most of these communities are characterized by a relatively high incidence of infant and child mortality and water-related diseases, poor sanitation and environmental hygiene, and severe inadequacy of basic amenities, in particular the lack of sanitary toilet facilities and safe drinking water. In general, these problems are more acute among shanty than slum communities.[1] Few of these communities have effective community-level organizations to initiate development activities to improve their quality of life. Often they also lack the assistance of trained community development workers to service their needs and to help in the formation of community organizations. Against this background the UNICEF-assisted project for Environmental Health and Community Development in the Slums and Shanties of the City of Colombo was conceived and put into operation. The project was implemented during the 1979 to 1983 period. The total cost of the project included a government commitment of 10.54 million rupees (R 26 = US$1) and a UNICEF contribution of US$900,000.

Objectives of the Project

The long-term objectives of the project were to reduce the infant and child mortality and morbidity from water-related diseases and to correct the nutritional deficiencies in the slum and shanty communities. The project consisted of four principal objectives, namely,

the provision of physical amenities; the institution of
health and health education programs; the creation of a
trained cadre of community workers, and the establishment
of community organizations for eliciting the inhabitants'
participation.

Physical amenities. The project aimed at providing
safe drinking water facilities, sanitary toilets, and
bathroom facilities for approximately 15 percent of the
slum/shanty population by 1983. The physical targets were
to provide one toilet per five dwelling units, one bathroom per eight units, one standpipe per ten units, and the
conversion of 3,200 bucket latrines into sanitary toilets.

Health services. Health education programs through
interpersonnel communications, group talks, mass media,
and institutions such as maternity homes and schools
formed the main activities under this project component.
Immunization campaigns, nutrition programs, promotion of
family planning, special programs for mothers, "little
mothers" (girls of marriageable age), and youth, and personal hygiene instruction for children were the important
elements in this sector.

Community workers. Recruitment and training of a new
cadre of officials (called health wardens) to work with
the communities were other important objectives. The original target was to train 150 health wardens (HWs), but
this number was later reduced to 100. HWs were to be
trained in community health, health education, and community development in general; after the training they were
to work with the communities to promote basic health care
and initiate community development activities. They were
to serve as the basic link between the communities and the
project authorities.

Community organizations. The project envisaged the
organization of selected slum/shanty communities into 300
community development councils (CDs). These grassroots
nuclear organizations were expected to engage in the
proper maintenance of common physical amenities, health
care, and environmental hygiene and other economic and
social activities to improve the quality of community
life. They were to be the principal instrument for
achieving community participation in the project implementation. The project's long-term objective was to build
viable and self-reliant communities having the organizational capacity as well as confidence in their abilities
to solve the basic problems relating to their livelihood.

Representatives of the CDCs and the project officials
at the district level serve as members of district devel-

opment councils. Elected representatives from the district councils and the key officials in the overall project administration make up a city development council,
which was to be the main body in charge of coordination
and project monitoring. In this way a participatory
three-tier development council system was to be put into
operation.

The project was implemented through the existing
official institutions and channels, in particular through
the Colombo Municipal Council (CMC) and the Common Amenities Board (CAB). Although the Public Health Department
of the CMC handled recruitment and training of HWs and
supervision of the work of HWs, health education programs,
and the CDCs, the CAB handled the provision of physical
amenities to the communities. The services of other
agencies were obtained when required for specific work
assignments, e.g., Women's Bureau for the initiation of
income-generating activities for women and National Youth
Services Council to provide leadership training for youth.
A coordinator for slum and shanty projects was to be
appointed in the Urban Development Authority, who was to
facilitate interagency coordination.

Methodology of the Study

The study focused on the operation of the project in
the field, in particular, on the interaction between the
project and the communities and the changes brought about
by this interaction.<2> Two principal methods of investi-
gation were used: (1) interaction with health wardens who
serve as the link between the target communities and the
project authorities, to gather information on the work
carried out in their respective communities and their
judgment on the project's operation in the field; and (2)
a comprehensive field survey of a sample of fifteen slum
communities under the project to gather information on the
interaction between the project and the communities and
the community views on the impact of the project. An in-
depth study was carried out in seven of these fifteen
communities using participatory methods of interaction
between the community and the study team.

The information gathered by these two methods was
supplemented by discussions with project officials and
other key informants and data gathered from official
records and publications. Furthermore, field investigations were carried out in a community not benefited by the

project (a nonproject sample) for the purpose of comparison with the project sample.

PROJECT IMPLEMENTATION

The project was implemented through the existing
administrative machinery of the municipality and of other
state agencies rather than by a separate implementation
machinery. This approach enabled the project to operate
with minimal overhead costs and to build up the implementing capacities of the existing agencies. In this process,
however, the project experienced several constraints such
as the lack of adequate interagency coordination and of
sufficient coordination between agencies and officials
within the municipality.

The programs on health, health education, activities
of CDCs, and the operation of the three-tier CDC system
came under the supervision of the Municipal Health Department. The provision of physical amenities was handled by
the Common Amenities Board (CAB). The Urban Development
Authority (UDA) approved the locations where physical
amenities were to be upgraded. Other agencies such as the
Women's Bureau and the National Youth Services Council
handled selected aspects of the project such as income-
generating projects for women and leadership training for
youth. Although the original project envisaged the
appointment of a coordinator for slum and shanty upgrading
in the UDA, who was to be responsible for facilitating
interagency coordination, the appointment was not made
during the project period. Lacking overall coordination,
the project ran into several implementation problems especially during the first half of the project period. In
particular, different agencies did not always deliver
services into the project areas; some services had seeped
into the nonproject areas.

In some instances the CAB had carried out upgrading
of physical amenities in sites in which CDCs had not been
formed, whereas the communities that had organized into
CDCs had not received the amenities. This situation not
only created a credibility gap between the project personnel and the potential beneficiaries, but it also violated
a basic principle in the project, namely, that a measure
of social preparedness on the part of the communities is a
prerequisite to receiving services. The CAB appeared to
have considered the selection of sites for upgrading of
amenities as a prerogative that could not be compromised

with requests emanating from the CDCs. In 1981, for
example, of the forty-four sites where work had commenced,
twenty-seven were not scheduled sites (that is, they were
outside the project area). The activities of the CAB and
the UDA lacked coordination. In some instances, the new
amenities constructed by the CAB were demolished by the
UDA within a few months to pave the way for other urban
redevelopment programs. Moreover, the CAB was providing
physical amenities using private contractors, and the
quality of the construction work was often found to be
poor. Members of many communities complained that substandard material had been used in the construction work.
Most of these problems arose during 1979 and the early
part of 1980 when CDCs had not been established in most
slums. According to the CAB, provision of common amenities was urgently needed in some areas because the prevailing insanitary conditions, and the work could not be
postponed until CDCs were formed.

Similarly, the Women's Bureau had initiated income-
generating activities in locations in which CDCs had not
been formed. The women selected for vocational training
were mostly from outside the project area. Moreover, the
use of the Women's Bureau for initiating income-generating
projects for women from low-income households was opposed
by the charity commissioner of the Colombo municipality,
who considered that such activity was his concern.

As the project got under way and a new cadre of
development workers (HWs) began to develop close links
with the communities, problems began to develop within the
municipality itself. Only the Health Education Unit had
been directly involved in the project implementation.
Other departments, as well as some officers within the
Health Department such as the Public Health Inspectors
(PHIs), began to stake their claim in the implementation
of the project. These pressures led the Health Department
in mid-1981 to remove the HWs from the supervision of
assistant health education officer (AHEOs) and to place
them under the PHIs. The result was that many HWs began
to be engaged in routine health and sanitary activities
(for example, the inspection of eating houses) at the
expense of their work with the communities. Lacking regular interaction with HWs, many CDCs also became inactive.
This situation proved a setback to the project. It took
virtually one year for the municipality to realize that
the project had suffered. In mid-1982, the situation was
corrected and HWs were replaced under the supervision of
the AHEOs. However, the coordination of the activities of

HWs was made difficult because of a distinction made between the male and female HWs for administrative purposes. Male HWs reported to the medical officer (MO) whereas female HWs had to report to the assistant medical officer (AMO) dealing with maternity and child care. Moreover, the administrative system failed to recognize the special nature of the work carried out by the HWs, that is, the fact that their work was with the community and included evening work when the residents were in their homes.

Most of these problems were overcome in time, and in the second half of the project period, particularly after mid-1982, the project implementation distinctly improved. In 1981, the CAB set up a special project unit to implement the UNICEF-assisted projects. The provision of amenities was increasingly concentrated on the project area where CDCs had been formed. UDA permission was sought before work began on the provision of amenities for a given location. The system of using private contractors was abandoned, and the CDCs began to be involved in the construction of amenities. This policy change led to a marked improvement in the quality of construction.

A coordinating committee was set up under the mayor of the municipality to review the project's progress at six-month intervals. Key officials of the municipality and the other implementing agencies formed the membership of this committee. The project implementation capacities of the different agencies (health department of the municipality and the CAB) and interagency cooperation had improved over time. Some administrative problems, however, remained such as the unnecessarily bureaucratic framework surrounding the community development workers (HWs).

AN OVERVIEW OF PROJECT PERFORMANCE

At the time of the study, the project had covered about 300 slum/shanty housing developments in which 279 CDCs had been formed. We were able to gather information on 260 communities covering 281 projects in which CDCs had been formed (about 93 percent of the total). The evidence strongly suggests that, although not all project targets have been achieved, the general performance of the project in relation to the targets appears to be quite high. The project has broken new ground in the field of urban slum development in Sri Lanka.

Of the 260 slum communities on which data were collected, 228 (88 percent) had received assistance under the
project for upgrading common amenities in the form of
either new construction or rehabilitation of existing
facilities. The total amenities provided, including both
new construction and rehabilitation, amounted to 1,280
toilets, 566 bathrooms, and 789 standpipes. No doubt the
provision of these facilities had a significant impact on
the communities. Enhanced community access to sanitary
toilets and to safe drinking water is an outstanding contribution of the project. The total number of households
that benefited from these facilities, assuming all households that received the facilities are beneficiaries, can
be estimated to be 11,686; that is a total population of
about 70,000 (assuming an average household size of six
members). This beneficiary population amounts to nearly
12 percent of the population of the city of Colombo.

The amenities provided under the project amount to
one toilet per nine households, one bathroom per twenty-
one households, and one standpipe per fifteen households.
This average performance represents a considerable short-
fall in relation to the project targets of one toilet per
five households, one bathroom for eight households, and
one standpipe per ten households. In three of the municipal districts, the average realized ratios are particularly low--one toilet per eleven households and one bathroom per twenty-five households. In many housing projects, congestion in use characterizes the existing amenities.

Health and health education programs have provided
fairly wide coverage. Immunization programs had been
implemented in 229 communities, that is, 88 percent of the
communities for which data were collected. Films on
health, nutritional education programs, and mothers' programs had been implemented in 80 percent of the communities. Little mothers' groups had been formed in 46 communities representing 18 percent of the total.

One hundred and twenty-three health wardens (HWs)
were recruited and trained under the project; the original
target of 150 was later scaled down to 100. Thirty-two
dropped out over the years, and 84 continued in the project at the end of 1983. This group is an important
source of human resources built up under the project
through a process of direct exposure to and interaction
with slum communities. HWs constitute the most important
link between the community and the project authorities.
For the first time in a government-sponsored urban devel-

opment project, a cadre of catalytic agents directly working with the communities at the grassroots level has been created.

A survey conducted by the Common Amenities Board revealed the existence of only 265 CDCs in contrast to a project target of 279. As many as 300 CDCs may have been set up at one time because official records refer to such a number. However, some of these barely began operations and left no record of their existence. Of the 260 CDCs about which we gathered information, 152 (58 percent) have been reported as active in that they hold regular meetings; 50 (19 percent) are relatively inactive, having irregular/occasional meetings; and 58 (22 percent) are no longer operating. However, community participation in the CDCs has been reported high in only 24 percent; an average level of participation is reported in another 33 percent. Active leaders, that is, those who take initiative and display commitment to community work, are reported in only about 11 percent.

The interaction between the health wardens and the communities has sparked a number of initiatives by the communities. The more important are shramadana (organization of voluntary labor) campaigns for cleaning the environment, which have figured in 197 communities (76 percent) and religious activities (mainly organization of sermons), which have figured in 189 communities (73 percent). Skill training programs have been conducted in 133 communities (51 percent of the total). Sports, cultural, and children's programs have been implemented in approximately one-third of the CDC communities. Other activities of CDCs include adult education, preschools, art circles, self-employment projects, and registration of marriages.

District development councils have been set up to serve as forums for interaction between the representatives of CDCs and the project officials in the districts. A city development council is in operation in which the key project officials and representatives from CDCs (selected from the District Council) meet to review the overall operation of the project. Initially this apex body had been functioning without CDC representatives; since 1983, the CDCs have also been represented in the City Council. The preparation of an annual implementation plan is an important activity of the three-tier development council system. This plan sets out the list of activities for each month to be carried out in each of the CDC communities.

Although the project was intended to cover both slums
and shanties, slums have been the focus. With the exception of the shanties in Henemulla and Summitpura, the
project has been confined to slums. The conditions in
shanty communities are in general worse than those for the
slum communities in almost all respects--access to amenities, health and sanitation, housing conditions, and education. Most shanty dwellers are squatters on private
lands or public land reservations, which do not qualify
for upgrading under the project.

FINDINGS OF SAMPLE FIELD INVESTIGATIONS

To evaluate the impact of the project and to draw
useful lessons from its operation, field investigations
were conducted in three sample slum communities. Sample A
consisted of ten communities reported to be relatively
active, having initiated a range of activities, and having
active CDCs. Sample B consisted of five communities that
were either less active or inactive. Sample C consisted of
a nonproject community that had not benefited from either
this project or similar external intervention. An attempt
was made to compare the conditions in the three samples
using certain key indicators and to examine how far the
project inputs could explain the differences.

A differentiated socioeconomic structure with a clear
division of the slum community into low-, middle-, and
high-income groups can be observed in all three samples.
However, the samples differ significantly. Although households below the poverty line in samples A and B (those
earning less than R 800 per month) constitute about one-
third of the total, in sample C the corresponding figure
is 41 percent. Shanty-type improvised/temporary dwelling
units characterize 44 percent of the households in C,
compared with 34 percent in B and 22 percent in A. Hence,
the average socioeconomic condition of the households
appears higher in samples A and B than in C. The
socioeconomic situation in A is distinctly better than
that in B.

Over 90 percent of the households in all the samples
use common toilets. However, the project has directly
resulted in a conspicuous difference between the conditions in the project and nonproject samples. In C, unsanitary bucket lavatories predominate (93 percent of the
households use this type). Moreover, severe congestion
characterizes the use of lavatories: An average of sixteen

households (involving 80 individual users) share one
bucket lavatory. The catch pits in these lavatories provide breeding grounds for flies and filariases mosquitoes,
and buckets overflow when not cleared regularly, creating
a health hazard. In contrast, as a direct outcome of the
project almost all households in sample A and 94 percent
in B use sanitary (water-sealed) toilets, and the house-
hold/toilet ratio is seven in A and eight in B.

In sample C, the household/standpipe ratio is as high
as forty-nine. Because of the severe congestion, households use the roadside standpipes for drinking water as
well as for bathing and washing. The community has no
common bathrooms. On the other hand, the project has
provided an average of one standpipe for ten households in
A and for nineteen in B. All housing projects in the
sample B and 70 percent of sample A have been provided
common bathroom facilities, and the household/bathroom
ratio is fifteen in both samples.

Although a distinct improvement can be seen in the
project communities in regard to common amenities, the
available facilities fall short of the targeted levels.
The project aim of one toilet for five households and one
standpipe for ten households has been realized only in 40
percent of sample A and 20 percent of sample B. The target
of one bathroom per eight households has been realized in
only 20 percent in both samples. Inadequacy of facilities
and congestion characterize the majority of the housing
developments in the two project samples.

Physical condition and cleanliness of the common
amenities depended on three factors (1) the quality of
construction, (2) user/facility ratio, and (3) community
participation in regular maintenance and cleaning. The
quality of construction, which had been generally poor
when the private contractors were used, showed a distinct
improvement since 1983 when the communities began to be
involved in construction and repair. Participation of
communities takes the form of supervision and overall
execution of the work and the supply of unskilled labor.
Payment for skilled labor and construction materials are
provided by the Common Amenities Board (CAB) under the
project.

User/facility ratio is particularly high for bathrooms in practically all communities resulting in faster
deterioration and frequent breakdown of water taps. Fifty
percent of the bathrooms in sample A and almost all in B
were dilapidated. Maintenance and cleanliness are also
affected by the user/facility ratio, but a more important

factor is the active operation of the CDCs. In sample A
in which the CDCs are on the average more active, the
amenities are observed to be cleaner than in B.

In project communities in which CDCs are active, the
interaction between the HW and the community has been
relatively high, and there has also been relatively high
rate of community participation in the health education
programs. Some 65 percent of the households in sample A
have met the HW serving the community, 70 percent have
watched films, and 30 percent have participated in discussions pertaining to health and sanitation (with mothers,
little mothers, adults, and youth). In contrast, only 11
percent have met the HW in sample B; 40 percent have
watched films, and the number participating in discussions
is less than 6 percent. About 63 percent of the households
in A who have participated in health education programs
have reported that they have benefited from these programs; the corresponding figure for B is only 30 percent.
HWs' activities in health education have varied with the
degree of activeness of the community (CDC) concerned.

Information collected on selected preventive health
care practices (use of toilets by children, washing hands
before meals, cleaning teeth, and boiling water for drinking) shows that the participation in samples A and B is
distinctly better than that in the nonproject sample C;
the people in sample A perform better than those in B on
all indicators. These differences are partly the result
of the availability and utilization of project inputs. In
child care practices (immunization and monitoring child
growth), all three samples record high levels (generally
over 80 percent) reflecting the effectiveness of the
national health programs in reaching these communities.
Sample A records a marginal improvement over the others,
perhaps a result of higher utilization of project inputs.

An exception to the general trend observed in the
relative performances of the samples is in infant feeding
practices. Sample A records a higher rate of bottle feeding (41 percent of the cases), compared with 29 and 27
percent in B and C, respectively. Perhaps the explanation
of these differences has to be sought in factors outside
the project, principally the socioeconomic characteristics
of the communities concerned. The relatively higher
income levels in sample A have presumably permitted the
households a greater choice of infant feeding practices
and a greater market orientation in meeting infant consumption needs. Within A, the rate of bottle feeding is
somewhat higher in communities in which lower-middle-class

families and working mothers, engaged in semiprofessional
work, are an important segment.

With regard to family planning, no significant varia-
tion can be seen among the three samples. Their average
rate is about 40 percent. However, in 50 percent of
sample A, the rate is observed to be in the range 50 to 65
percent, and this appears to be partly a result of greater
activity in family planning education in this community.

Children's health in A is found to be distinctly
better than that in B and C. Reported cases of malnutrition amounted to less than 1 percent in A compared with 5
and 18 percent in B and C, respectively. The average
infant mortality rate for the 1979-1983 period was forty-
one per thousand in sample A compared with forty-eight in
C and sixty-five in B. The child death rates show a similar pattern, 0.7 percent in A, 2 percent in C, and 2.5
percent in B. A conspicuous difference can also be
observed among the samples in the importance of water-
related diseases in infant and child deaths. Although in
A only 7 percent of the deaths could be attributed to
water-related diseases, the corresponding figures are as
high as 25 percent in B and 30 percent in C. Analysis of
cases of sicknesses in the family during the six months
preceding the field survey revealed that although diarrhea
accounted for only 11 percent of the reported cases in A,
corresponding figures are 21 percent in B and 24 percent
in C.

Preschool attendance is low in all three samples. The
rate, however, is much higher (28 percent) in A compared
with the rates in others (12 percent in B and 19 percent
in C). On the other hand, school attendance is quite high
in all three samples. Here again, the rate in A is higher
(83 percent) than in others (74 percent in B and 79 percent in C).

The better performance of sample A people in health,
health practices, and preschool and school attendance
appears to result from three main factors: (1) the relatively higher socioeconomic status of households; (2) the
existence of active CDCs; and (3) the greater interaction
between the HW and the community. The relatively higher
socioeconomic status appears to have favored greater
absorption of project inputs. The incidence of infant and
child deaths is highly correlated with the socioeconomic
status and the income levels of households. Eighty-five
percent of total deaths have occurred in households with
monthly income of R 1,000 or less, and 61 percent have
occurred in families in which the family head is a

laborer. In sample B, CDCs have remained inactive, interaction between the HW and the community was low, health
education programs have not made much headway, and the
health situation of the communities has failed to improve
markedly as a result of the project. In fact, the nonproject community C performs better than sample B from the
project community on some indicators, and on others the
two samples do not show a significant difference. This
result seems to show that the provision of physical amenities is a necessary but not a sufficient condition to
bring about the desired changes to benefit the children;
the close interaction between the HW and the community and
the active operation of the CDCs are also important factors.

COMMUNITY DEVELOPMENT COUNCILS

The reported participation of households in community
development council meetings and other activities was 69
percent in A compared with only 10 percent in B. In 60
percent of B, the participation rate is 0, meaning that no
meetings of the CDCs have been held and no activities have
been initiated by the CDCs. In fact only 26 percent of
the households in B were aware of the existence of CDCs.
This awareness ratio was 86 percent in sample A. In the
community's perceptions, the main activities of CDCs had
been obtaining amenities and maintaining them, making
representations to authorities about further needs, con-
ducting welfare activities including religious activities,
and leading shramadana (self-help) campaigns. Inadequacy
of common amenities was identified as the most important
unsatisfied need. Provision of drains for waste water
disposal and lampposts for the gardens and improvement of
garbage disposal were among the other important needs
identified. Although 82 percent of the participating
households in A considered the CDCs to be a success (or to
have the potential for success), only 17 percent in sample
B considered this to be true. Leadership problems, dis-
unity within the community, and indifference by the members were cited as the main factors in the limited success
of the CDCs.

The in-depth investigations carried out in seven CDC
communities revealed that the relative success of some
CDCs was a result of the small size of the community, the
high degree of economic and social homogeneity, and the
existence of a previous tradition of working together. In

general, the smaller the community, the greater is the
scope for developing a measure of cohesiveness and neigh-
borly relations among members. A small community can more
easily meet at frequent intervals to discuss common issues
and problems, to evolve a group spirit, and to manage
affairs.

Coupled with smallness, a high degree of economic and
social homogeneity characterized these communities; at
least, no sharp disparities separate the economic and
social statuses of the members. This characteristic
greatly facilitated interaction among members, and there
was less likelihood of sharp differences or conflicting
interests in the identification of common needs. Two of
the successful communities were predominantly lower-
middle-class communities, consisting largely of salaried
workers or those of similar economic and social status.
The third was primarily a low-income working-class community without sharp differences in income levels.

In each community, group activities of various forms
were held even before the formation of the CDCs. In the
first two, successful mutual aid schemes had been in operation; in the third community a series of group actions
were initiated when dwellers faced the threat of eviction
from a private landowner. The community had successfully
overcome the threat. This factor created a tradition of
working together among the residents.

The relatively poor performance of the other four
CDCs could be attributed to two main factors. First,
either the community was too large, or it was divided
among two or more separate housing projects. When more
than one housing project was covered by a CDC, the amenities were often not equitably distributed, making some
residents better off than others. Those bypassed felt
discriminated against and rarely participated in CDC activities. The needs of different housing projects had not
been properly met through a single CDC. In a relatively
large-size project, the CDC had contacts with only a section of the community and neglected the rest. It may be
noted that a part of this community was a shanty. In
another community, the CDC leadership was dominated by
private owners who had used the CDC to agitate for the
supply of private facilities (without much success, however). The interests of this group did not coincide with
other dwellers.

In the communities with relatively poor performance,
a significant gap existed between the CDC leadership and
the rank and file membership. The leadership came either

from one housing project or from a particular social
stratum or from a section of the community (or from both
sources), and was not generally accepted by the community
as a whole. CDCs failed to hold meetings for several
months, and even when occasional meetings were held, community participation was quite low. The attendance at the
discussions that we held with these communities was generally less than 50 percent of the households.

The more active CDCs have undertaken a range of activities besides the proper maintenance of common amenities
and evolved a community cohesiveness and a group spirit of
working together to pursue common interests. Even the
currently less-active or inactive CDCs had initially been
active but had gradually become inactive over time. Having obtained the amenities and initiated schemes to maintain them, they could not conceive a further role for them
and fell into a state of stagnation. Even some of the
more active CDCs appear to have failed to initiate new
activities apart from an occasional religious activity or
a shramadana campaign. Even these CDCs could fall into a
state of stagnation unless a new sense of dynamism is
introduced into them. This revival requires that HWs
interact with them more intensively and explore areas for
group action as a continuous process.

HEALTH WARDENS

Health wardens are an important resource developed
under the project. They have acquired useful experiences
by working with the slum communities and stimulating them
to initiate development actions. Considerable potential
exists for more effective utilization of the skills and
experience of the HWs. The existing uncertain and bureaucratic framework in which they operate is hardly conducive
to using their experience and skills better for the benefit of the project. There is a danger of a continued high
dropout rate. Already 32 percent of the recruits have
dropped out.

Lack of promotional prospects has created a sense of
uncertainty among the HWs. This problem needs to be corrected by introducing a higher cadre so that those whose
performance reaches a certain specified standard can be
promoted. Simultaneous with such change, the designation
of a health warden needs to be changed to reflect more
fully the nature of their work (for example, community
development officer/assistant). At present, the HWs are

subject to rather anomalous office rules that provide no
incentive for work. They must work normal office hours,
but they also are expected to work with the communities in
the evenings (when the residents are in their homes). The
project activities require frequent and intensive interaction with the communities in which HWs need to spend a
good part of their time rather than in offices. Hence
their working hours need to be adjusted to include evenings for about three days a week and to make Saturdays or
Sundays working days in place of a weekday.

The existing system of monthly progress assessment of
HWs is unscientific. It attempts to set out a rigid
guideline as to what a HW should do, the nature of the
interaction between the HW and the community, and by
implication, what even a community should do. This
amounts to a top-down approach to community development.
HWs tend to concentrate more on easier activities avoiding
harder tasks, and they give more attention to the quantity
of work than to the quality. Marks are awarded on the
basis of HWs' reports rather than on assessment of the
field situation. The reported and the actual situation
can differ substantially. Finally, the scheme is based on
an implicit assumption that all housing projects can be
treated alike for the initiation of the listed activities.
However, they differ considerably in regard to the conditions and circumstances that favor community mobilization.
It is, therefore, suggested that the scheme be abandoned
and replaced by a system of group assessment carried out
in quarterly workshops.

At present there is no systematized learning program
for HWs. The existing monthly meetings are more reporting
exercises and not learning sessions involving reflection,
analysis, and conceptualization. HWs need to go through a
continuous process of experiential learning. For this
purpose, it is suggested that quarterly review and reflection workshops (lasting two to three days) be held for
groups of twenty to twenty-five HWs, in which they present
their work to others, reflect on and analyze experiences,
and critically assess each other's work.

CONCLUSIONS AND IMPLICATIONS

Our analysis of community views and perceptions about
the project revealed the people's very positive outlook
and readiness for change. They perceived the possibility
of a progressive improvement in their living conditions by

a process of graduating from one level of needs (and their satisfaction) to another and the need for mobilization of community resources to facilitate the process.

Most communities suffer from inadequate access to common amenities (bathrooms, standpipes, and toilets). It is crucial that support be provided to these communities to achieve a minimum level of basic amenities. Since the nature of the problem differs from one housing project to the other, it would be necessary to study the specific situation in each one with the participation of the communities and to take necessary remedial actions. Even though the ratios of households per facility laid down in the project document appear reasonable, we suggest a more flexible approach to determine the ratios (within certain limits) in consultation with the communities and to suit the conditions in the particular housing project.

Installation of drains for water disposal, improvement in garbage disposal, cementing of paths and compounds/open yards of the housing projects, and provision of a common lamppost for the housing projects were other physical amenities that the communities indicated that they need. Housing improvements, which also emerged as another important need, should be integrated into the community development program. These improvements are particularly important for those living in dilapidated or improvised structures under congested conditions. Housing improvements could operate as an important catalytic force to mobilize the community resources for productive investment and to decrease waste in consumption.

At present, amenities are provided in an ad hoc manner. HWs should work together and formulate an integrated plan for upgrading physical amenities and for making housing improvements for each community. The provision of amenities can then be undertaken in accordance with this plan. Such a plan would also enable the communities to know beforehand what facilities would be available under the project for the next three years or so and what community contributions would be needed to implement the plan.

The communities identified a number of economic activities that they could undertake: consumer activity (for example, cooperative procurement of essential goods), thrift and credit societies, a community development fund, and skill-training and income-generating projects.

Health and health education programs would be greatly
facilitated by the selection and training of a community
health volunteer for a group of households not exceeding
about fifty (for best results there should be a volunteer
for about twenty-five households). Such a volunteer could
reach the poor and vulnerable sections of the community
and also administer first aid and treatment of minor ail-
ments within the community itself.

Finally there is a need for a more selective, poverty-oriented approach. Inadequate access to physical amenities has provided a common issue for community mobilization. But beyond obtaining common amenities and their
maintenance, the interests tend to diverge given the differentiated socioeconomic structures of the slum communities. Hence, a total or a general community approach is
likely to be less effective as a means of community mobilization. There is a need for a sharper focus on the
poorer households. The benefits accruing to the bottom
half (or even bottom two-thirds) should be adopted as an
important criterion in project formulation, implementation, and monitoring. This criterion suggests that greater
attention should be paid to the mobilization and organization of the poorer households in the slum communities in
which common amenities have been provided; that in the
selection of slum communities for future programs, greater
attention should be paid to those in which poor households
predominate, and that an attempt should be made to extend
the program to shanty communities, which are generally
worse off than slum communities. Even when technical
factors prevent the provision of upgraded physical amenities, these communities can be mobilized and organized for
self-reliant development activities and for the provision
of primary health care services.

NOTES

1. Shanty dwellers are often squatters on private,
government, or municipal land (usually on reservations
made for public purposes such as roads). Many of these
sites are marshy lands or canal/river banks that can be
inundated by floods. Dwelling units are typically impro-
vised/temporary structures made of various nondurable
materials. In contrast, slums consist mainly of permanent
structures (subdivided or in tenements) that are deterio-
rated, overcrowded, and lacking in basic amenities.

2. This chapter is a shortened version of an unpublished manuscript entitled "UNICEF Assisted Project on the
Environmental Health and Community Development in the
Slums and Shanties of the Colombo City: An Evaluation
Report," prepared by the authors in 1984. The financial
assistance provided by UNICEF for undertaking the study is
gratefully acknowledged.

7

Block Grants Project
in Surabaya

*S. Tarigan, Soedarjo, and
Saukat Sacheh*

INTRODUCTION

Surabaya, Indonesia's second largest city and port,
has a population of 2.5 million, though the actual number
of people requiring services at any given time exceeds 3
million. The city is gradually recovering its prewar
status as Indonesia's primary industrial center and now
accounts for about 30 percent of the country's jobs in
manufacturing. The city also services a hinterland of the
most densely populated rural areas in the world. Thus
land is scarce, contributing to traffic congestion and
high urban population density. Many kampungs (low-income
neighborhoods) have densities exceeding 1,000 persons per
hectare in single-story dwellings. Most kampungs are in
low-lying areas and experience frequent flooding.

Geography and density have created the conditions for
acute sanitation problems. Because Surabaya has no sewer
system, over 60 percent of human waste goes into ditches,
canals, and rivers. About 70 percent of the solid waste
is similarly disposed of. Only 17 percent of the people
have access to piped water, and an additional 25 percent
buy from vendors; the rest must use wells or open water
courses. Basic education needs are better met: About 95
percent of school-age children have access to primary
schools, though teacher shortages are estimated at 30
percent. Illiteracy is still between 20 and 30 percent,
primarily among women over 40 years and recent rural
migrants.

As regards health services, immunization is available
to only 40 percent of the under-fifteen population;
influenza affects 14 percent of the population and diar-
rhea/gastroenteritis another 10 percent. Infant mortality

125

is high for the city as a whole and undoubtedly higher for
kampung areas.

NATIONAL POLICY BACKGROUND

National development policy in Indonesia is based on
the concept of regional planning and growth, with the
overall objectives of equity and social justice. Cities
are viewed as having certain functions in overall regional
development depending on the characteristics of the region
as a whole. No specific policy can be characterized as
urban in focus or character. This is reflected in the
government structure, which has no agency specifically for
urban affairs above the directorate level. The Directorate for Urban Development of the Department of Home
Affairs is primarily concerned with the development and
guidance of municipal administrative structures.

However, an overall national program is aimed at
improving urban environmental conditions, notably sanitation. One component of this program is the Kampung
Improvement Programme (KIP), which provides upgrading of
neighborhood (kampung) structure. On one hand, KIP is
implemented at the city level, with national technical and
financial assistance, and it is thus not considered a
national program nor even a citywide program since it is
provided only to selected lower-income neighborhoods.
Despite its limited objectives, KIP coverage can be extensive, and in Surabaya it covers nearly one-half of the
city's population. On the other hand, since KIP in one
form or another is available to all Indonesian cities, it
might be considered as a de facto national policy for
certain types of urban neighborhoods.

Indonesia has no specifically urban social policy.
Social policy in areas such as health, nutrition, education, and community development provides for standardized
approaches to specific problems nationwide and does not
differentiate between urban and rural areas or conditions.
Social programs are typically delivered as packets containing a number of activities and are allocated evenly
across the country according to administrative divisions.
This allocation procedure has ensured that all parts of
the country have received all social programs but has also
resulted in lower population coverage for cities, in which
population per administrative division is usually considerable higher than in rural areas. Some of the supporting
activities of social programs, such as publicity, informa-

tion, or training, are also sometimes of limited relevance to urban conditions.

Evolution of the Kampung Improvement Programme

Although it has colonial antecedents, the modern form of KIP began in 1969 in the cities of Jakarta and Surabaya. The program began on a self-help basis, with the city government providing 50 percent of the financing. Although this form of KIP is still being implemented in Surabaya, the program has been expanded considerable since 1973 with the assistance of the World Bank and the Asian Development Bank and with bilateral assistance. Responsibility for financing the program also shifted to national and city governments. Although changes in the source of funding and expanded coverage reduced the role of communities in KIP, they did enable neighborhoods to receive KIP irrespective of the financial capacity of the population. Expanded funding also enabled standardization of components such as drains and roads and the inclusion of facilities such as health clinics and primary schools.

In the late 1970s the objectives of KIP began to be expanded to include social and economic factors in neighborhood development as it became clear that physical improvements alone did not necessarily lead to socioeconomic improvements. The present conception of KIP is thus KIP terpadu (integrated KIP) which includes social and economic components coordinated at the city level.

Repelita 3 (Third Five-Year Plan) Experience

Major lessons learned from examining the delivery of urban social services in Repelita 3 were concerned with coordination and the adaptation of nationwide programs to urban conditions. Indonesia has planning boards at the national level (Bappenas, the Badan Perencanaan Permbangunan Nasional or National Development Planning Agency) and provincial and city levels (Bappeda, Badan Perencanaan Pembangunan Daerah or Provincial/Municipality Development Planning Agency) to approve and coordinate the activities of all sectoral departments at the level in question. However, actual planning and program formulation are done individually by sectors. In other words, sectoral agencies prepare standardized packets in accordance with national allocational guidelines; these then are sent to

Bappeda to be combined into an overall annual program for
a city and passed on to the province. The provincial
Bappeda performs a similar exercise and passes the provincial program to Bappenas for final approval.

Since this process involves allocation or programming
and not planning, the UNICEF-assisted program personnel
attempted to influence city allocations by coordinating
the sectors involved in special efforts for the selected
KIP kampung, to ensure priority for the selected neighborhoods. At the city level, this scheme worked reasonably
well after some initial problems; however, at the provincial and national levels, the relevant sectors often had
different allocational priorities. The sectors were also
particularly reluctant to allocate additional packets
required to ensure full coverage of the selected neighborhoods.

The UNICEF-assisted kampung program was initially
implemented in four cities--Surabaya, Ujung Pandang, Yogy-
akarta, and Cirebon. In 1983 the program was expanded to
also cover Medan, Semarang, and Bandung. Further expansion to four more cities is scheduled for 1985. Demand
for the program is high among other cities. Expansion in
1983 was based on the methodologies developed in the initial four cities. Relatively few problems were encountered beyond those that effect community-level programs
generally.

GENESIS AND EVOLUTION OF THE PROJECT

Since 1979, UNICEF has been supplying funds for Block
Grants Project in Surabaya, with initial delivery of funds
beginning in 1980. The funds have been used entirely for
projects formulated and implemented by the residents of
low-income kampungs. Over the course of the Third Five-
Year Plan, the program has enjoyed strong political support from national and local governments, though it has
not always been possible to translate this support into
effective implementation, usually because of labor shortages at the municipal level. Other significant constraints include limited management capability at the
community level and community perceptions that do not view
infant mortality, nutrition, and sanitation as significant
problems.

These constraints notwithstanding, the Block Grants
Project can be considered an overall success as measured
by increased community awareness of social problems, grow-

ing levels of participation in kampung projects, and mobilization of community resources. The program has also
contributed to the development of a useful forum for
intersectoral coordination. Furthermore, the project has
demonstrated replicable mechanisms for implementation of a
convergent Kampung Improvement Programme (KIP) consisting
of physical and social components and has led to improved
maintenance of physical components in most of the concentrated kampungs. Until 1983 when significant expansion
occurred, the program had been implemented in seven kampungs selected by the city government from among areas
covered by KIP.

Overview of the Project

Block grants are best viewed from the perspective of
UNICEF's overall assistance to urban programs in Indonesia. A general objective of this assistance has been to
develop mechanisms for convergent delivery of basic social
services for children and mothers among the urban poor.
Since the bulk of services are delivered through government sectoral agencies, block grant assistance is necessarily supplemental.

The manner in which block grants have been supportive
has been modified over the course of Repelita 3, but, with
varying emphases, four objectives have been present
throughout: (1) to compensate for deficiencies in sectoral coverage; (2) to assist in the delivery of basic
services through enhancing community participation; (3) to
encourage flexible and innovative local initiatives to
overcome problems peculiar to particular areas; and (4) to
enhance local administrative and implementation capacity.
The midterm review of the urban program generalized these
objectives as a gradual decentralization of the development system aimed at linking national sectoral programs at
one end with community-based development at the other.

Administratively, convergence of delivery and attain-
ment of the other objectives were to be facilitated by a
coordinator chosen from among the senior municipality
staff in Surabaya--the head of the Health Department. In
addition to coordinating the delivery of sectors other
than his own, this individual was expected to involve
himself actively in the enhancement of community participation to support sectoral activities and to respond to
local needs. Block grants provided the justification and
necessity for this frequent and detailed involvement in

kampung affairs. Block grants also differentiated the
concentrated kampungs by requiring a special programming
process apart from the established programming exercise
carried out for the city as a whole. This process
included sectoral programming and produced special sectoral submissions from the concentrated kampungs.

During the initial stages of the program, the process
leading to achievement of the objectives was clearly
stressed. Participation of communities and sectors in the
programming exercise became the operational objective, and
the program came to resemble closely a community development effort whose success was measured by levels of community participation. This emphasis on process necessarily
diverted attention from the content of projects and justified funding of some activities that, although highly
participatory, were very indirect routes to the overall
objectives of UNICEF assistance and at times of question-
able utility to kampung residents. Even though a preoccu-
pation with the process may have obscured substantive
objectives, it did provide an invaluable experience and a
clear awareness of the obstacles to the delivery of services. Most important, the early experience resulted in
replicable programming and delivery mechanisms for block
grants.

Funding of the project came entirely from UNICEF,
though the national and city governments did provide some
of the staff and office space. During the 1980-1984
period, 43 percent of block grant funds have been spent
for garbage removal projects, 21 percent for kindergartens
and playgrounds, 22 percent for community centers, 6 percent for public libraries, and the balance for income-
generating projects, sports equipment, and so on. On the
other hand, 30 percent of sectoral projects consisted of
primary health care, school health, training, immunization, and water supply; 19 percent of nutrition; and 51
percent of supporting activities such as nonformal education, community development, and other operational support
to build management capacity of the local government appa-
ratus.

In the master plan of operations, the implementation
of the urban program only stressed the importance of local
government capacity building on surveys/studies and pro-
gram/project formulation exercises, which was an extension
of earlier cooperation with Directorate of Urban and
Regional Planning in the field of training for urban
social planners. At the same time, significant amounts of
money were earmarked for direct assistance to an initial

four cities, with possible expansion to seven. Responsibility for allocation and management of these funds was assigned to a steering committee. Funds would be transferred directly to the cities based on the results of programming workshops, and each city would have a coordinator to oversee activities at that level.

The steering committee has yet to be established, primarily because of organizational changes within the Ministry of Home Affairs. The functions of this committee have been assumed by the Directorate for Urban Development (Binakota), which as secretariat of the technical committee now handles the actual allocation of funds. Binakota also arranges the annual sectoral meeting between city officials and national departments to ensure that city sectoral proposals for the concentrated kampungs are included in project budgets.

At present, the urban program has become almost entirely a Department of Home Affairs activity. This can be attributed largely to the administration of block grants, which have been seen as requiring frequent monitoring and which require detailed information on a large number of novel projects. This is a positive development, one that has changed Binakota's orientation from routine administrative supervision to active promotion of social services to the urban poor. The effect of this activist orientation can be seen particularly in the nationwide physical KIP, which now includes the processes of integrated delivery of services and community participation.

Block grant programming must pass through a formidable number of governmental layers and agencies (see Figure 7.1). Even though efforts have been made to streamline the administrative aspects of the process, approximately six months are still required between the start of community meetings and the transfer of funds to the city.

Project Administration

Beginning with the level of initial community meetings and moving upward involves the following levels and agencies. Rukun Warga/Rukun Kelaurga (RW/RK, neighborhood association) is an established administrative subdivision; it is not a governmental level as such but a legally established neighborhood association. Its head is elected but unpaid and works on a part-time basis. Some administrative functions are undertaken at this level, notably management of garbage collection in some cities. This

Figure 7.1 Urban programming and implementation structure in Surabaya

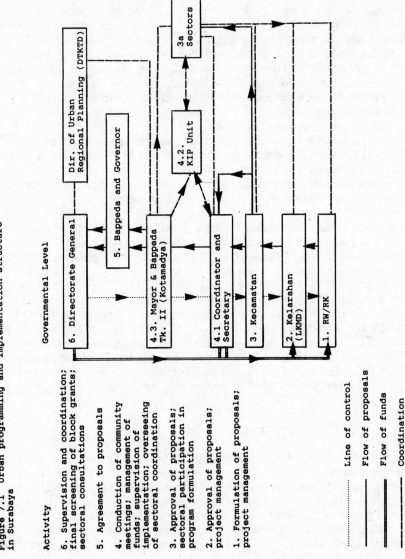

Activity

Governmental Level

6. Supervision and coordination; final screening of block grants; sectoral consultations

5. Agreement to proposals

4. Conduction of community meetings; management of funds; supervision of implementation; overseeing of sectoral coordination

3. Approval of proposals; sectoral participation in program formulation

2. Approval of proposals; project management

1. Formulation of proposals; project management

.... Line of control

————— Flow of proposals

▬▬▬▬▬ Flow of funds

––––––– Coordination

unit typically consists of 400 to 800 households, or 2,000
to 4,000 people and is frequently the unit of coverage for
block grant projects. In Surabaya these associations are
well-developed institutions, and most block grant projects
are developed and implemented at this level.

The kelurahan (village) is the lowest level of the
formal administrative hierarchy, and its head, the lurah,
is a civil servant. A wide range of local activities are
managed at this level; the lurah is responsible for coordinating all sectoral and development activities in his
area. An active lurah with an informal approach is often
the key person in the success of block grant projects,
whereas an obstructionist lurah can defeat the efforts of
the most cooperative and energetic neighborhood groups.

In the programming process a kelurahan-wide meeting
is held to discuss and ratify the proposals from the RWs.
In most cases this meeting merely compiles and standardi-
zes the proposals for the lurah's approval and submission
to the next level of government. In a few cities with
active coordinators the kelurahan meetings provide a forum
for elaboration of the program's goal and for refinement
of proposals.

Lembaga Ketahanan Masyarakat Desa (LKMD, or neighborhood resilience council) is perhaps best translated as
village social council, the term for the organization it
replaced. As a legal entity, the LKMD through its ten
sections is supposed to be responsible for all social
activities in the kelurahan. Its membership is voluntary
and unpaid, and an office is usually provided by the kelurahan. All block grant projects usually are considered to
be under the supervision of the LKMD or one of its sections. The LKMD in theory provides an established organizational potential for implementation of local projects
and in some cases is a very effective group. The LKMD
also provides a legal and political umbrella for innovative activities.

The Family welfare organization (PKK) is formally one
of the LKMD sections, though efforts are under way to
elevate it to a separate entity. PKK is by far the best
established and most active of semiofficial kelurahan-
level organizations, almost invariably more so than its
parent organization, the LKMD. Headed by the lurah's
wife, the PKK is a women's organization, though as its
name suggests its objectives and activities are not solely
concerned with women. The organization participates in
the implementation of a variety of UNICEF-assisted programs. PKK also receives significant amounts of block

grant money, usually for a variety of income-generating projects and/or for skills development. In some cities these projects have included good links with sectoral programs, such as cases in which the proceeds from economic activities are used to extend the supplementary feeding program.

The kecamatan (subdistrict) is the largest of a city's administrative divisions and is composed of a variable number of kelurahans. Some city-level dinas or departments have staff posted at this level, notably health, nonformal education, and sports. This level is not a unit for block grant allocation or management but is important since sectoral participation in programming begins here. It is also presently the final stage of programming prior to overall approval by the city government. Proposals are submitted separately for sectoral and block grants at this level. The kecamatan is currently the unit selected for handling intensive programs within the city. Coverage within the kecamatans varies from city to city, ranging from two to all kelurahans.

In the kotamadya (municipality), lokakaryas or programming workshops were a prominent annual feature for the first three years of the program. The workshops were attended by representatives from all administrative and community units involved in the programming process, including sectoral representatives from the KIP unit and city and provincial Bappedas and national-level staff from the Binakota and UNICEF. Usually about 100 people attend. The purpose of these meetings was to examine the proposals submitted through the kecamatan for practicality, accordance with guidelines, suitability for block grants, and acceptability for sectoral submissions.

In the initial stages of program development, lokakaryas were undoubtedly a useful and necessary forum for advocacy, coordination, culling and refining (for block grants), and standardization (for sectoral proposals). These objectives were not always fulfilled for the following reasons.

1. None of the community members involved in initial project formulation attended the workshops, thus precluding direct feedback. With the exception of representatives of the LKMD and PKK, all in attendance were government officials.

2. The communities' perceptions of problems often differ considerably from those of program planners. Altering these perceptions is a major community development objective. However, the perceptions of poor communities

are too firmly rooted in objective conditions of powerlessness to be readily modified by lokakarya experiences.
Communities are nearly always inclined to propose activities in those areas over which they have some expectation
of control and immediate benefit.

3. In the lokakarya format, problem identification,
prioritization, and project development were derived from
data collected for the intensive areas. These expectations were seldom realized, partially because of the pro-
hibition of new proposals but, more important, because the
data were being employed too late in the program process.
The available data were frequently inappropriate or difficult to use. Annual data collection was handled by the
kelurahan, and although the data were accessible at the RW
level, they were secondary and highly variable in accuracy. The surveys conducted by the city with DTKTD assistance were more accurate but seldom included information
for units smaller than kelurahans.

4. The most intractable constraint is the social and
political situation of poor communities. The nature of
these situations varies between and within cities based on
a large number of historical, social, ethnic, and economic
factors. However, one feature common to all cities is a
national policy that all access to communities must be
through the established administrative hierarchy and that
development activities must be conducted in a manner that
contributes to the development and strengthening of that
hierarchy of administrative capacity. However, structures
whose primary function is routine administration are very
awkward channels for transmission of community and pro-
gram-specific advocacy of the types produced by lokakaryas. The heavy reliance on officials can also be counter-
productive to the objective of fostering community self-
reliance.

Lokakaryas have not been used since 1982. The decision to stop them was based primarily on these four con-
siderations; furthermore, it was aimed at reducing the
time between community participation and the delivery of
funds. The kecamatan is now the level for overall program
compilation. Examination of the operation of the program
during 1983 clearly indicates that the absence of lokakarya has reduced the time for the delivery of services.

The Coordinator, Secretary, and Municipal Steering
Committee. In accordance with agreements between UNICEF
and each city, the mayor appoints city-level staff to the
positions of coordinator, secretary, and member of the
Municipal Steering Committee. To facilitate convergent

delivery the coordinator chairs a city-level steering committee composed of the sectors receiving UNICEF assistance. This committee also has responsibility to oversee block grant activities, though in practice this function is solely the responsibility of the coordinator and secretary. In Repelita 3 these individuals received salary subsidies as compensation for increased workloads.

The steering committee and coordinator make up a nonstructural arrangement operating under the authority of the mayor in a fashion similar to that of the KIP unit. This setup has proved to be a workable and replicable arrangement, particularly for administering block grants. However, the arrangement relies heavily on individuals and short-term agreements: The coordinator's normal responsibilities necessarily limit the time available for block grant activities, and long-term support for implementation of the program thus remains problematical. On the other hand, in instances in which it is running smoothly, the program has demonstrated a flexible and relatively fast response to social problems. The role of coordinator has also attracted the attention of cities outside the program, and a substantial number of cities have requested that they be included.

A wide variety of factors affect the success of block grant delivery, but the characteristics and energy of the coordinator have proved to be a key variable during Repelita 3. The most important characteristic has been the coordinator's and secretary's willingness to participate in community deliberations and to maintain continuing awareness of local conditions. The extent to which coordinators embody these characteristics is clearly reflected in block grant programming and implementation, since the coordinator must both advocate projects directed to certain problems and assure himself of the feasibility of community initiatives. The position is time consuming and few successes are immediate; it is not surprising that a few coordinators prefer to manage the program from their desks.

The coordinator cannot participate in the majority of community meetings to prepare proposals and is therefore expected to further check the proposals resulting from lokakaryas and now kecamatans. In the past there has been extensive national-level participation in the checking phase. National-level intervention is currently being reduced as proposals have increasingly been prepared in accordance with guidelines of Ministry of Home Affairs. In some cases city officials appeared to be deferring deci-

sionmaking and field investigations to national-level
staff.

Department of Home Affairs. In the programming process, Binakota, in conjunction with the coordinators,
prepares specific guidelines and priorities for block
grants, usually annually, to accommodate the shifting
emphases of UNICEF but also in response to problems
encountered through monitoring activities. Binakota ini-
tiates the scheduling of the annual program cycle and
participates in the programming exercises, though the
extent of this participation is declining as the program
matures. Upon receipt of final proposals, Binakota
requests the necessary funds from UNICEF after satisfying
itself that the projects are viable and follow the guidelines.

Department of Public Works, Directorate-General Cipta
Karya, Directorate of Urban and Regional Planning (DTKTD).
For urban programs UNICEF has had a long and (before Repelita 3) exclusive relationship with this directorate.
DTKTD is responsible for national macrolevel planning and
assists provincial and municipal governments with the
preparation of master plans. It also provides technical
assistance for the collection and analysis of the data
necessary for these planning activities. The bulk of this
planning is spatial and oriented to physical infrastructure programs.

Though not an agency normally responsible for training, DTKTD's primary input to the program is the urban
social planning training course that has been conducted
annually in Bali for the last ten years. The course originally had little direct relevance to block grants; however, it has recently been modified to include community
participation in a programming module. The DTKTD activity
of direct relevance to block grants was the systematic
collection of data on the seven cities. These data were
then used to prepare multiyear programs for each city,
which are specific and detailed, though necessarily vague
about the contents of block grant projects.

UNICEF. As part of an overall program of advocacy,
UNICEF has supplied several inputs: (1) consultant services to Binakota and DTKTD, though the DTKTD position has
been vacant since 1982; (2) equipment and supplies for
national and city levels; (3) audiovisual materials; (4)
training in Indonesia and abroad for camats (civil servants who head kecamatans or subdistricts), and lurahs;
(5) funds for block grants; (6) salary subsidies for the

coordinator, secretary, and city staff involved in the
program.

BENEFICIARY PARTICIPATION

In accordance with the national policy, all organizations involved in programming and implementing the block
grant projects were official or quasi-official, with the
attendance of government officials. Formal and informal
participation of community leaders was nonetheless quite
high, particularly when project location was the issue.
Project sites were invariably chosen by the community in
meetings attended by the project coordinator.

In terms of block grants, the implementing agency was
the community itself. For sectoral programs, the community meetings decided on location of implementation but
had no choice of agency. Since all sectoral programs used
the cadre, the community provided the list of candidates
for training and thus indirectly influenced the choice of
individuals. Most projects used existing community leaders, all of whom had been chosen or agreed to by the community. Selection of project beneficiaries/clients was
done simultaneously with choice of project type and location since identification of target groups was necessary
to justify funding. Community resources were allocated at
the same time that the location was chosen. The resources
committed varied from labor to money, depending on the
type of project.

Participation by the poorest people as a group is
difficult in Indonesia. Administrators and the people
themselves are very reluctant, for political and other
reasons, to single out a group as poor. As a result kampung residents are very unlikely to point out a neighbor
to be part of a target group. In turn, members of disadvantaged groups do not demand for a service or assistance
in terms of such definitions. Therefore, the coordinator
must identify target groups, and he too is constrained to
use acceptably ambiguous terminology. In any event, target groups were identified but not with the precision that
foreign experts might have liked.

PERFORMANCE IMPACT

During its early stages, the program did not show a
clear focus as to the type of project receiving support.

Guidelines were gradually sharpened in response to field experiences as it became clear that certain projects could not be implemented or did not lead to anticipated objectives. Present program guidelines limit projects to three priority components: sanitation, direct services to children, and income-generating activities. Earlier guidelines did not mandate certain types of activities but attempted to limit certain uses of the funds allocated. The present guidelines are clearer, easier to apply, and more comprehensible to communities, though the choice of priorities is still under discussion.

Improved sanitation was a low priority objective in the early stages of the program and was seldom included in block grant proposals to some extent because it is a standard component of the physical KIP. The projects currently funded are provision of gerobaks (garbage carts), bak sampah (garbage bins), local drains, water-supply-related equipment, and project-support communications packages, though the latter are still being developed.

Waste and disposal management is a major problem for all Indonesian cities, particularly those in low-income areas. All cities lack adequate facilities and transportation for final disposal. Management of existing resources is usually poor. Block grants were used intensively in 1983 for acquisition of carts. It is too soon to gauge the success of recent efforts, but small past projects and KIP unit experience point to the several constraints. Maintenance is frequently poor and user fees inadequate to cover costs of repairs, particularly in very poor areas. Management of pickup scheduling at the community level is inadequate, with sporadic service reinforcing residents' natural inclinations to dispose of waste in drains and canals, and pick up by the city is poor. Public habits and lack of awareness of the consequences of disorderly disposal limit the usefulness of available physical facilities.

These constraints were usually discussed at length during the programming process and efforts were made to ascertain local disposal options as much as possible. However, even if these efforts have positive results, ultimate success rests in the hands of ill-equipped city agencies. On the other hand, the management and maintenance problems encountered by the physical KIP have often been attributed to lack of community participation in the planning process. Instead, the components are delivered and the communities left to figure out what to do with them. The block grant approach is intended to provide the

community with a sense of ownership, which will in turn
lead to better maintenance. The Surabaya experience has
shown that a participatory approach can lead to expanded
coverage and better mobilization of community financial
resources. In the short period of implementation, user
fees have already generated enough money to purchase additional gerobaks.

Water supply is a minor part of block grant projects
and limited to collection containers near wells or public
taps. Maintenance of these has been good. Direct services
to children have consisted of supplies for kindergartens
and playgrounds. Kindergarten supplies have been put to
effective use and are well maintained, and upgrading of
buildings has also been supported, with positive results
for children. Playgrounds have suffered from poor maintenance because of the limited support of the community.

During Repelita 3, a large number of small income-
generating projects were funded with block grants. Each
type of project faces constraints peculiar to the activity
and location. However, we can identify some general problems, which may be called structural, that all projects
face. Kampung residents seek a livelihood in an economy
that is basically static, beyond their control, and at
best expanding at the rate of population increase; it is
largely an economy composed of similarly poor people. Thus
marketing opportunities are not expanding in per capita
terms, and the best that income-generating activities can
hope to achieve is very marginal readjustments of a fixed
amount of resources.

Small increments can, however, have significant
impact on problems like child nutrition and health in
cases in which parents are aware of such problems. Income-
generating programs are important in cases in which sectoral programs provide information that cannot be utilized
because of a lack of resources. An example of how this
might work is a mother participating in the nutrition
program who would be able to obtain better quality food
with increased income. Fragmentary field observations
indicate that these linkages do occur, though how consistent and widespread they might be are unknown.

Income-generating projects also face a wide range of
operational constraints, which are perhaps best discussed
in the context of the specific activities funded through
block grants. For example, cooperatives have had only
limited success, and UNICEF-assisted cooperatives are no
exception. The major problem is management, the improvement of which requires time and personnel beyond the

resources of program staff. Perhaps because of agencies' reluctance to fund cooperatives, the majority of the block grant funded activities are running satisfactorily, particularly those managed by the PKK.

Workshops (Bengkel) funded in Repelita 3 include those for carpentry, welding, and vehicle repair. By block grant standards these involve large proportions of a city's allocation and, with the exception of those in Surabaya, have encountered great difficulties since their inception. The major difficulty is a lack of managerial and bookkeeping skills. Whether the necessary resources to overcome these difficulties are justified by the benefits of the activity is an issue under consideration. Skill training for youths is the primary benefit of functioning bengkels, and in Surabaya, the bengkels produce equipment for other block grant and sectoral projects.

Block grant assistance to small traders has provided some of the best linkages to sectoral programs such as UPGK (Usaha Perbaikan Gizi Keluarga or Family Nutrition Improvement Programme) and PKK, and funds have been allocated to further the activities of groups trained under these programs. The assistance provided to the groups is expected to be paid back to managing organizations usually the kelurahan/LKMD or PKK. These projects have been frequently monitored and two primary benefits result in cities in which the projects are well managed. All money is repaid with interest, typically at a rate of 2.5 to 3 percent a month, and the PKK uses this money for community activities, usually the nutrition program. The second benefit is an improvement in the capital position of the individual, who no longer is dependent on daily loans or credits at very high interest rates, usually 5 to 10 percent per day. Actual increases of income are very small and are unlikely to improve for the structural reasons outlined.

A good deal of overlap occurs between assistance to community centers and the rehabilitation of structures for kindergartens, though a few structures were not used for both purposes. These buildings are frequently in use for PKK activities and other community functions. The appropriateness of using block grant money for this purpose has been questioned because funds are available from other sources such as Inpres Desa (District Development Fund) for these. It was also felt that in some cases block grant support was used for nonessential aspects of the building. No such buildings were funded in 1983.

Other block grant projects primarily include provision of sports equipment, musical instruments, and libraries. these projects are very popular and almost invariably
are suggested first at community meetings. Discussions of
priorities and environmental problems at length over four
years have not in any way diminished their appeal. These
facilities initially formed a large part of block grant
projects and by 1982 were coming to resemble a sectoral
packet. They are now excluded from program guidelines
since the objectives they were hoped to achieve have not
materialized. The expectation was that sports and cultural activities, being highly participatory, would provide occasions for motivating the people, particularly
unemployed youths, to make environmental improvement. The
resultant patterns of cooperation would then be directed
to other social problems. In short, these were well-
established activities and were considered to be an easy
entry point. The fact that communities had already supplied these facilities without any of the anticipated
results should perhaps have injected a note of caution
into the expectations. In any event, none of the expectations was realized, and most of the sports equipment was
lost or broken. In defense of this type of support, in a
few documented cases sports activities did lead to cooperative efforts in other areas. However, the successful
attempts reflected intensive efforts by full-time community workers over an extended period of time.

Libraries were the other popular choice for community
projects. Assistance was provided for purchasing furniture and a book selection determined by the Department of
Education. These facilities are rarely used. Management
of the facilities has been difficult to arrange, and most
lurahs keep the books locked up to avoid their loss. The
books provided were also of limited interest to children,
the one group in poor kampungs that might have the time to
read them.

IMPLICATIONS OF EXPERIENCES

At the present time the urban social services projects are considered a part of the integrated KIP or KIP
terpadu. However, integrated delivery of physical and
social components has yet to be realized, though there is
widespread recognition of the desirability of such an
approach. The major obstacle to integrated, or even convergent, delivery is the existence of separate, parallel

institutional arrangements for planning and delivery, leading to separate programming and implementation cycles.

As a result of overseeing block grants implementation, the capacity of Department of Home Affairs' Directorate Binakota to facilitate the delivery of social services has clearly increased. The benefits of this capacity are not limited to UNICEF-assisted programs since the information and contacts from frequent communications with the field assist them in their other activities. Their most notable success has been their ability to establish self-sustaining programming methodologies, thus reducing the need for intensive national-level guidance.

However, some deficiencies can be identified. Although a monitoring system does operate, the incentives necessary to encourage kotamadya staff to develop more comprehensive and project specific information systems have not been found. It would appear that national-level agencies have limited ability to overcome local staffing inadequacies. Resources for activities such as camat-lurah training are limited and are applied piecemeal.

The major constraint on the allocation of funds is the limited management ability of communities and their leaders, particularly when community groups are being encouraged to undertake new activities. Future block grant programming should, therefore, incorporate the provision of management or bookkeeping skills deemed appropriate to local needs. The current practice in cities with innovative coordinators has been to drop projects whose success is problematical, and, in cities with less active coordinators, communities themselves are expected to figure out ways to overcome operational constraints. Both approaches reduce the effectiveness of the program, and more serious efforts should be made to support innovative projects.

Advocacy from outside the community has been a crucial element of program success throughout the program. These inputs, when available, have come from the coordinator of UNICEF and the Department of Home Affairs staff. The reduced need for these inputs is a measure of program success, but, should the program be expanded to new cities, existing personnel levels are inadequate, particularly in terms of assistance for daily implementation problems. The time of coordinators is limited, and all cities could benefit from increased support provided at the local level. The existing program cannot provide this support, and efforts should be made to provide such assistance.

All block grant money has come from UNICEF. The city governments are also committed to provide funds for administrative expenses, although actual payments have been sporadic. The block grant approach to enhancing community participation has proved workable for both the UNICEF-supported program and other government programs. As the program matures, becomes institutionalized, and perhaps expands, it would be appropriate for the government of Indonesia to ensure the long-term viability of the program by taking increasing responsibility for funding, as it has done for the Kampung Improvement Programme.

8

Improving Urban
Settlements for the Poor:
Case Studies of Dandora
and Chaani Projects in Kenya

James O. Kayila

INTRODUCTION

In its 1974-1978 development plan, the government of
Kenya noted that there was a massive drift of people from
rural to urban areas and that many of these people could
not find formal employment in their new environment
because they did not possess necessary skills. The urban
economy was not expanding fast enough to cope with the
large population growth. Thus the growing number of inhabitants placed an additional strain on available urban
services, and these people could not afford even a single-
room accommodation with shared facilities at the market
rent rates.[1] The only alternative accommodations were
squatter settlements that lacked basic standards of shelter and sanitation. In the late 1970s, one-third of
Nairobi's population was estimated to be in this category.
Existing arrangements for supplying urban houses over the
years do not seem to have solved the housing problem;
setbacks include not only the rapid population growth but,
more important, increases in building costs and shortage
of development funds.

As in other developing countries, the central and
local governments in Kenya initiated several projects to
improve the socioeconomic situation in urban settlements
inhabited by low-income groups. Such projects were initiated in Dandora and Chaani settlements. This chapter
attempts to examine the dynamics of implementation of
Dandora Community Development Project in Nairobi and
Chaani Upgrading and Site and Services Project in Mombasa.
The evolution of these projects is discussed, and their
main objectives and activities are identified. The performance of the projects concerning basic urban services

145

to the settlements and the extent and modes of community participation are also analyzed.

DANDORA COMMUNITY DEVELOPMENT PROJECT

A study carried out by the staff of Nairobi City Council in 1973 had recommended that formulation of a housing program was essential to meet the needs of the city, which was estimated to grow from about 600,000 people to between 3 or 4 million by the turn of the century. Such a housing program was to be based on standards affordable by the various income groups of the population. The report stressed the need to limit housing subsidies to the lowest-income groups and to maximize the use of inexpensive local building materials and unskilled labor particularly in connection with self-help schemes. It advocated a program that included an increase in the proportion of the city's total resources invested in private housing and the reallocation of public housing investment toward lower-income groups; improvement of existing squatter settlements and preservation of existing housing, except where those were hindering necessary public improvements; provision of sites with basic services to accommodate lower-income groups; and encouragement to aided self-help housing schemes, cooperative and private building companies, and individuals to provide housing under revised standards and regulations.<2>

The Dandora Community Development Project in Nairobi was the first comprehensive development effort in Kenya to provide shelter, community facilities, and other promotive facilities for income generation and was intended to benefit low-income urban dwellers. Formerly a private farm, the Dandora site was brought, subdivided, and laid out as a site and service scheme in which land and the basic infrastructure and garbage collection systems could be provided for people who would construct their own houses.

The project was divided into five phases involving 6,000 plots and was to provide, in addition to the traditional sites and services, community facilities such as public markets, primary and nursery schools, public open spaces, community and sports centers, and light-industrial buildings. The project plan also provided for adult literacy and cooperative efforts, as well as health improvement programs through maternal, child care, and nutrition activities. Thus, apart from the physical improvements of the dwelling houses, the project had built-in economic and

social components intended to raise the status of the
low-income target group. One other objective of the project was that in the long term, the technical assistance,
expertise, and experience gained in the project could be
used to guide the government and other local authorities
in planning and executing future low-cost housing projects
in an effort to cope with the rapid population growth and
the high demand for urban housing. The project was
planned to cost over 250 million Kenyan shillings (KSh)
and to benefit about 50,000 persons.

Although the site and service approach had been tried
since 1970 in Nairobi, Mombasa, Kisumu, and other towns,
the Dandora project was the first large-scale attempt by
the government of Kenya and the City Council of Nairobi to
implement a cheap solution to the shelter and service
needs of the urban poor.<3> The comprehensive nature of
the project and the determination and interest of both the
government and the local authority in Nairobi led the
World Bank to fund 55 percent of the project. The project
was launched in 1975, and by the end of that year section
heads in the project unit had already taken up their management duties.

Development Approach

Apart from the infrastructure and community facilities to be developed, each plot had to be provided with
either the usual wet core (toilet and shower facilities
and kitchen) or a wet core and one living room. The allotees were expected to develop their own plots in accordance with some predesigned plans, but variations were
allowed provided prior approval was obtained by the individuals concerned. More than 16,000 people applied for the
6,000 plots in Dandora and successful applicants were
selected by computer balloting. Each applicant was
required to produce a birth certificate, identity card,
statement of income (allowed range was between KSh 250 and
KSh 680 per month) and evidence of residence in Nairobi
for a minimum of two years. An applicant was also
required to be the head of a family, and persons who owned
other plots in Nairobi were excluded.

The allotees were to develop their plots gradually,
starting with one living room and building additional
rooms later. The allotees were allowed to lease some of
the rooms they did not want to enable them to earn extra
incomes, which they could use for loan repayments. Loans

of up to KSh 6,400 were given to the allotees to help them
carry out the construction.

Many of the allotees joined building groups to pool
their limited resources for financing construction. The
groups collected monthly contributions from their members
to finance construction of one room at a time. They also
pooled their materials and loans for better management.
The groups were also formed to share labor; members would
help each other to build. In Phase 1 alone, fifteen
building groups consisting of 158 members had been registered between March and December 1977. The Dandora Amal-
gamated Groups Society with fifteen members had also been
formed by December 1977 to facilitate smooth running of
the groups, to help in the construction of buildings for
community use, and to investigate individual group problems.<4> These groups played an important role in giving
social as well as financial support and cohesion during
the unfamiliar and difficult process of construction by
beneficiaries.

Project Performance

Despite a cost overrun of KSh 40 million caused by
delays, inflation, and improved designs for infrastructure
developments, the Dandora project is, on the whole, a
great success. The construction on only 10 plots in Phase
1 has remained incomplete, and 2 percent of the plots were
sold five years after the allocation. In Phase 2, improved
infrastructure standards for roads increased costs and
with them the cost allocation to the allotees. Despite
this, only 12 percent of the allotees in Phase 2 were in
arrears with their repayments and only about the same
percentage sold their plots. In other phases development
was continuing.

Social workers in the project unit have worked very
closely with the allotees, helping them obtain business
loans that have enabled them to improve their economic
status. A special welfare fund has also been set up to
help those who experienced exceptional financial difficulties in developing their plots. A number of nongovernmental organizations such as UNICEF, the National Christian
Council of Kenya, the Catholic Secretariat, and the Undugu
Society also have made contributions to augment government
and council efforts to develop the Dandora community. The
nongovernment organizations (NGOs) have provided adult
literacy classes, nursery schools, libraries, multipurpose

centers, and special adult skills training programs in the
area. Though it is difficult to quantify, a change can be
said to have occurred in the life-style of those who were
allocated plots and were living in Dandora. Some have
developed management capabilities they never had before
and can now obtain loans directly from banks and other
financial institutions to finish their projects or start
small-scale businesses.

A survey carried out by the project consultants,
Senga, Ndeti, and Associates between 1977 and 1980
revealed that nearly half of all dwellings on plots in
Dandora Phase 1 were fully sublet to other tenants and
that in only about 20 percent were the sole occupants
allotees and their families. The remaining houses were
partly sublet by owners.<5> Although the tenant population
is large, the longer the allotees stay at Dandora the more
likely they are to bring their family members to join
them.

It was also reported that most of the household heads
in Dandora were employed; a larger portion of the wage
employments were located either in the city center or in
the main industrial area. However, the location of Dandora in relation to work places required many working
residents to walk long distances or to spend a large portion of their income on transport. Overcrowding was also
reported; members of over 90 percent of all tenant households slept in rooms also used for cooking.<6>

Despite these weaknesses, nine out of ten households
had access to piped water. The residents also generally
agreed that they live in a relatively healthier place than
their previous residence. The rents paid by tenants
(around KSh 250 per month per room) are said to be higher
than anticipated, but this increase has helped enhance
incomes of the allotees, enabling them to meet monthly
charges. On the whole, therefore, the Dandora project has
succeeded in providing real physical, social, and economic
support for the urban low-income groups, and hence the
projects replicability was advocated.

Implementing Agency

A Dandora Community Development Department was established in 1975 within the City Council of Nairobi to
implement the Dandora project. In 1978 the department was
renamed the Housing Development Department (HDD). The HDD
has been the council's executing agency for the Dandora

development project as well as all other housing development programs undertaken by the local authority. The
department integrates management and finance and technical
and community aspects in its planning and implementation.
It has three principal divisions through which services to
the target groups are provided. It is headed by a director who is responsible to the council through a special
Housing Development Committee. The director is assisted
by a deputy who is responsible for personnel and legal
sections. Each of the three divisions is headed by an
assistant director.

The Administrative Unit is responsible for directing
and coordinating all activities for overall administration. Headed by the deputy director, the division deals
with budgeting and overall supervision of consul-
tants/contractors. It also interacts with other council
departments, government ministries, and departments on all
matters relating to programming and implementation of the
project.

The Technical Division supervises detailed planning,
engineering, and preparation of tender documents for site
infrastructure, wet cores, and community facilities. It
ensures proper supervision of construction stages and
provides technical staff with specific building skills to
improve performance and service delivery. The division
ensures that the workshop sheds are provided at reasonable
rents, and technical assistance is given in the form of
machine selection, maintenance of tools, and product
development. It also assists in bookkeeping, production
planning and marketing, and short-term capital loans to
new entrepreneurs.

The Finance Division is responsible for keeping all
project accounts, developing accounting and management
systems, preparing quarterly financial reports and annual
audited project accounts, operating and administering the
materials loan fund, and collecting monthly charges pay-
able by the allotees.

The Community Development Division is responsible for
publicizing the project and performing related public-
relations functions, soliciting and processing applica-
tions for residential plots for low-income city dwellers,
orienting and training allotees prior to the occupation of
the plots, working with families during construction
stages, and assisting residents in developing institutions
and programs to enable them to create a genuine and cohe-
sive community.

The Legal Support Unit, which falls directly under the deputy director, has a principal counsel. It works in liaison with the town clerk's department to provide legal advice and carry out legal work for the HDD. Its responsibility includes scrutinizing the consultants, contacting tender documents, and preparing offer agreements to the allotees and eviction notices for delinquent allotees.

Lessons Learned from Dandora Project

The success story of the Dandora project can be attributed to the allotees' readiness to provide shelter for themselves. The allotees have been motivated by the opportunity offered, and they had to work hard to own land and urban houses. Although the completed phases of Dandora tend to have more tenants residing than the number of allotees, the development of these houses has greatly helped to ease housing demand within the lower rent category in Nairobi. The acute shortage of low-income housing has enabled Dandora to attract people who are compelled to pay as high as one-third of their income for housing in Dandora. Despite this and the distance from work places, renting a house in Dandora has continued to be popular as city dwellers struggle to get some reasonable shelter for themselves.

The formation of building groups has demonstrated the effect of a cooperative approach in dealing with problems and issues faced by those who seek shelter in site and service schemes. It has also helped in generating a sense of belonging among the people who did not know each other or have affiliation before but who have been brought together with common problems and therefore needed to share experiences and expertise in finding solutions. The encouragement of social interaction and sense of community among group members in the project area helped to increase informal mutual assistance in the early stages of the project and facilitated the extension of group collaboration in activities unrelated to the project.<7>

When people attempt to solve their own problems rather than relying too heavily on the government or any other institutions, the latter tends to play only a peripheral role as a facilitator and a provider of guidance when necessary. In such situations, development objectives are achieved through the people's own initiatives.

CHAANI UPGRADING AND SITE AND SERVICES REPORT

In 1976 the government of Kenya and the municipality
of Mombasa decided to upgrade the Chaani settlement under
the country's World Bank-funded Second Urban Development
Programme, which included development projects in Nairobi,
the capital city, and Kisumu, the third largest town. The
Chaani project was to involve 1,485 plots including 941
existing structures and 544 plots for site and service. It
was the first integrated scheme initiated by the government and the municipality to bring about significant benefits to low-income population in Mombasa.

Genesis and Evolution of the Project

This project was initiated as a component of Kenya's
Second Urban Project. The aim of the Chaani project was
to replicate the urban shelter project implemented in
Dandora and to apply lessons learned from that to improve
the conditions in Chaani. Chaani was chosen because it
was the most densely settled and uncontrolled development
area with the lowest building quality in Mombasa. For
these reasons, it was rated as the highest priority area
for the implementation of an upgrading scheme. In fact,
Chaani represented a larger and more immediate problem to
Mombasa as was evidenced by reports of "bulldozer demolition" by the municipal law enforcement staff.<8>

Objectives

The broad objectives of the Chaani project were as
follows:

1. Settlement Upgrading. To provide basic infrastructure including paved and unpaved roads,
   water, and sewerage systems.
2. Site and Services. To prepare surveyed plots
   and provide them with water, sanitary facilities, and unpaved access roads.
3. Plots for Market Sale. To generate a surplus of
   plots to be serviced and sold on the open market
   to attract and promote mixed development and
   meet the low-cost housing needs of other income
   groups.

4.   Community Facilities. To provide primary
      schools, a community center, markets, refuse
      collection and disposal systems, and electricity
      for domestic use and for street lighting and to
      improve the effectiveness with which the exist-
      ing public health, nutrition, and family plan-
      ning programs are serving the urban poor.

The World Bank has been actively involved in financing similar projects in Kenya and other Third World countries and had been requested by the government to provide
resources to engage consultants in planning and formulating suitable project proposals for Chaani, Mikindani, and
Miritini in Mombasa under the urban program. The consultants carried out studies that assessed the needs in the
project area and made recommendations on the appropriate
strategies for the provision of site and services within
the context of slum and squatter improvement. They also
carried out physical and engineering plans for the study
area.
      The government agencies that collaborated in planning
and developing the Chaani program were the Ministry of
Works, Housing and Physical Planning, the Mombasa Municipal Council, the National Housing Corporation, the Ministry of Local Government, the Ministry of Lands and Settlement, and the Ministry of Finance and Planning.
      A loan agreement between the government of Kenya and
the World Bank provided that under the Second Urban Project the World Bank would finance 72 percent of the cost
of the project and the other 28 percent would be met from
local funding by the government.

Project Implementation

      According to the implementation chart for the Chaani
project, work was scheduled to start at the beginning of
1978 with land acquisition, aerial mapping and soil surveys, and detailed project designs; it should have ended
with the development of infrastructure, on-site services,
and superstructure so that by the middle of 1980 the project team could move on to the Mikindani site. The implementation period was charted to take thirty-one months.
However, the implementation progress has been slow, and
the project is already four years behind schedule. The
delay started with land acquisition and payment of compensation that took a long time to settle; this was followed

by delays in the recruitment of project staff and appointment of contractors for site mapping, surveys and development of site services, community facilities, and other
structures.

The delays in the implementation of the project have
had some serious financial consequences brought about
mainly by runaway inflation. Increases in cost caused by
the delays resulted in lower standards being adopted and
the elimination of clustered wet cores for the existing
structures. These changes will result in lower environmental standards than those originally planned.

Capabilities and Resources of Implementing Agencies

The functions of the Ministry of Works, Housing and
Physical Planning (MWHPP) in respect of the project
included physical planning, cadastral surveys, housing
policy, legislation, and budgeting and supervision of
expenditure on housing. The ministry also executed, where
applicable, construction work through the National Housing
Corporation. The Ministry of Lands and Settlement (MLS)
was charged with the acquisition of land for development
and with the valuation and assessment for compensation. It
was also responsible for the allocation of government
plots for development and the issue of title deeds for
land ownership. The Ministry of Local Government (MLG) was
responsible for overseeing and financing operations of
municipal, county, and town councils. It also advised and
assisted these local authorities on administration, training, accounting, and financial arrangements. The Ministry
of Water Development (MWD) is responsible for the development of water resources throughout Kenya and manages water
supply systems in a number of urban areas. It assisted
urban authorities by giving policy direction and development plans for water and sewerage installations and staff
training.

The Mombasa Municipal Council (MMC) was involved
through its Housing Development Department (HDD), which
was formed specifically to handle all matters relating to
housing development projects. This department has a
single committee, the Housing Development Committee (HDC),
whose members include the mayor, the deputy mayor, the
chairmen of other standing committees, the Mombasa district commissioner and the permanent secretaries, and
nominees from Ministry of Works, Housing and Physical
Planning, the Ministry of Local Government, the Ministry

of Finance and Planning, and the National Housing Corporation. This diverse membership ensures immediate linkages
and interrelationships between the agencies and the project. The committee cannot sit and deliberate on any
matter without government representation.

The nongovernmental agencies involved in the project
in one way or another include the Family Planning Association of Kenya (FPAK), the Medical Research Centre of
Nairobi, and the National Christian Council of Kenya
(NCCK). These bodies work within the community to provide
information related to the project and community training
and, in some cases, to lobby for funds for specific community activities from donor organizations.

The Housing Development Department, the main coordinating and implementing agency, has several sections that
include engineering, architecture and planning, quantity
surveying, community development, and communication. The
diversity of the disciplines required for the department
is intended to enable the team to look at all aspects that
would bring about an effective community development.
However, because of a shortage of qualified personnel and
restrictions on new recruitment, out of 104 established
posts for the department, 30 were vacant in June 1983.
The situation is likely to remain the same since the
embargo on recruitment by local authority was still in
force at the time of this study.

The only beneficiary organization in Chaani is the
Chaani Village Committee. There are fifteen members of
this committee under a chairman, and each committee member
represents about 250 plot owners. The Chaani Village
Committee was formed during the implementation of the
project and did not participate in the planning process.
Although the members were supposed to be elected by the
beneficiaries, they were actually nominated by community
development officers, in collaboration with the councillor
for the area.

The factors that led to ignoring the beneficiaries in
project identification are not stated by those involved.
One factor could have been the assumption by the planners
that the urban poor could not articulate their needs in
the best manner possible. Indeed, this was the predom-
inant feeling of some of the beneficiaries interviewed by
the author. The beneficiaries were not requested to contribute money, labor, or land. Most of the work was
executed by contractors with their contingents of paid
workers. However, the beneficiaries were expected to be

fully responsible for the physical improvement of their
houses.

Performance and Impact of the Project

The performance and impact of the upgrading project
in Chaani may be viewed from three main dimensions—
physical, sociopolitical, and economic.

Physical outcomes. The Chaani settlement was originally a scene of spontaneous and haphazard housing development whose layout lacked sound physical planning. Most
houses were constructed of cheap local materials. The
houses were owner built for self-accommodation, but extra
rooms were rented to other low-income persons working in
the industrial area at Changamwe and the Port of Kilin-
dini. Some of the structures were so closely clustered
that they posed serious health and fire hazards, apart
from making access extremely difficult.

In Chaani, the displaced owners were invited to apply
for plots and were subject to the same allocation procedures as other applicants except for the minimum-income
requirement. Most beneficiaries in this category felt
that the compensation given was inadequate. The project
provided for the allocation of plots to applicants by a
ballot system. Allotees of residential plots were to be
granted long-term leases of thirty years by the Municipal
Council. They were expected to reside on their plots, but
they could lease extra rooms to raise additional household
income. Sale or transfer of lots in the sites and services areas or in the infill plots within five years was
to be done only by the Housing Development Department,
which would pay compensation for improvements and either
reallocate the plot to another person or sell it on the
open market.

Although the plots are being surveyed and demarcated
and the owners have registered at a fee of KSh 600 per
plot, no allocation certificate has yet been issued to any
beneficiary. This delay has had several repercussions for
the beneficiaries: Those who wish to start building their
houses cannot do so; moreover, all major repairs to existing structures are suspended with the aim of providing
loans to owners to upgrade or build new structures in
approved materials. Though standards for buildings in the
project were lowered considerably, many beneficiaries
still find the cost of such materials as cement blocks too
high for them. The ban on repairs to the existing struc-

tures also led to the collapse of some of these during the
recent heavy rains in the region.

The Chaani area has a very weak soil structure, and
the engineering designs for the roads have to take this
into account. Compared to the original state of roads,
the completed network is indeed an impressive face lift
for the area. The layout is structured around a primary
distributor road shaped like a loop and provides major
internal circulation and connects all main neighborhoods
and community facilities. The Kenya Bus Service in Mombasa is already running a bus service through Chaani at
half-hour intervals throughout the week. This service has
gone a long way toward alleviating transportation problems
in the area. The residents interviewed were very happy
with the road network as completed and the bus service
operations.

The drainage ditches along the roads were constructed
to carry storm water and not domestic waste water or sewage. However, some residents empty their domestic foul
water into these storm water drainage systems. If this
situation continues unchecked, it is likely to result in
some serious environmental problems. Piped water supply
is another major infrastructure planned for the project
area. The original policy was to supply potable water to
all households through individual connections to meet a
consumption level up to some 70 liters per capita per day.
However, since the standard of most structures even after
upgrading would remain relatively low, it was necessary to
modify this objective. The site and service areas would
have their own on-plot connections whereas the upgrading
areas would have connections to shower and toilet units.
Each unit would consist of showers and toilets. Fifteen
such units were to be constructed.

These objectives have not yet been met, and the previous system of water kiosks still exists. In this system, individuals rent the kiosks from the Ministry of
Water Development and sell water at 20 cents per 20 liter
container. Other intermediate suppliers buy from them and
sell to domestic users. These intermediaries normally
wheel the water around in tins of 20 liters in handcarts
that carry 10 or more tins and sell these for as much as
60 cents a tin. The system is likely to continue until the
planned connections are available.

Social impact. The education policy for the area was
to enroll 85 percent of all school-age children. Four
primary schools were planned, and two have been completed.
The schools are of very high standard compared to what

existed previously. Though completed and ready for use, the schools are not yet operational, partly because of the lack of water and electricity connections. The program does not include the provision of any nursery and secondary schools, but sites have been reserved for these. Two day-care centers are housed in a council-acquired structure, and one is built on a self-help basis and run by the parents themselves. It is felt that one secondary school cannot adequately serve the need of the area.

The general policy on health was to improve the effectiveness of the existing health, nutrition, and family planning program serving the Kenyan urban poor. Support for the improvement of these services includes home visits, staff training, monitoring of nutritional status, prevention of malnutrition, and evaluation of benefits. The performance of the new facilities is yet to be seen. Although the construction of a health subcenter is complete, it is still nonfunctional. The new and upgraded centers will endeavor, among other activites, to provide preventive, curative, and environmental health services.

The upgrading project was intended to furnish loans originally estimated at a maximum of about KSh 24,000 per plot owner. When the loans are given, construction and upgrading are to be completed within eighteen months. However, the increase in construction costs and the limited time available might lead to failure to improve the situation of the urban poor in Chaani. Many people may be forced to sell their plots and revert to squatting in the neighboring areas. This development is indicated by the tendency of displaced households to opt to squat after mismanaging the compensation.

A multipurpose community center has been completed as planned and will start operating when water and electricity are connected. It will house the community library, and its activities will include literacy classes, youth development and women group activities, and sports activities. It could house a nursery school to be run by the council.

Two markets were included in the project plan: Each will cover an area of 0.8 hectare, including open space. One of these markets was about 90 percent complete by June 1984. The construction of the new structure is of a high standard compared to that of the previous one. The markets will provide stalls for enterprising beneficiaries in Chaani with the aim of improving their income levels.

The objectives for refuse collection and disposal included the provision of hard stands and storage bins and

the collection to be financed through the project. These
objectives have not been met, and garbage is still disposed of on an individual basis, by burning it or leaving
it to rot in heaps or ditches. Consequently, garbage is
still part of the Chaani environment, a factor common to
many urban environments in which systems for collection
and disposals are inadequate.

The plan provided for street and security lighting to
be installed at major communal and pedestrian access
areas, that is, on footpaths alongside roads and parking
areas. The poles for the lights, spaced 30 to 60 meters
apart, have already been installed and underground con-
duits laid. However, the connections have yet to be made
for the lights to start functioning. Nevertheless, the
beneficiaries interviewed were happy and had high hopes
that these lights would alleviate the security problems
within the area.

Unanticipated Consequences. Although only twenty-six
structures (4.2 percent) had to be demolished to make room
for infrastructure and services, the displaced beneficiaries feel that the compensation paid was insufficient.<8> They claim that they were facing hardships in
attempts to resettle. This situation might have been
compounded by the delays in issuing certificates of allotment to enable those who wish to build to start. The money
paid in compensation has lost value over the last five
years because of inflation. Large plot owners will not get
the same size plot but a standard size (350 square
meters). Those who had rented structures have also suffered loss of rent because of the subdivision of original
plots.

As a result of the ban on major repairs, some structures have collapsed completely, and some owners have
continued to live in part of the collapsed structures at a
fairly high risk. Moreover, the standards of building to
be applied in Chaani are still considered too high for
many of the poor who feel that their meager resources will
not enable them to buy enough cement blocks to build a
house within the given time.

Activities in upgrading have been delayed because the
letters allotting plots have not been issued. Of the
beneficiaries interviewed, 90 percent complained that the
most critical problem at the moment was their inability to
build, which to many meant continual loss of rent. The
morale of the beneficiaries was reduced further because
promised loans were apparently not forthcoming. The project unit division for community development assured them,

however, that the loans would be given later. However, the
time and the amount of loans were not specified because
they were being reexamined in the light of other problems.

Primary schools, a clinic, and a community center,
which were reportedly completed about a year ago, remained
nonfunctional at the time of this study. Similarly, the
council had not started maintenance of the newly constructed road network in the area. Some parts of the
roadside drainage system were already getting filled with
sand, thereby defeating their original purpose (that is,
to act as a storm water drainage system to keep the place
free of stagnant water that could be an environmental
nuisance.)

It was originally announced that a wet core and
kitchen would be built for the site and services infill
plots and clustered wet cores for the upgrading area. The
beneficiaries have been informed that these will now not
be possible and that those concerned should build their
own wet cores and kitchens. It was not clear whether the
cash loan levels would be raised to cover the cost of
these units now to be built on a self-help basis.

CONCLUSIONS

The 1978-1980 period for the Chaani project implementation was long enough to see it completed. As a result
of delays, cost overruns will be inevitable unless the
original design standards are reduced or some work eliminated. The beneficiary morale may also be weakened, which
will affect the shelter improvement process by the plot
owners.

When the Second Urban Project in Chaani was launched,
it was hoped that successes and lessons of the First Urban
Project at Dandora would be easily applied. Little seems
to have been thought about how these lessons could be
adapted to suit the socioeconomic conditions of Chaani to
enable the implementing agencies to adopt approaches for
successful project implementation.

For example, the Dandora site had almost no community
base before the start of the project and most of the
people allocated plots were drawn from other areas of
Nairobi and met for the first time after the allocation
was done and the permission to move to the site granted.
In no way could the community have been organized and
involved in the project formulation stages since it just
did not exist. Only after taking their plots did the

beneficiaries start to organize themselves into building
groups to pool financial resources and labor for construction work. The project community development staff then
helped the groups to organize their efforts and gave them
technical advice in the organization and management of
their affairs. In Chaani, neighborhood communities had
existed long before the project initiation, and they
should have been fully briefed and involved in all stages
of project planning and management. The lack of their
adequate involvement in project formulation and implementation was a key factor that impeded successful implementation of the project.

In Dandora, the neighborhood committees under area
chiefs were increasingly used to ensure an orderly life
and security in their areas. These committees have helped
settle minor disputes between individuals, and the communities have joined hands with the government to ensure
that law and order is maintained in the area for their own
benefit.

In the past, planners tended to ignore the public
completely when formulating complex projects designed to
benefit the community. They always thought that they knew
what the people wanted and acted as judges to determine
and design how to go about implementing this. However,
the modern approaches to planning for public services call
for a complete understanding of the social and economic
environments and the constraints and opportunities existing at the time of evolving a project. Given the availability of limited resources, especially finances, the
project beneficiaries logically are involved so that both
private and public resources are coordinated and applied
to produce maximum results.

For community participation to be viable, however,
sufficient groundwork must be undertaken involving the
release of information and explanation of the proposals to
the communities targeted. This kind of awareness must be
created during the early stages of project management so
that the beneficiaries know their roles in the project.
The implementing agencies have to identify the opportunities and specific areas of popular involvement that contribute to the success of the project. These decisions
should have been a function of the project management team
of the Mombasa municipality, but seemingly the institutional arrangements for managing the project were only
made after the project had been formulated, and thus a
firm base for participation could not be established.

NOTES

1. For an overview of urban service deficiencies in Kenya, see James O. Kayila, "Urban Management in Kenya," in G. Shabbir Cheema, ed., Managing Urban Development: Services for the Poor (Nagoya: United Nations Centre for Regional Development, 1984), pp. 127–140.
2. City Council of Nairobi, Nairobi Metropolitan Growth Strategy vol. 1 (Nairobi: City Council, 1979).
3. Ibid.
4. Senga, Ndeti, and Associates, "Monitoring and Evaluation Study of Dandora Community Development Project" (Nairobi, 1980), mimeo.
5. Ibid.
6. Ibid.
7. Ibid.
8. "Kenya Second Urban Project," vol. 1, Government of Kenya, 1977.

9

Upgrading Olaleye-Iponri Slum
in Lagos Metropolitan Area

Paulina Makinwa-Adebusoye

INTRODUCTION

Persistent housing shortages in the Lagos metropolitan area in Nigeria have necessitated a radical departure
from the time-worn strategy of total slum clearance and
resettlement of displaced persons. After more than half a
century of resettlement schemes that made no appreciable
impact on housing and other needs of the urban poor, planners now seek to upgrade slums by infusion of municipal
services such as treated water and electricity supply.
Olaleye-Iponri, a vast slum in the Lagos metropolitan
area, is the first testing ground for this new approach,
which is further distinguished by its emphasis on neighborhood participation and self-help.
    Modern planning in the metropolis began in 1928 with
the creation of the Lagos Executive Development Board
(LEDB) in reaction to insalubrious environmental conditions that bred fatal epidemics.<1> Since then, a variety
of planning and management authorities have cleared slums,
built housing units, and provided sites and services for
thousands of residents in the metropolis. However, because
of continual massive in-migration, demand outstrips the
supply of services and the urban poor inhabit areas lacking in an adequately treated water supply, drainage, good
roads, dependable electricity, and areawide solid waste
removal and disposal facilities.<2> It has, therefore,
become necessary that "large scale slum clearance should
be postponed till a more adequate supply of housing was
available."<3>
    Activities to redevelop Olaleye-Iponri began in April
1983; these included widening and paving five major roads;
providing community clinics, a town hall, and a market;

providing public toilets, maintaining existing drains, and constructing additional ones; increasing the supply of pipeborne water; resettling some residents displaced in the course of implementing the project; and preparing service sites for prospective houseowners.

Since its inception the upgrading project has recorded several successes, notably the mobilization of neighborhood resources. From planning to execution, project directors involved the community through the bale (chief), the representative councillor (local government), and representatives of the already existing community development association (CDA) and the association of market women. In addition, the main storm drainage system, known locally as the "canal," has been redredged and widened with expected dramatic results. For the first time, most of the residents of this swampy slum do not need to vacate their homes during the rainy season.

The urban poor in Lagos tend to inhabit self-imposed segregated areas characterized by overcrowding and shortage or total lack of amenities. Other indices of poverty are low income, low nutritional status, and, more important, lack of access to power. This description was agreed upon at a recent National Conference on the Urban Poor in Nigeria.<4> After considering these indices and their interactions, the conference agreed that at 1984 prices the poverty line could be drawn at a monthly disposable income of 380 naira (N380.00)<5> for an average household of five. With this definition, between 53 and 60 percent of urban households in Nigeria are poor.

UPGRADING OLALEYE-IPONRI

With its haphazard layout and insalubrious environment, Olaleye-Iponri is typical of several other slums within the Lagos metropolitan area. The main objective of the upgrading project is to improve the quality of life of residents through implementation of project activities listed in the introductory section of this chapter. Specifically, the project aims at providing urban services to meet immediate needs of residents of Olaleye-Iponri, encouraging community participation through existing neighborhood groups such as women's associations and community development associations, which would help the poor become more self-reliant.

Choosing the Olaleye-Iponri Slum

As part of the implementation of the second phase of
the master plan, several slums were identified within the
metropolis. Olaleye-Iponri was chosen for upgrading
because of its easy identification within well-defined
boundaries and its central location, which makes it
readily accessible to participating government and nongovernmental organizations. In addition, its heterogeneous
inhabitants--a mixture of Yoruba, Igbo, and Edo migrants--
have an active development committee ready to participate
fully in any effort to upgrade their community. This sense
of common interests is no doubt brought about by shared
poverty and lack of urban amenities. In fact, the slum is
popularly known as Olaleye village.

Socioeconomic Setting

The Olaleye-Iponri slum is located off Western Avenue, a major artery that links the mainland at Ebute Metta
to Lagos Island. It is bounded on the northwest by Western Avenue, on the west and south by a railway track, on
the northeast by the Alaka Estate, and on the east by a
large earth drain, the canal, which separates it from a
high-class residential area, the Railway Yard. This slum
is characterized by overcrowded shanties built of corru-
gated iron sheets, planks, and plywood and set haphazardly
without adequate land for vehicular movement, drains,
ventilation, and natural light.<6>
     Pipeborne water is available in the area, but most
houses lack indoor plumbing. The few public water taps
are grossly inadequate for a population of about 20,000.
Electricity is available subject to incessant low voltage
or blackouts--a deficiency shared by other parts of the
metropolis. There is a community hall at Iponri. The two
existing markets are small, and many of the residents sell
assorted wares in front of their houses. Although there
are schools, churches, and mosques, the area lacks a post
office, police post, or fire station or any organized open
space for recreation. Facilities within housing units are
similarly inadequate. In Table 9.1 the existing conditions within houses in Olaleye-Iponri are summarized.
     The unsatisfactory method of disposing of domestic
refuse and human waste constitutes a major health hazard
for this area. Furthermore, the combination of shanties,
overcrowding, and the absence of a fire station increases

Table 9.1 Facilities in houses in Olaleye-Iponri, 1983

Facility	Number	% of Total
Kitchen		
Shared	624	82.87
Individual	17	9.43
None	58	7.70
Total	753	100.00
Bathroom		
Shared	695	92.30
Individual	48	6.37
None	10	1.33
Total	753	100.00
Toilet		
W.C.	33	4.38
Bucket type	273	36.25
Pit latrine	204	27.10
None	243	32.27
Total	753	100.00
Water		
Pipeborne water	287	38.11
Well	332	44.10
None	134	17.79
Total	753	100.00

Source: Table 6, Final Report on Olaleye-Iponri
Urban Renewal Plan, May 1984, mimeo., pp.15-16.

the danger of major fire outbreaks. In fact, one such
fire destroyed a large part of Olaleye village in November
1983.

A contributory factor to the general squalor of this
area is the tenant status of most residents. Nearly 90
percent are migrants to Lagos although many have been
residents for over thirteen years.<7> Many of these are
very poor, usually earning below N 2,000.00 per year, that
is, below the poverty line as previously defined. Their
educational level is also significantly lower than the
average in Lagos. Most of the residents are illiterate
and/or primary school dropouts. A 1983 survey of Olaleye-
Iponri revealed that of the total sample of residents
interviewed, 30.77 percent were illiterate whereas another
12.44 percent had not completed six years of primary
school.<8>

Legal bottlenecks have also contributed to the
squalor. Successive governments of Lagos state had failed
to approve building plans for the area thereby forcing
landowners to build shanties as a device to safeguard
ownership of land while also earning some revenue.
Consequent nonrecognition by the government is a contributory factor for the sparsity of amenities.

Participants

This new approach to urban renewal was spearheaded by
officials in the Urban Renewal Committee of the Urban and
Regional Planning Division of Lagos state and United
Nations Development Program (UNDP) staff who were con-
tracted by the United Nations Centre for Human Settlement
to work on the Lagos metropolitan master plan. They are
joined in this effort by officials from other Lagos state
ministries, specialized agencies, and UNICEF. Because of
the project's emphasis on community participation and
self-help, residents of Olaleye-Iponri, through their
community development associations, bale (chief), and
representative councillor (local government), are also
active participants.

CAPABILITIES AND RESOURCES OF IMPLEMENTING AGENCIES

From the preceding section on participants, three
groups of implementing agencies appear to be involved in
the Olaleye-Iponri project, namely

1. Nongovernmental organizations (NGOs), including the Olaleye-Iponri community development associations, and market groups and other residents.
2. State government ministries and specialized organizations, especially the Urban and Regional Planning Division, which acts as project catalyst and is supported by other relevant ministries and boards charged with the provision of services and other infrastructural facilities; and
3. International agencies such as UNDP and UNICEF.

The Division of Urban and Regional Planning is responsible for policy planning and for coordination of activities of other groups. Members of this division are protagonists of the new strategy, and, given their training, background, and enthusiasm to try a new approach, they are no doubt competent in managing the administrative work involved and have succeeded in imbuing residents of the target area with their enthusiasm.

Responses to questionnaires addressed to officials representing other state ministries and boards indicate that these are well-trained technocrats and experts in their chosen fields, capable of carrying out assigned project activities.<9>

UNICEF is well placed to perform all its self-assigned tasks directed toward women and children in the target area. Most residents know about the organization. Although UNICEF follows its own defined objectives, it interacts on a regular basis with the officials of the division of Urban and Regional Planning of Lagos state.

The heterogeneous residents of Olaleye-Iponri are united for the time being in their determination to join forces with the state and local government officials and any nongovernment organization to improve their environment. However, given the well-known inclination of urban Nigerians to view government as a Father Christmas, present enthusiasm may wane in the future. Indeed, the success or failure of the present project will depend largely on sustaining residents' present level of enthusiasm.

Coordination and Funding

All groups of participants are represented in seven working groups to execute specific tasks of the upgrading

project. Coordination of efforts is achieved through
regular meetings called by the Urban Renewal Committee and
attended by highly placed officials of all the cooperating
ministries and specialized boards, representatives of
participating nongovernment organizations, and representatives of Olaleye-Iponri residents.<10> The position of
the Urban Renewal Committee directly under the governor's
office rather than as an appendage of a ministry under-
scores the importance attached to this urban renewal
scheme. Thus placed, the Urban Renewal Committee can
readily avail itself of expertise from all state ministries and specialized bodies. For the same reason, the
committee is readily perceived and accepted as the overall
coordinating body responsible for not only the Olaleye-
Iponri project but also similar schemes in the metropolitan area.

Capital for project activities such as roads is provided by the state government through annual budgetary
allocations to the appropriate ministries and boards.<11>
NGOs and residents of Olaleye-Iponri also contribute in
various ways. For example, the Lagos State Market Development Board is the body responsible for funding, overseeing, and subsequently managing the proposed market,
whereas the proposed clinics will be funded by the Olaleye
and Iponri community development association. As its
contribution, UNICEF has earmarked up to N 10,000.00 per
year to equip each clinic when completed.<12> The sources
of funds for project activities are listed in Table 9.2.

Residents of Olaleye-Iponri contribute money, labor,
and materials to projects. To supplement efforts of the
State Ministry of Environment, which has recently completed a block of flush toilets, UNICEF aids landlords in
erecting vented improved pit (VIP) latrines by providing
technical advice; the landlord supplies materials and
labor. To further reduce costs, some residents have been
trained by UNICEF to build the special concrete slabs used
in their construction. UNICEF also sponsors volunteers
from the community to take short courses at the nearby
School of Health Technology to heighten participants'
awareness of environmental sanitation. Other important
sources of revenue are various rates, such as the water
rate, collected by the Lagos Mainland Local Government
Council from Olaleye-Iponri residents.

Table 9.2 Funding of Olaleye-Iponri project activities

Activities	Source of Funds
Market	Lagos State Market Development Board
Clinics	Olaleye-Iponri community associations. UNICEF spent up to N 10,000 per year per clinic for equipment.
Classrooms and library	Lagos mainland local government; State Ministry of Education
Roads and drains	Lagos mainland local government; Works Management Board; and Lagos State Ministry of Works (the environmental section)
Public toilets	Lagos mainland local government; Ministry of Works
Public water taps	Lagos State Water Management Board

Source: Final Report on Olaleye-Iponri Urban Renewal Plan, May 1984, mimeo., p.35; P. K. Makinwa-Adebusoye, "Survey of Participating State and Local Government Officials," Olaleye-Iponri, Lagos, 1984.

Political Support

Support for the upgrading scheme has been tremendous especially at the local level. This enthusiasm is readily explained by the fact that all community leaders were identified and fully involved in defining broad policy guidelines and drawing up the program of action for the project. Formation of community development associations in most neighborhoods within the metropolis was encouraged and effectively utilized to gather political support at the grass-roots level for the former civilian government of Lagos state. These associations in Olaleye-Iponri serve as a ready forum for launching the urban renewal scheme. Furthermore, information elicited through informal discussion and the structured questionnaire reveals that many residents are aware of the advantages of this minimal renewal effort, which guarantees secure tenure and a healthier environment. Over 70 percent of those interviewed noted changes, especially the widened roads and the redredged canal, and 35 percent had participated in effecting these changes.<13>

Since the Lagos state government is, under existing laws, the lawful owner of all land within the state, the Olaleye-Iponri upgrading scheme is rightly perceived as being state government-sponsored, a fact that ensures support of NGOs and local participants. Under the political and administrative setup currently operating in the country, state governments are answerable to the federal government. It is therefore reasonable to assume that the decision of the Lagos state government to upgrade the Olaleye-Iponri area receives the political support of the federal government. Recent pronouncements originating from the Federal Ministry of Works show a shift from previous policy of construction housing units for the public. In the future the role of the federal government in urban housing will be limited to provision of site and services at affordable prices. Thus the days of federal government subsidies for housing appear to be over. Efforts to conserve existing housing through upgrading decaying residential districts, as in Olaleye-Iponri, is therefore to be encouraged.

BENEFICIARY PARTICIPATION

Before the project was undertaken, two prominent community organizations existed in Olaleye: the Council of

Elders and the community development committee (CDC). The
former consisted of representative elders from all areas
who came together periodically to deliberate on political,
social, economic, and other aspects of the community.
Decisions reached by the council were made known to the
entire community either through the district elders or the
bellman who announced the decisions from place to place.
The community development committee was more broadly based
and included people chosen from different districts. The
CDC acted as the intermediary between residents and the
state government by relaying its and Council of Elders'
decisions to the government while also making the government's views known to the community. On the advice of the
project planners (the neighborhood upgrading team of the
Division of Urban and Regional Planning), the CDC was
enlarged to include representatives of the Council of
Elders, market groups, women's organizations, and youth
and religious groups.

This enlarged CDC held consultative meetings with
planners to identify the needs felt by the community and
comment on proposed project activities. Objections raised
at one such meeting resulted in the shifting of the site
of the proposed market. Project planners and UNICEF officials also gave a series of lectures to Olaleye-Iponri
residents. UNICEF's concern for women and children of the
urban poor was visibly demonstrated by the daily distribution of food to afflicted residents after the fire in 1983
and through a series of meetings with women's groups on
aspects of public health.

Participation in Funding and Implementation

A strategy of total urban renewal for the Olaleye-
Iponri area would almost certainly have resulted in the
evacuation of present residents who could not be expected
to afford the price of newly laid out plots or decent
housing of the kind public authorities and private devel-
opers would choose to build. This realization is one
reason for residents' present support of the continuing
improvement scheme. The fact that most residents find
Olaleye-Iponri a convenient place to live is also important.

Most of the land in Olaleye-Iponri was privately
owned by a few families who sold or leased part to present
residents. Owners of prime property (in the heart of the
metropolis like that in Olaleye-Iponri) on which stand

unapproved buildings (those built without prior government
approval) have good reason to be skeptical of urban
renewal efforts because they fear that they could lose
their property to the government. In the Olaleye-Iponri
area, however, landlords as members of the community
development association were party to the decisionmaking
process from the planning stage to the adoption of program
activities. They are, therefore, aware that the project
poses no threat to landed property and that tenants are
assured of continued occupation of rented units at present
low rates.<14> Whenever it has become necessary to
acquire land for public buildings such as clinics and
market stalls, consultative meetings have been held and
owners have been allocated new, comparable sites in the
area. In a few cases in which no new site was available
in the immediate vicinity, owners have accepted land allocations elsewhere within the Lagos metropolitan area. A
good example is the case of the African Church, which has
been allocated another piece of land outside Olaleye-
Iponri to build a church house. In short, the solidarity
being shown reflects the residents' perception of present
activities as immediately beneficial.

Effective participation of Olaleye-Iponri residents
in the management of ongoing activities is ensured through
membership of five to seven community-nominated persons in
each of the seven special task forces identified in Table
9.3. Each task force is responsible for one or more of
the following areas: (1) roads, water, transportation, and
electricity; (2) the community hall, clinic, and public
toilet; (3) market and day-care centers; (4) recreational
areas; (5) relocation and land matters; (6) finance and
community relations; and (7) primary school. The Finance
and Community Relations Committee has the largest number
of community representatives; twelve members of the community including the bale (chief), the councillor (at the
local government level), the head of Market Women's Association, and other acknowledged community leaders are
members of this committee, which also includes officials
from the Ministry of Local Government and Community Development and the mainland local government.

Motivation for Participation

Residents of the Olaleye-Iponri area currently are
strongly motivated to participate in project identification, implementation, and evaluation. The series of pre-

Table 9.3 Responsibilities of groups participating in the Olaleye-Iponri Project

Project	Implementing Agencies	Work-Monitoring Agencies
Roads and drainage	Olaleye-Iponri community; Works Management Board (Ministry of Economic Planning and Land Matters) (MEPLM)	Community development committee (CDC); Works Management Board
Refuse disposal	Olaleye-Iponri community; Waste Disposal Board	CDC; Waste Disposal Board
Water	Ministry of Environment; Water Board	Water Board
Transportation	Ministry of Transport; Works Management Board	Ministry of Transport; Works Management Board
Community hall	Local contractor; Olaleye-Iponri community; Some UNICEF assistance	MEPLM; CDC
Clinic	Ministry of Health; Local contractor; Olaleye-Iponri community; UNICEF	MEPLM; CDC
Public toilets	Olaleye-Iponri Community; UNICEF; Mainland local government	CDC; UNICEF; Mainland local government
Market	Olaleye-Iponri community; MEPLM; Market Development Board	CDC; Market Development Board
Daycare center	Olaleye-Iponri community; UNICEF	CDC; UNICEF
Playgrounds	Olaleye-Iponri community; Ministry of Youth, Sports, Welfare	CDC; Ministry of Youth, Sports, Welfare
Electricity	Ministry of Works; Electricity Board	Electricity Board

Source: Compiled from Neighbourhood Upgrading Project, Olaleye village, Interim Report, May 1983, mimeo., pp. 37-38.

project lectures, a film show, and consultative meetings
between government planners, NGOs, and the Olaleye-Iponri
community development committee and Council of Elders
ensured that tenants and landlords fully grasp the meaning
of the type of urban renewal planned for the area and its
effects on various groups. Landlords welcome the renewal
scheme because it does not threaten their property whereas
tenants are aware that the renewal scheme will not lead to
any increase in rents in the immediate future or, worse
still, forceful ejection from their dwelling units.

Furthermore, the subcommittees in charge of various
project activities include, as members, community residents who are the immediate targets and beneficiaries,
thus making it obvious that participants are primarily
helping themselves through the improvement of their community. For example, the market committee includes market
women who will be allocated stalls when the proposed market is built.

The tremendous and highly visible impact of some of
the ongoing activities under the scheme is also a strong
motivating factor. One example will suffice: Men and
materials from the State Ministry of Environment have
recently reopened the large earth drains that for years
had been silted with refuse and human waste. The immediate result is that during the year's rainy season no family living in the traditionally flooded parts of Olaleye-
Iponri had to vacate its house as in previous years. The
inexpensive, hygienic, and aesthetically pleasing VIP
latrines have similarly proved to be an instant success
with the landlords, some of whom have erected VIP latrines
in their houses to the obvious pleasure of tenants.
Finally, as responses to the survey of residents show,
Olaleye-Iponri residents have become highly motivated
because of the newly found sense of pride in their community as a result of the upgrading project.

PROJECT IMPACT AND POLICY IMPLICATIONS

Project Impact

To date, few of the major activities planned for the
upgrading of Olaleye-Iponri slum have been fully
implemented. It is, therefore, too early to judge the
success or failure of the project by specific activities.
However, one achievement is the adoption by the state

government of this new strategy of minimal urban renewal,
which provides upgrading by introducing basic infrastructural facilities and public utilities in place of the
usual total urban renewal; the latter policy would have
necessitated evacuation of the inhabitants of the area.
The beginning made on some activities is also impressive.
As an emergency measure to eliminate some of the worst
health hazards, a block of public toilets has been erected
near the market. At the same time as the public toilets
were being installed, UNICEF officials were assisting
individual landlords who could afford them to build VIP
latrines in their houses. The first of these VIP latrines
was commissioned with great publicity and fanfare, and it
has been followed by the installation of several more in
private houses.

As already mentioned, the major earth drain lying
along the northeast/southeast boundary of this slum has
been redredged with the result that all the habitable
parts of the Olaleye-Iponri villages are now dry land, and
no residents have been forced by flooding to evacuate
their homes during this year's rains.

The dramatic impact on the Olaleye-Iponri areas of
both the siting of the public and private toilets and the
opening up of the earth drain cannot be overemphasized.
Besides reducing health hazards and generally improving
living conditions, residents perceive these projects as
demonstrations of the positive impact that the intervention of well-meaning outsiders can have in a slum area.
These projects have also generated several positive though
intangible consequences, notably the willingness of residents to cooperate (demonstrated by donations of cash and
materials) with any government or nongovernment organization that may express a desire to ameliorate the living
conditions in the area. In fact, this project has succeeded in mobilizing community resources usually outside
the reach of established government agencies.

Visits for project identification, consultations, and
the ongoing activities have together had tremendous impact
on residents' outlooks. A new social orientation can now
be found among Olaleye-Iponri residents, which emphasizes
the creation of a salubrious neighborhood. For example,
since the completion of the public toilets and the reopen-
ing of the drain, individual landlords in the community
have established vigilant groups who mount a nightwatch to
ensure that residents do not dump human waste substances
in the drain. As a sign of the new sense of pride in the
neighborhood, some landlords have rebuilt their houses

with more solid material in attractive and comfortable
designs.

Policy Implications

Because a very large proportion of Lagos state residents live in substandard conditions,<15> the lessons
emerging from the Olaleye-Iponri upgrading project will
obviously become useful inputs to future slum-upgrading
projects. The Olaleye-Iponri scheme is nonintensive with
minimal government intervention and aims at mobilizing the
entire community to action.

Although major public projects are not yet completed,
the achievements mentioned indicate that this strategy is
an economically sound and socially acceptable approach to
slum upgrading, which should be extended to other slums
within the metropolis. Since conditions in various
blighted zones differ, there will be need to study the
peculiar characteristics of such slums and modify the
Olaleye-Iponri strategy accordingly. However, the political, economic, and social gains accruing to the government
and the resident beneficiaries of the Olaleye-Iponri area
obviously weigh heavily in favor of slum upgrading instead
of total slum clearance and redevelopment, which tend to
aggravate housing problems. Results so far indicate that
the Olaleye-Iponri pilot scheme is worth trying in other
metropolitan slums.

Politically, this approach to slum improvement wins
friends for the state government, which is portrayed (to
Olaleye-Iponri residents) as a benevolent body interested
in improving the lot of the underprivileged class and the
urban poor.

In concluding, some cautionary concerns must be
voiced. Although the pilot scheme at Olaleye-Iponri seems
to have made a good start, it is too early to judge
whether the project is a success or a failure. The ongoing
project activities, especially the redredging at the canal
and the increase in the number of toilet facilities, have
brought about some improvement in the living conditions of
the people. This benefit is short term; for it to be
permanent, both participating agencies and beneficiary
participants need to keep up their initial enthusiasm and
commitment to the scheme.

Project organizers must be aware that the provision
and maintenance of services for the urban poor may lower
the tempo of beneficiary residents' enthusiasm for self-

help. Too often, community projects are transferred to the
government for continuation and sustenance--a manifestation of the dependency syndrome. A way ought to be found
to increase the community's interest and active participation in the upgrading projects. Officials from international agencies such as UNICEF have demonstrated strong
commitment to the project by providing sufficient financial allocations. It is to be hoped that this commitment
will outlive future changes in personnel.

The upgrading project is economically feasible. It
will eventually cost the state and local governments much
less than would total evacuation and redevelopment of the
area. For example, the provision and rehabilitation of
roads and the construction of community facilities such as
the clinic and the market are expected to cost about N 3
million.<16> This amount is a small fraction of the cost
of building the low-income and middle-income housing under
a total redevelopment scheme. Furthermore, the total cost
to the government is further reduced by the contribution
of nongovernmental agencies such as UNICEF.

Several social benefits arise from the upgrading
scheme. In comparison with total urban renewal, the Olaleye-Iponri project has not disrupted day-to-day living in
the affected area. A total of ninety-two buildings are
marked for eventual demolition, and about 1,000 persons
will be displaced to provide infrastructural facilities. A
total slum clearance and redevelopment scheme would have
necessitated evacuation of about 20,000 persons who might
have been rendered homeless, at least temporarily. Even
though this project has mobilized community residents to
action, total slum clearance would have been solely a
government affair and invoked residents' opposition.

NOTES

1. After an earlier influenza epidemic that claimed
many lives, the bubonic plague raged in central Lagos
between 1924 and 1930. LEDB was set up to combat environmental squalor in 1928, the year that the highest number
of deaths from the plague was recorded. See Lagos State
Development and Property Corporation (LSDPC), 50 Years of
Housing and Planning in Metropolitan Lagos: Challenges of
the Eighties (Lagos, 1978), p. 7.
2. In spite of large capital outlays by the colonial
government (before independence) and in recent years by
federal and state governments, the public sector accounts

for only an estimated 4 percent of the total metropolitan housing stock. (LSDPC, op. cit., p. 20.)

3. UNDP subcontractor, Wilbur Smith and Associates with UNDP project staff and Lagos state government, Master Plan for Metropolitan Lagos, vol. 2, p. 281.

4. Report issued at the end of the National Conference on the Urban Poor, University of Benin, Nigeria, 17-19 April, 1984.

5. One Nigerian naira (N) is equivalent to about US$1.35.

6. Factual data on the current situation in Olaleye-Iponri originate from the Lagos state government, the Urban and Regional Planning Division, and the United Nations Centre for Human Settlements; Final Report on Olaleye-Iponri Urban Renewal Plan, May 1984, mimeo., 51 pages.

7. P. K. Makinwa-Adebusoye, "Survey of Beneficiary Participants," Olaleye-Iponri, Lagos, 1984 (unpublished manuscript).

8. Ibid.

9. P. K. Makinwa-Adebusoye, "Survey of Participating State and Local Government Officials," Olaleye-Iponri, 1984 (unpublished).

10. This is documented in the attendance register of these meetings and in Makinwa-Adebusoye, "Survey of Participating Officials," op. cit.

11. Makinwa-Adebusoye, "Survey of Officials," op. cit.

12. Final Report on Olaleye-Iponri, op. cit., p. 35.

13. Makinwa-Adebusoye, "Survey of Beneficiary Participants, op. cit.

14. A recent survey of residents of Olaleye-Iponri shows that no landlord (landlords' and tenants' response) intends to increase rents as a result of recent developments in the area. Makinwa-Adebusoye, "Survey of Beneficiary Participants," op. cit.

15. According to one source, slums and squatter settlements provide shelter for more than half the population of metropolitan Lagos. See, Joseph Igwe, "The Urban Poor in Nigeria," paper presented at the National Conference on Urban Poor in Nigeria, Centre for Social, Cultural, and Environmental Research, University of Benin, 17-19 April, 1984, p. 6.

16. Final Report on Olaleye-Iponri, op. cit., p. 39.

10

Hyderabad Urban Community Development Project

William J. Cousins
and Catherine Goyder

INTRODUCTION

This case study of the Urban Community Development (UCD) Project in Hyderabad, India, describes how the project attempts to improve the living conditions of people in slum areas through a process of self-help. This project is of interest to UNICEF, urban planners, and social workers.

The provision of minimum essential services to children and mothers is a central concern of UNICEF. Such services may benefit children: directly, through the improvement of their environment in terms of health, sanitation, and education so that their potential growth and development are enhanced, and indirectly, through increasing family income so that parents can provide better for their children's future. Because children make up about half the urban slum population, social change must begin in the basti (neighborhood) in which they live. This is what the Hyderabad project is attempting.

Community development seems to have had little impact upon urban policymakers except in some isolated situations such as that in Baroda. It is hoped that this study will help them see the potential of urban community development for building systematic linkages between physical improvements, social services, and people's participation.

The Municipal Corporation of Hyderabad with UNICEF assistance is currently extending the project to cover all slums in the city. This case study is an opportunity to help those and other urban planners to reflect upon their past experience as they plan for the future. The analysis of the Hyderabad experience can be useful not only for

that city but also for other cities attempting to improve
slum conditions through the community development process.

We are learning that the solution to the slum problem
lies neither in slum clearance public housing schemes nor
in rehabilitation settlements on the outskirts of cities.
Although each of these approaches has merit in appropriate
situations, each also brings other problems in its wake.
For example, people used to living much of their lives
outdoors in single story dwellings do not easily adapt to
the new patterns required in multistory dwellings; and
those used to living within walking distance of their work
face new problems of transportation and reduced job opportunities for family members if resettled in remote housing
projects. A third alternative is to give people security
on the land that they occupy and gradually help them to
improve their living accommodations, basic social services, and incomes.

In Hyderabad, a city with a population of about 2.2
million, this third approach is being tried successfully.
The Municipal Corporation and the Hyderabad Urban Development Authority have decided that the city slums can real-
istically be improved in situ wherever possible. They
also plan to develop sites and services schemes and new
industrial townships on the city's outskirts.

While plans for expansion are being developed and
implemented, the time is appropriate to reflect upon the
past work of the Hyderabad Urban Community Development
Project. This study is not an exhaustive evaluation—the
insufficiency of baseline data prevents this—but it
attempts to analyze systematically the accomplishments and
methods used. Both the strengths and weaknesses of the
project are scrutinized in an attempt to identify replicable elements that could be tried elsewhere.

This study is based upon participant observation,
project reports, field workers' diaries, and interviews
with the project staff and the residents of a sample of
the slum localities covered by the project. Many sites of
project activities were visited, and discussions were held
with representatives of some voluntary groups and basti
welfare committees in the project areas. These were supplemented by interviews with people in the city who have
had contact with the project in various capacities. It is
hoped that this UNICEF study will be helpful to the Municipal Corporation of Hyderabad, stimulate people's initiatives for slum and shanty town development, and, at the
same time, provide case study material for other practi-

tioners and policymakers in the field of urban development
and planning, both in India and abroad.

A PARTICIPATORY APPROACH TO COMMUNITY BUILDING

Hyderabad was chosen as one of twenty cities for the
central government's Urban Community Development Pilot
Project initiated by the Ministry of Health, Family Planning, and Urban Development in 1967. The city is India's
fifth largest, and, although it may lack the more acute
problems faced by the larger metropolitan areas, it is
growing fast and has a sizeable slum population, though it
is proportionately smaller than that in the larger cities.
It includes twin cities: (1) the old city and the modern
commercial and residential areas of Hyderabad, and (2) the
old British cantonment area of Secunderabad. The whole
area is known as the city of Hyderabad.

Hyderabad was the seat of the nizam until the state
was joined to the union in 1948. In 1956 it became the
capital of the newly formed state of Andhra Pradesh. The
city population remained fairly constant in the first
decades of this century but experienced two growth spurts:
first, after joining the union, and second, in the 1960s,
with the influx of coastal Andhra people after the formation of the new state. The population is now just over 2
million.

The Old City and the Slums

The old city was built in 1589 and was designed by
Persian architects on a model of Isfahan, Iran. Today it
is in decline because of the out-migration of the jagir-
dars (big landowners) who left for Pakistan in large numbers after independence. As a result, the old city lost
its economic base and has never really recovered.

The Urban Community Development Project chose to
concentrate on this part of the city. The area is a maze
of narrow streets and lanes thronged with pedestrians and
slow-moving traffic. Many houses are old and near collapse, physical facilities are inadequate, and little
space is available for recreation. The Muslim influence
is evident in the large number of mosques, the cafes and
bakeries, the shop signs in Urdu, and women in burqas
(veil), many of whom are in purdah and seldom go out. The
congestion level is very high around the Mir Alam Mandi

vegetable wholesale market, but almost deserted open
spaces exist around some of the old palaces still in private hands. The density in the old city is 33,356 persons
per square kilometer as compared to 9,494 in the city as a
whole.<1>

The project population in the old city was 82,389 in
23,679 households in 1971. Muslims account for 70.8 percent of the population, which is stable and traditional,
82.72 percent having lived in the area for more than 20
years.<2> Seventy percent of the population is classified
as lower middle class, and the remaining 30 percent are in
the lowest income group, the average monthly income being
only 219 rupees (R). Only forty-five registered industrial units are in this area,<3> mainly small-scale workshops and cottage industries manufacturing products such
as joss sticks, matches, balloons and toys, trunks and
suitcases, wood products, leather goods, plastics, and
traditional work such as embroidery, bangle making, and
silverware.

Recent data are not available. However, a 1972 study
defined 50 percent of the city's dwelling units as
slums.<4> The development plan defines slums as "areas
where buildings are unfit for human habitation by reason
of dilapidation, overcrowding, faulty arrangement and
design of buildings, narrowness of streets, lack of ventilation and light."<5> By these standards large areas of
the old city could be classified as slums. The city has a
housing shortage and considerable overcrowding, indicated
by a sample survey covering 245,750 households of which
105,730 lived in one room and 72,435 lived in two rooms.
Household size in 1970 was 5.88 for families living in two
rooms and 4.58 for those living in one room.<6>

Essentially two types of slums can be found in Hyderabad: the old housing areas now in a dilapidated condition
and the hutment areas (squatter settlements or shanty
towns) that have been developed more recently. In this
study, most of the slum areas are of the latter type since
they house the poorest people. A survey carried out by
the Municipal Corporation in 1973 located 283 slum areas
in the twin cities with a population of 272,713.<7>
According to current estimates, about 300 such areas exist
with a population of around 300,000 people. The project
now covers 52 of these areas with an estimated population
of about 60,000.<8>

Slum areas are noticeably concentrated on the eastern
side of the city, in the old city, and around the Musheerabad area, as well as in the industrial area of Sanath-

anagar toward the north. They vary in character, some
being long-established hutment colonies, especially in the
old city where land was provided for the servants and
laborers connected with the large houses and the court.
Land was also provided for Muslim families who sought
refuge in the city from other states. Some localities
were settled by migrant families, usually Scheduled
Castes, who migrated to the city as long as fifty years
ago. Some are in the more recent industrial areas in
which workers need to be near their work and no alternative housing has been provided.

History of the UCD Project

During the 1958-1959 period, although some interest
was apparent for starting an urban community development
project in the city, no action was taken until an outline
scheme was prepared by the government of India, following
the ideas formulated in the Third Five-Year Plan and the
recommendations of the Rural-Urban Relationship Committee
(1966). The plan mentioned the need for each city to
mobilize its own resources to help create better conditions for its citizens and emphasized the need and potential for urban community development.[9] The Rural-Urban
Relationship Committee, set up to examine the role of the
municipal government, reported that the people did not
realize that the municipality was there to serve their
needs. The report suggested that constant discussion of
local problems was necessary to help people verbalize the
needs they felt should be provided, to motivate change,
and to encourage people to exercise their own initiative
in planning and carrying out improvement projects. Technical and welfare resources should then be directed to the
people to assist them in meeting their needs.[10] The
ministry then formulated a scheme based on these recommendations, which was viewed as a continuation and expansion
of the experimental work already begun in Delhi (1958),
Ahmedabad (1962), Baroda (1965), and Calcutta (1966).

The pilot project began in Hyderabad in December 1967
following a two-month training course for the project
staff at the Faculty of Social Work at Baroda University.
Ward 22 was chosen by the municipality as the starting
place for the pilot project. The Engineering Department
of the Municipal Corporation was to carry out extensive
slum improvement work alongside the project, and the dif-

ferent departments of the corporation were asked to assist
in the project.

After three years the project ceased to be a central
government scheme and was transferred to the state government; the project was expanded in 1970 to include part of
Ward 17 and again in 1974 to cover half of Ward 1 in Musheerabad and Wards 6 and 11 in Secunderabad. Thus between
1967 and 1974 the project tripled in size.

Objectives and Approach

The project was designed to function as part of the
Municipal Corporation and was viewed as a link between the
people and the Municipal Corporation. The staff was given
scope to develop activities according to the expressed
needs of the people and was given a mandate to include
activities not normally covered by the Municipal Corporation.

The original scheme was based on the philosophy of
self-help first introduced into the rural development
program. The aim was to create stronger communities in
problematic urban areas with their own leaders who could
plan, finance, and carry out self-help projects. To bring
this about, local voluntary organizations were to be
strengthened and basti welfare committees established.

As part of this study, the project staff was asked to
share its views about the aims and objectives of the project. Several felt that their work was directed toward
bringing about overall human development in all aspects of
life. One community organizer (CO) wanted to bring about
social awareness among the people so that they could learn
to identify and solve common problems and to share available resources and thus improve conditions for all the
community. The COs felt that both individual and community help were needed and that one should not be carried
out at the expense of the other since both were important.
All COs felt that economic development was essential and
that without it social programs would have less lasting
significance. They also believed that such programs
appealed to the people more directly, whereas long-term
development schemes required more subtle and difficult
community work.

This points up the essential difference between the
need that the people felt and the planners' views of the
changes they wished to introduce. The people wanted immediate results to relieve their pressing problems. Their

realization of other needs would come later, and these would require long-term changes in the community itself. They felt that once their immediate needs had been met, other social changes could be brought about over time through the close relationship between the project staff and the people. This approach sounds like classic community development theory, except that it resulted from the empirical experience of the project staff.

At the same time it reflects a change in the thinking of the project staff, a change based upon experience over time. The project leader pointed out that in the 1960s the focus was upon indirect benefits, such as education, health, maternal and child health, and nutrition--the kinds of things envisaged by UNICEF. Today, in his view, the Urban Community Development Project focuses more upon schemes giving immediate economic benefits.<11>

Methodology and Planning

The early work of the project was based upon a set of procedures discussed during the weekly staff meetings. First, the UCD department had to be established as an integral part of the Municipal Corporation and contact made with the various departments so that their maximum cooperation could be ensured. The second task was to acquire detailed knowledge of the project area and identify local problems. The third task was to work alongside the Engineering Department, which was to carry out an intensive slum improvement program. Fourth, it was necessary to build up the existing local organizations and start new ones, especially basti welfare committees and mahila mandals (neighborhood associations), and eventually to help them initiate self-help projects to meet local needs.

The community organizer's job was to establish personal contact and rapport with the local people and to gain their confidence. One CO described her task as "friend, philosopher, and guide to the people," a well-known phrase from the Rural Community Development Programme. The COs worked in pairs: The men concentrated on building up basti welfare committees and contacting the male population, and the women talked with the females and developed women's and children's activities. The work of each group was similar; the only difference was the emphasis placed upon working with one sex. This approach was

particularly necessary in a largely Muslim area where many
women observed purdah.

Building up strong communities meant understanding
the local system and the nature of local conflicts and
factions: COs had to bring differing groups together to
resolve conflicts and prevent communal feelings because
the project could only work effectively if the people were
united. All the COs spoke Telugu and Hindi, and all but
three members of the staff were fluent in Urdu, the language of the Muslim community. These three were able to
learn Urdu over time, and no real language barrier arose
because most Urdu speakers also understood Telugu or
Hindi.

Some local people were only interested in the project
insofar as it could solve their own family's problems.
Even though many individual problems were beyond the scope
of the project, the project personnel attempted to assist
families, for example, in finding homes for orphans and a
means of livelihood for widows. The emphasis was upon
group work, and family problems of only the poorest members of the community were taken up. In the early stages
of the project the COs spent most of their time in the
field. Later, some time was set aside for local people to
meet the staff members in their offices to discuss programs. Some COs also set up small offices for a few hours
a week in their areas either at the headquarters of a
local organization or in a community hall so that they
were available to discuss local problems on the spot.

The working conditions were strenuous for the project
staff, especially for the men who had to put in more hours
early in the morning or in the evening when the male population was available. The women were able to put in extra
work during holidays and evenings, whenever extra functions took place or the community needed them. Further,
their organizational abilities were exploited to the full-
est, and they were expected to assist in other municipal
programs, sometimes outside the project areas.

When the project was expanded, each group added a
part of Ward 17. Since 1974 four of the COs have been
engaged in work in Secunderabad and Musheerabad. Initially
the COs spent six hours a day in their areas with one day
a week in the office. Later, however, the COs were forced
to spend more time in the office doing clerical and administrative work because of the shortage of adequate clerical staff. As a result their field work suffered. In the
early stages staff meetings were held every week, but
these were later held less frequently because of the pres-

sure of work, so there was not as much guidance on field work problems.

Finance

Originally, the basic budget pattern of the pilot project in urban community development consisted of R 50,000 per year plus a separate grant of R 15,000 for local development activities to be used on a matching-grant basis. Initially, 50 percent of the expenditure was met by the central government, and the remaining 50 percent was shared between the state government and the municipality. After three years, 50 percent was provided by the state government and 50 percent by the municipality. The project was later operating on a budget of R 290,000, of which more than two-thirds was spent on staff.

These figures indicate that community development projects are people intensive with most of the budget being spent on staff and that they can be relatively inexpensive if the people actively participate. About 60,000 slum inhabitants are currently being reached by this project at an annual cost of R 290,000, or less than R 5 per person. Thus community development can be a very low-cost component of the development package.

Project Staff

The project began with a full staff quota of eight community organizers, headed by a project officer. No director of urban community development was appointed because this was the only project in the state. After the first few years one female community organizer (CO) was transferred and not replaced. The remaining community organizers have stayed with the project since it began. At present the project is seriously understaffed. Funds were sanctioned to recruit new staff for the expanded project, but no staff members have been appointed yet because of the recruitment difficulties that have plagued the state government since the Telengana agitation. Two of the community organizers are acting as deputy project officers to supervise the projects in Musheerabad and Secunderabad, but their promotions have not been recognized officially or their salaries adjusted accordingly.

All staff members have university degrees and back-grounds in the Rural Community Development Programme from

which they were recruited. The community organizers spent
up to ten years working in that program as social education organizers. No member of the staff is a professional
social worker, although they have had long experience in
organizing and dealing with groups of people.

To assist in the two new projects, eight volunteer
social workers were recruited. Half of these were trained
social workers seeking experience in UCD work, and the
rest had only passed matriculation. In addition, the
project has recruited a large cadre of volunteers to teach
in balwadis (nursery schools) and sewing centers and to
help in running different activities. The teachers, who
also help in other activities, are mainly local women, and
only a few have had previous training and experience. The
project organized training courses for them. A recent
sifting process was carried out, and a number of volunteers were retrenched in an effort to raise the standard
of work. Because the remuneration rate is low, recently
raised from an honorarium of R 75 to R 100 per month, it
is not easy to attract staff of a high enough caliber and
so the standard of work varies. All volunteers are also
expected to carry out community work in their locality,
but for this type of work more trained and experienced
community workers are needed.

APPROACH AND ACTIVITIES OF THE PROJECT

In 1976 the project covered three areas that included
a total population of 225,600 persons of whom about 60,000
were slum dwellers living in about fifty slum colonies.
The rest of the inhabitants belonged to the lower middle
classes whose living conditions, especially in the old
city, needed improvement. By the end of 1976, after much
discussion and planning, the Municipal Corporation of
Hyderabad, the state government, the Department of Social
Welfare, government of India, and UNICEF agreed that the
project should be expanded with UNICEF assistance.

At that time approximately 300 slums existed in Hyderabad containing about 300,000 people. The Municipal
Corporation of Hyderabad gave the Urban Community Development Department responsibility for coordinating the major
programs in the slums--slum improvement and slum clearance, health and family planning, and supplementary nutrition. Thus, the perennial dream of the community develo-
per--program coordination--might actually be realized
there. Further, the special officer of the municipality

emphasized that this program was not just for slum people
but for the total city with special emphasis on slums.

Flexible Approach

The project followed an integrated approach to the
development of the slums and middle-class localities of
Hyderabad and concentrated its efforts mainly on slum
areas. Resources from the lower-middle-class area, especially volunteers and voluntary organizations, were utilized to carry out development work in the poorer localities. One aim of the project was to complement the work
done under the slum improvement scheme with self-help
projects directed toward meeting some of the social and
economic needs of the people. It also attempted to discover and channel resources from municipal and government
departments and nongovernmental agencies to enable people
to improve their living conditions. Another aim was to
encourage self-reliance by setting up voluntary organizations within the communities themselves, so that the
people could organize their own developmental activities.
The project staff tried, with a good deal of success,
to maintain a flexible approach to people's needs, and a
number of activities were started at the request of the
local people. Over the years, in response to the people's
desires, the project began to emphasize programs of direct
economic benefit, whereas in the beginning it emphasized
more social welfare activities such as health, nutrition,
and child care. According to community development theory,
this flexibility should be at the heart of the community
building process; yet in practice, it is very difficult to
maintain. The necessity for forward planning for programs
and budgets and the need for indexes for monitoring and
evaluating too often lead to the establishment of fixed
targets, and these bring in their train an increasing
rigidity. Thus the needs of the people tend to become
subordinated to the bureaucratic needs of the project that
originally set out to help them. The success of the Hyderabad project in maintaining a high degree of flexibility
is a rare accomplishment and one of the sources of its
strength.

Budget

The project operated on a total budget of R 290,000
per annum of which more than two-thirds was spent on
staff. The project, like all community development projects, was therefore staff intensive. At the same time,
it was comparatively inexpensive for the Municipal Corporation, since the cost of projects was shared among the
community, the project, and voluntary organizations. For
example, the cost of a community radio installed in Jagjeevan Nagar was R 450, and it was shared by the local
basti development committee, which paid R 100, the Rotary
Club of Hyderabad, which paid R 200, and the project,
which paid R 150. This approach has become standard for
the project and has enabled it to mobilize resources for a
large number of slum people with a small budget; its
annual operating cost per person is less than R 5. This
experience shows that community development, properly
managed, can be an extremely inexpensive component of the
development package because it provides a means of actual-
izing and focusing effectively a variety of resources.

Staff

Another major strength of the project has been the
ability of the project staff to achieve so much with so
few resources. Much of this has been the result of its
commitment, the close teamwork that has developed over
eight years of working together, and the leadership of an
inventive and insightful project officer. All the original staff were in government service--as rural community
development workers--before joining this project. Thus,
this element may be replicable if the staff selection is
good. Nevertheless, it is remarkable that the project has
been able to retain intact both its original approach and
its original staff for eight years. Certainly the relationships built up over the years among the project staff
and between them and the people have been largely responsible for some of their most substantial achievements.

Local Volunteers

One reason for the project's present low cost is that
it is seriously understaffed. The project employs only
seven community organizers, the project officer, volunteer

social workers, and a large cadre of volunteer teachers.
Although the use of local volunteers enables the COs to
extend their work at low cost and to root it in the local
community, the work sometimes suffers from a lack of sufficient fulltime professional workers.

People's Needs

During the last eight years the community organizers
have worked alongside voluntary groups and basti welfare
development committees to encourage a large number of
self-help developmental activities to meet the needs of
the people. Since it was discovered that the people's
main needs were for adequate physical amenities and
schemes of economic benefit, emphasis was on meeting these
needs.

Physical Amenities. To supplement work carried out
under the slum improvement scheme, twenty-three wells were
dug or renovated, eighteen community halls built, and two
housing colonies erected at a cost of R 3,500 per house in
one colony and R 5,000 per house in the other. Experience
indicates that people are much more inclined to undertake
such improvements themselves once they have security of
tenure.

Self-help Housing. Self-help housing is more appreciated by the urban poor than is government housing. In
the industrial area of Sanathanagar, for example, various
types of housing were found: small squatter huts, self-
help pucca houses, and government housing built by the
Social Welfare Department with loans supplied by the Life
Insurance Corporation. In the government scheme, the
tenants paid for the houses on a hire/purchase system.
Householders in the self-built houses had a very different
attitude to their houses and to house repair. The tenants
in the government housing did not perceive these houses as
their own, even though they were buying them on
hire/purchase terms. If the roof leaked, the owners were
not prepared to carry out the repairs themselves, whereas
the people who had built their own houses naturally
assumed that they were responsible for maintaining them.

The first self-help houses were built gradually:
Often a family first lived in a hut; then they borrowed
from a moneylender to construct a pucca room. When this
was completed, family members could sleep in the room and
use the hut for cooking. They added to the room when
money became available. Even though this incremental

approach to housing was more conducive to aiding upward
mobility than the provision of public housing, until 1977
only two small self-help housing schemes had been undertaken.<12>

Then, after much discussion, the secretary of housing, municipal administration and urban development of the
state government asked the Urban Community Development
Department to take responsibility for the construction of
some 13,000 houses for slum dwellers who had been given
pattas (deeds) for the land on which they are living. The
project staff has adopted a self-help approach to this
task. When asked if they were frightened by the enormity
of this task, one staff member replied, "We're not building any houses; the people are. There are 13,000 families
and each one is building its own house. Why should it be
a problem? One family, one house like Devanagar." And
this is actually how it is; like Devanagar multiplied 650
times.<13>

A town planning wing and an engineering wing have
been added to the UCD department. The planners design the
new layout of the slum with equal-sized plots, once the
residents indicate their desire to participate. Both human
and technical problems must be sorted out in realigning
lanes, sewer lines, and laying out each plot. The engineers furnish model house designs and give technical supervision and assistance throughout the building process.<14>

The department has recruited a new staff member to
work in areas in which housing is being built. He is
called a basti sahayak (slum helper). He is a high school
graduate who is paid R 200 per month, and he is expected
to live in the slum community in which he works. Each
basti sahayak works with about 100 families. His first
tasks are to get to know the families and then act as a
liaison between them and the project. He notifies project
personnel when technical people are needed and facilitates
their work in his area; he notifies project personnel when
a family has completed a stage of its work and is ready
for another loan installment. He also helps people identify and take action on other community needs. Once the
housing project is completed, he will be a leading community development worker because housing is seen as a means
rather than an end in the community development process.

The method of financing the project is not new, but
the scale is certainly significant, as is the self-help
emphasis. Eight commercial banks with eighty-six branches
have agreed to lend up to R 4,000 to each family with the

pattas as security. The family contributes about R 1,000
in cash, kind, and labor. Most unskilled labor is used for
digging foundations, carrying bricks, and similar jobs.
The people are given credit for the amount that would
normally be paid for contractor's charges (7 percent) and
Public Works Department (PWD) overhead for supervision (8
percent). This 15 percent of the total cost comes to R 750
and is justified by the fact that the people themselves
fulfill these functions.

Schemes for Economic Improvement

Experience in this project suggests that involvement
of slum dwellers in health and nutrition programs will not
be really effective until family incomes have improved.

Small Loans. Schemes of economic benefit have
increased rapidly now that the nationalized banks are
providing small loans for slum dwellers. So far 1,050
small loans have been given as well as larger loans to
enable cycle-rickshaw drivers to purchase their own rickshaws. These loans provide direct assistance to the poor.
The interest rates are lower than those of money-lenders.
They are not charity and therefore enhance the self-
respect of the borrowers. Further, work in this field
needs to be directed toward some of the poorest families
in the project areas.

Cooperatives. The organization of cooperative
efforts has not been easy. Of all the cooperative schemes
introduced, Shri Mahila Griha Udyog Lijjat Papad Cooperative is the most encouraging. This cooperative has succeeded because of the attention paid to careful management
and strict quality control and to finding secure marketing
outlets for its products.

The cooperative scheme introduced in Jagjeevan Nagar
has been effective in reducing the exploitation of middlemen. Any schemes undertaken with this aim can have great
impact on the economic position of the urban poor, but
they usually encounter the opposition of the middlemen
whose own positions are threatened.

Vocational Training. Vocational schemes appear to
have had considerable impact. No attempt has been made to
find jobs for the trainees of these courses except for
women trainees from sewing centers. Instead, the emphasis
has been on furnishing young people with marketable skills
to enable them to find employment themselves.

Educational Activities

The organization of balwadis has had considerable
impact both on the education of the young and on their
parents' attitudes toward education and child development.
A number of nonformal education programs for women have
been successful, particularly classes for sewing and for
nutrition.

The project has accomplished a different kind of
nonformal education in helping the city planners and policymakers learn more about the nature of their slum inhabitants and the need for direct public participation in any
scheme for slum improvement. The right of the urban poor
to live in the city and not be transferred to the city
limits has also been established; this has meant a shift
away from costly slum clearance schemes toward slum
improvement schemes. Although these changes are not
entirely the result of the examples set by the UCD project, urban community development has played an important
role in the development of the city.

SIGNIFICANCE OF THE PROJECT

The Hyderabad project is significant for several
reasons:

1. It demonstrates that the classic community
    development approach to the problems of the
    urban poor can be effective both in providing
    improved social services cheaply and in meeting
    some basic problems of poverty.
2. It also shows that despite the central problem
    of poverty, enormous potential economic
    resources can be found in most slum communities,
    which can be utilized with the help of sensitive
    community workers.
3. It shows that one key to success in community
    development is the staff and its approach. In
    fact, the selection and training of staff are
    probably the most important elements in any
    community development program.
4. It demonstrates the importance of the effective
    coordination and use of both internal and exter-
    nal resources.

5. It also demonstrates the importance of certain
   basic links in the development process: integration of physical improvements within the community development process; systematic linking of
   voluntary organizations with slum communities;
   and systematic linking of slum residents with
   financial institutions in the formal sector of
   the urban economy.

Linkages

The exploration of the linkages in the development
process will illuminate the other generalizations.

Integration of Physical Improvements. The reconstruction of a slum community according to a planned layout requires the willing cooperation of the residents so
that they give up part of their plots or part of their
buildings so that straight lanes may be made or drainage
lines laid. Not infrequently, engineers have come into
slum areas selected for political and technical reasons
and arbitrarily installed water or drainage systems or
constructed low-cost housing without consulting local
residents. The attitude of the people then is "you built
it, so you can maintain it." This is one explanation for
the maintenance problems that affect many housing and slum
improvement projects. When community workers indicate
when and where the people are ready for these improvements
and act as liaisons between the people and the engineers,
the changes are more likely to be welcomed, understood,
and long lasting.

Linking of Voluntary Organizations with Slums. In
any city many resources besides governmental ones are
underutilized. Some of these are well-established local
branches of international service organizations such as
the Lions and Rotary Clubs; others are national bodies
such as the Lijjat Papad Cooperative. Still others are
local groups ranging from university service organizations
to neighborhood sports and cultural groups. One of the
goals of the Hyderabad project is to identify and systematically involve such groups in slum development activities.

Linkage Between Slum Residents and Financial Institutions. Much of the economic activity of the urban poor
takes place in the informal sector of the economy, indi-
cating that the existing linkages are insufficient. Some
studies have shown that there are inadequate understanding

and awareness of the important functions fulfilled by the
urban poor in the economy of cities.

In addition to the innumerable services performed by
such people as domestic servants, fruit and vegetable
vendors, snake charmers, and so on, any large city has a
host of slum family-based enterprises. These enterprises
are usually labor intensive and often feed larger enterprises in the formal sector. They range from beedi-making
and agarbatti-making to leather work, basketry, textile
creation, and carpentry to metal work and even light
industry. If these service enterprises cease to function,
serious lacunas would develop in both urban social life
and urban economy.

An important contribution of the Hyderabad project
has been to persuade banks to extend loans to selected
categories of slum workers, for example, loans to cycle
rickshawallas (rickshaw drivers) to enable them to purchase their own rickshaws. Rickshaw drivers are now able
to make loan payments at a lower rate than that of their
previous rickshaw rentals, and, as owners of their
vehicles, they have a different stake in the economy and a
different possibility of increasing their family incomes.
Further, for the first time they have the experience to
dealing with a bank--an experience previously confined to
middle-class citizens. This link immediately decreases
their marginality as citizens and draws them more into the
formal system. By the same token, this approach is new
for the banks, which probably initially feel that they
have an opportunity to perform an act of charity. But
closer analysis shows that such loans are good banking
business. The experience with small loans seems to indicate that the rate of recovery is very high if the groundwork is done properly.

In addition, a considerable amount of aggregate capital may be involved in such transactions. For example, in
the plan to assist 13,000 slum dwellers to build their own
houses, the 13,000 loans of R 4,000 each result in a R 52
million investment from the urban poor. Even if only half
this goal is reached, it is still more than R 25 million.
These figures make one wonder what is meant by the informal sector of the economy.

Organizing the Poor

One consequence of community development programs,
which is insufficiently understood, is the organization of

the poor per se. It is usually couched in terms of organizing poor people to undertake self-help activities to
improve their lives. Shrewd politicians use this organization for their own ends, or, if they are in power, they
are quick to recognize the potential political threat of
such organizations. This threat may lie in the emergence
of new leadership from below or in the additional pressure
placed on municipal governments as poor people demand
services that they feel are rightfully theirs. The experience of the disciples of Saul Alinsky in the United
States and of the war of poverty are examples of this
fact.

This implication, which is important for community
development projects such as that in Hyderabad, involves a
paradox. On one hand, the urban poor become more integrated into the formal sector of the economy and into the
accepted mainstream of social life: They become more a
part of the status quo. On the other hand, as poor people
learn to identify and work together to meet their problems
and needs, they begin to call for help, which they feel is
their right as citizens. They begin to see the services
that result from this process as their own and not simply
those of the municipal corporation. The implication is
that poor people and municipal authorities more and more
begin to see the urban poor as legitimate citizens fulfil-
ling important functions and having power, rather than as
merely nuisances or objects of charity.

Replicability

The fashionable expectation used to be that successful pilot projects should be completely replicable elsewhere. Because none were, they were criticized as inadequate or ill planned. This cloning model is now rejected
as simplistic, unrealistic, and unnecessary. Previous
projects have suffered too much from the block-pattern
fallacy, that is, a standard pattern of staffing, programming, and budgeting used in every situation and infinitely
replicated throughout the land. This approach leads to
inflexibility and unreality.

The new approach involves looking for elements, not a
total scheme, of replicability: interesting ideas,
approaches, schemes that could be adapted in other projects. It may be an approach to selection or training, a
way of financing a scheme, an organizational innovation,
or a combination of these. The Baroda project has been

commented on as follows: "Well it could only be done in
Baroda and maybe one other city, because of the kind of
local pride you find there." This limitation does not make
it less valuable. The first step is to build imagina-
tively upon whatever local strengths or unique qualities
can be found in a community. The second step is to look
for elements in the Baroda project that could be tried
effectively elsewhere.

Thus UNICEF may not always come along just after the
state government has given pattas to slum residents in
other cities, nor will there always be an understanding
and supportive special officer running the corporation nor
an experienced and dedicated UCD staff. But there are
other funding sources, other good officers and staff; and
the pattas have proved to be important devices in motivating the poor to improve their housing. The project also
has established the precedent of individual bank loans and
self-help housing on a large scale as well as the innovation of basti sahayaks. Also, the UCD project has been
seen to play an important role in coordinating services in
the slums.

Most important, the twin cities of Hyderabad-
Secunderabad, together making up the fifth largest city in
India, represent a sizable universe in themselves. If the
UCD project has even modest success in improving the lives
of most of the slum residents in Hyderabad, this achievement has been outstanding in itself, a kind of replication
in situ. It will also have been a useful demonstration to
other cities: It is a commitment to link physical
improvements with social development and to improve all of
the slums in Hyderabad using the principles of self-help
and people's participation.

Hyderabad has some advantages over many other cities:
proportionately fewer slum dwellers in its population and
more available space; a political decision to give slum
dwellers the legal right to dwell on their land; and a
first-rate UCD program. At the same time, it is the fifth
largest city in India, and, if such a program can prove
successful here, it can have implications for many cities
smaller than Hyderabad.

POSTSCRIPT: FURTHER IMPLICATIONS

Additional data, collected after 1979, make it possible to verify certain hypotheses and to spell out certain implications of the Hyderabad project, such as impact

upon policy, scaling-up and replication, coordination, and linkages. In addition, it is possible to mention problems.

Impact on Urban Policy

When first describing the project, it was stated, "Community development seems to have had little impact upon urban policymakers except in some isolated situations, such as Baroda." In the past two years evidence indicates that those concerned with urban policy in India are beginning to consider the community development approach as exemplified in Hyderabad as a viable method for alleviating the problems of urban poor families. Expert committees discussed this in preparation for the seventh plan. In April 1985 a national conference, sponsored by the Ministry of Works and Housing and UNICEF, endorsed the urban basic services approach.

Scaling-up and Replication

When UNICEF became associated with the project in 1976, it covered three areas with a total population of 225,600 inhabitants of whom 60,000 were slum dwellers. One aim of the collaboration was to expand the project to cover all slums in the city. In 1985 this aim has nearly been attained. The project is now working in 477 slums and includes approximately half a million poor people. Nine thousand self-help houses have been built in 92 slums.

In six other major cities in India, Ahmedabad, Baroda, Kanpur, Pune, Aurangabad, and Vishakapatnam, UNICEF has been assisting community development programs.<15> In some cities, such as Kanpur, this assistance has meant strengthening a small existing community development project, and in other cases it has been assisting the municipal government to initiate community development projects. In Vishakapatnam, two community organizers—a man and his wife—were borrowed from the Hyderabad project to start a project. In a sense, this was the first real replication of the Hyderabad project. In addition, projects using the same approach have been initiated with UNICEF assistance in a number of small and medium-sized towns across the country. Between 1981 and 1984, UNICEF assisted the government in forty such projects; in the 1985-1989 period it plans to expand to 250 such projects.

Coordination

In the original plan of action agreed upon by the
Municipal Corporation of Hyderabad and UNICEF, the project
was envisioned to coordinate services for the urban poor
in the city. This dream has become a functioning reality
with most departments coordinating their activities for
the urban poor through the Urban Community Development
Department because it is practical to do so. Physical
slum upgrading, the United Nations Center for Human Settlements (Habitat) sponsored program, and improved health
care are examples.

Linkages

Although the major outside assistance to the project
in the late 1970s came from UNICEF, today the Housing and
Urban Development Corporation (HUDCO) has become the main
financier of self-help housing in place of the national
banks. In addition, the Overseas Development Agency (ODA)
of the British government has made a large grant to the
Municipal Corporation of Hyderabad to strengthen health
and sanitation programs. Thus acknowledged success brings
support. The physical manifestation of success, in the
form of thousands of self-help houses, brought public
recognition to the Hyderabad project. However, members of
the project staff feel that the success of the self-help
housing aspect was only possible because of the community
development approach and process and the credibility
established by their years of work.

Problems

Replication Without Dilution. Although the Hyderabad
approach is being replicated in forty towns and cities
across the country, the key question is whether the
quality of the approach can be maintained. A key variable
in Hyderabad's success has been the quality and motivation
of the staff. It is still necessary to find a systematic
way of identifying, selecting, and training staff who have
the qualities for successful community work. Another key
variable is training. There is still no satisfactory and

systematic way of training staff for new projects, though
one recognized part of that training should be some sustained exposure to the work of successful projects such as
Hyderabad. A third question is whether community workers
should be paid. Hyderabad went through a difficult period
when the basti sahayaks and community volunteers organized
into a union and demanded that they be paid according to
the regular municipal pay scale and be given all the benefits that accompany it. One lesson learned from this experience is that community volunteers should actually be
part-time workers who are compensated by the people they
serve rather than by the municipal corporation. This
method is based on the principle that the one who pays the
piper calls the tune: Community volunteers should look to
community members, rather than the government, for direction and rewards.

Means and Ends. The main reason that the Hyderabad
project has become so well known and widely replicated is
the spectacular success of its Habitat program, in which
9,000 self-help houses have been built. This model was
followed in the Vishakapatnam project--as a means of getting low-cost housing for the poor. The problem with
following the Habitat approach is that people see the
consequences of a long community development process by
highly skilled professional organizers and they are eager
to get those results, but they often lack the patience and
skilled staff to go through the required process. The
Vishakapatnam project differed in that housing was the
entry point, but the leaders of the project always emphasized the community development process and always planned
to broaden it to include other services for the poor. In
short, project leaders and the community members do not
always understand that community development is not simply
a means to a specific circumscribed end; it is also a
process that implies the broad goal of human and social
development. This process takes much time and skill and
cannot be short-circuited.

Monitoring and Evaluation. The Hyderabad experience
and the general approach have not been adequately evaluated systematically. The approach has been used in other
projects, such as Baroda Citizens Council, which were
forerunners to Hyderabad. However, except for the original Delhi urban community project, none has been studied
and evaluated in a sufficiently systematic and detailed
manner. Perhaps this book indicates a change for the
better.

NOTES

This is a shortened version of an earlier study by the authors entitled "Changing Slum Communities." It was condensed by the editor and includes a postscript written for this book by the first author.

1. Census of India, 1961, vol. 2, Andhra Pradesh, part 2 A, census population tables with the additional 1971 census total, New Delhi, Government of India.

2. Programme of Integrated Services for Children and Youth in the City of Hyderabad, UCDP, Municipal Corporation of Hyderabad, March 1974.

3. W. Khan, "Redevelopment of South Hyderabad—Employment Opportunities and Industrialization," UCDP Souvenir, Municipal Corporation of Hyderabad, 1970.

4. S. M. Alam and W. Khan, "Metropolitan Hyderabad and its Region—A Strategy for Development," 1972, mimeo.

5. Government of Andhra Pradesh, Directorate of Town Planning, "Development Plan for Hyderabad City," mimeo.

6. Census of India, 1971, series 2, Andhra Pradesh, part 4, housing report and tables.

7. Unpublished data, Municipal Corporation of Hyderabad, 1973.

8. This number has increased since this writing as the project is expanding.

9. Subhash Chandra and S. P. Punalekar, Urban Community Development Programme in India, New Delhi, National Institute of Public Cooperation and Child Development, 1975, p. 5.

10. Government of India, Ministry of Health, Family Planning and Urban Development, Report of the Rural-Urban Relationship Committee, vol. 1, June 1966.

11. Based on a meeting with Dr. Surya Rao on 2 September 1976.

12. C. A. Meade, Self-help in Hyderabad's Urban Development, unpublished M. Phil. thesis, University of London, 1975.

13. Devanagar was the first self-help housing experience of the project in which nineteen families built houses with the support of the local Rotary Club and the Department of Social Welfare.

14. Each house costs R 5,000, which includes a hand-flushed water-seal latrine of the type introduced into villages. These individual latrines, which cost approxi-

mately R 35 are a great improvement over community latrines.

15.   The basic services strategy adopted by UNICEF
and endorsed by the UN General Assembly is UNICEF's version of community development.   It is a means of systematically linking the efforts of the community with the formal service institutions in a three-tier system based on
community volunteers supported by paraprofessionals, who
in turn are supported by highly trained professionals.

11

Providing Urban Basic Services:
A Comparative Analysis

Clarence Shubert

Throughout the world, the standards and procedures for the delivery of urban services are very similar. The use of similar design standards for roads, sewerage, water supply, and electric power systems is seen as logical, practical, and technically required. Although in developing countries some modifications have been made for climatic reasons and financial constraints, the design standards used have usually been those brought in from developed countries. Similarly, hospital-centered health care, academically oriented education, and welfare systems for the poor have been modeled on those in the developed countries.

These standards for urban services are suited to neither the needs of the urban poor nor the overburdened city governments in the developing countries. Poor communities have little access to such services and lack the capacity to fully utilize them. Local governments lack the financial and management resources to provide high-standard urban services for the total population. Nevertheless, urban services for the poor should be provided. Currently the poor supply many of these services for themselves, or they simply do without.

During the last fifteen years, a variety of programs and projects have been started in an attempt to provide services particularly adapted to the conditions of the poor. Broadly defined, these are programs for the physical improvement of slums and squatter settlements and the provision of basic social services focused on the urban poor. The case studies presented in this book are illustrative of the projects of this type.

Services in cities are often not available to the poor. Unlike rural areas in which physical isolation and

207

lack of service facilities are problems, the urban poor
often live in close proximity to schools, hospitals,
piped-water systems, and other urban services, but they
cannot use them. Access to the services of the government
and the private sector is limited by legal, economic, and
social barriers. Sometimes the poor inhabitants are barred
from access to public facilities because they do not possess a legal residence. However, in most cases, simple
poverty keeps them from using the formal private-sector
services, and they lack the funds to provide adequate
subsidized government facilities.

This chapter is a comparative analysis of selected
aspects of the case studies of projects providing urban
basic services to the poor.<1> The following sections
examine political priority and policies toward the urban
poor; administrative structures for interagency coordination and linkages to the poor; and community participation
in project planning and management of urban services. The
performance of the selected projects in achieving stated
objectives is reviewed briefly, and finally funding availability, costs, and prospects for replication of projects
of this type are discussed. In the final section some
general conclusions are stated regarding the feasibility
of extending basic services to the masses of the urban
poor, and some of the technical, administrative, and
financial implications are pointed out.

POLITICAL POLICIES TOWARD THE URBAN POOR

The type and level of services for the poor are con-
tingent not only on recognition of their rights and needs
but also on political priorities. Political priority for
the urban poor results from pressures or concerns
expressed by various sources: demands for services from
poor communities, concerns expressed in the media, administrative problems created for government, or concern for
national or city prestige. In most cases, a combination of
these pressures and concerns shapes policies toward the
poor.

Policies toward the poor are seldom explicit and must
often be implied from actions. Such actions vary in
response to the source and type of pressure or concerns.
If the poor communities are mainly seen as a planning or
administrative problem, the approach may be to restrict
migration to cities, remove squatters, and/or clear and
redevelop their settlements. If prestige is the main

concern, merely hiding poor communities from sight may be
considered an appropriate response. However, when poor
communities are seen to have a legitimate role in the
city, particularly when inhabitants have land tenure security, physical upgrading and social services are being
provided.

In Kuala Lumpur the squatter population began growing
rapidly in the 1970s, and initial responses were to demolish squatter settlements and move the residents into high-
rise flats. However, this approach proved to be slow and
expensive. It was also forcing the relocated poor to
spend more on housing and transportation. Yet no policy
of legalizing or upgrading squatter settlements was developed. In 1979 two projects specifically providing social
services to the poor emerged: the parasite control project
and the Sang Kancil project (combining preschool centers,
maternal and child health clinics, and women's income-
generating projects). With the establishment of the Ministry of Federal Territory in 1979, an ambitious program
of organizational reform (Nadi) was initiated to coordinate and improve delivery of services to the urban poor
through some twenty agencies. However, because of rapid
personnel turnover, budget cutbacks, and the withdrawal of
UNICEF support, the program has substantially declined.
Although mid-rise walkup buildings have replaced high-rise
ones, resettlement of squatters in public housing is still
the dominant policy, and services to squatter areas are
limited and temporary.<2>

Indonesia has an explicit national program to improve
urban environmental conditions affecting the poor: the
Kampung Improvement Programme (KIP), which began in the
early 1970s.<3> KIP has provided basic physical improvements such as walkways, drainage, access roads, and public
water taps in urban kampungs of 200 cities. Kampungs,
traditional unplanned settlements, contain over half of
the urban population, including nearly all the urban poor
and are recognized as a legitimate form of urban residential settlement. KIP has received strong political,
financial, and technical support from national and international agencies, local governments, and the kampung
inhabitants themselves. The extension of social services
in urban kampungs also received strong policy support as
part of the integrated KIP and a program started in 1980.
However, the need for multilevel and multisectoral coordination and a high level of community participation has
limited it to only seven major cities by 1984. Nevertheless, nationwide implementation of both physical and

socioeconomic improvements through KIP is the main thrust
of policies affecting the urban poor. Sites and services,
low-cost housing, and construction of mid-rise apartment
blocks are also continuing, but these are seen as primarily serving middle-income groups.

In 1956, India began slum clearance and rehousing
plans, but two basic problems emerged: Most of the poor
could not afford ready-made housing, and the housing
improvements rarely provided the social and economic
improvements that poor families needed.<4> In 1972 policy
shifted from slum relocation to environmental improvement
in existing slum settlements. Public water taps, drainage, public baths and toilets, widening and paving walkways, and street lighting were provided. This program was
extended to all cities with more than 300,000 inhabitants,
or to an estimated 13.6 million slum dwellers by 1983. In
1976 basic social services were added to the slum improvements through the Urban Community Development Programme
(UCD). UCD is now active in forty cities and will be
carried out nationwide in the next plan period.

The massive migration of population accompanying the
independence of Pakistan created large settlements of
refugees in urban areas. Urban growth continued rapidly,
and about 25 percent of the urban population lives in
squatter settlements called katchi abadis. Katchi abadis
figured prominently in the elections in 1970 and 1977. The
residents of these settlements are active lobbyists and
draw considerable attention from the authorities.<5>
Although early attempts were made at clearance and rehousing, the main thrust of the government's policy since the
mid-1970s has been on-site improvement of katchi abadis,
particularly those located on government land. Since 1977
the Lahore Development Authority (LDA) has made physical
improvements in fifty slums and katchi abadis. In 1981 a
project for social development was started in seven katchi
abadis and four slums of Lahore. The Walled City Upgradation Project began in 1982. Although strong political and
financial support exists for physical environmental
improvements in katchi abadis and slums such as those in
the walled city area, the limited social services projects
have primarily depended on the support of international
and nongovernmental organizations and on the active participation of residents.

Seoul, Korea, has grown from 1.6 million people in
1955 to over 9 million in 1984. The rate of growth has
declined from 9 to 5 percent per year, but there are still
shortages of urban services, both physical and social.

Residents of squatter settlements are unable to pay for or legitimately demand urban services. Government programs to assist the poor have been mainly directed toward employment creation through public works projects or welfare for food, medical, and educational expenses. Projects for squatter clearance and rehousing in flats, for resettlement in new towns outside the city, and for upgrading on site have been carried out,<6> but no consistent policy on slums and squatter settlements has been established. Many areas have been designated for redevelopment, such as the Bongchun-dong site. However, redevelopment is essentially clearing squatter housing and constructing high-rise flats, most of which are sold to middle-income families. The delivery of social services specifically for poor urban communities has primarily been through a variety of nongovernmental organizations (NGOs).

Urban development in Kenya has emphasized investments in water supply, sanitation, low-cost shelter, primary and secondary education, and primary health care.<7> Kenya has been a leader in introducing sites and services and slum upgrading projects in Africa. In spite of these efforts, an estimated 50 percent of the inhabitants in some towns live in unplanned settlements with inadequate basic services. Since 1975 the government has carried out low-cost housing projects at Dandora in Nairobi and sites and services and slum upgrading projects covering 1,400 hectares in the three largest cities. These projects provide physical improvements including school buildings and health centers, but social services specifically adapted for the urban poor have not yet been developed.

Since 1950 Lagos, Nigeria, has grown at a rate of about 9 percent per year with the population far outstripping the provision of housing and services. Half of the 6 million inhabitants are considered poor. Slum clearance and resettlement were the main policies until the mid-1970s. Slum upgrading rather than clearance and rehousing has gained political support, especially in the affected communities. Although it is not yet an explicit policy, upgrading appears to be an encouraged approach.<8>

Sri Lanka has consistently been a leader in providing basic services for the poor, including universal free education, food subsidies, and subsidized health care. However, slums and shanty towns have continued to grow and now are estimated to contain half the population of Colombo.<9> The ceiling on residential property law, which was introduced in the early 1970s, resulted in transferring many slums first to the government and then to the residents. However, the physical environment (poor sanitation and lack of access to safe water and sanitary toilets) remained unchanged as did the generally low level of socioeconomic development in these communities. In the late 1970s the Urban Development Corporation began planning physical slum upgrading as well as substantial new housing development. At the same time the Environmental Health and Community Development Project began to provide health care, community organization, and nutrition training through the Municipal Health Department and sanitary toilets and water taps through the Common Amenities Board. Although these policies and programs have substantially improved the slums, most shanty areas have not yet been improved. Clearly the policy is to preserve and improve slum and shanty communities both physically and socially whenever possible.

Examining the case studies reveals a clear pattern of policy shifts that have been occurring in most countries at about the same time. Until the end of the 1960s resettlement, slum and squatter settlement clearance, and other methods to suppress the growth of poor urban communities were the main policies in most countries. In the early to mid-1970s the emphasis shifted to physical upgrading slums and squatter settlements. Except in Malaysia and Korea, in which agencies still hope to eventually clear and redevelop areas, upgrading on site has become the dominant policy. Particularly in India, Indonesia, Sri Lanka, and Pakistan, this approach has led to nationwide programs for physical upgrading of poor urban communities.

In several countries, social services are increasingly being included in upgrading schemes. India, Sri Lanka, and Indonesia have rapidly expanded this type of program but have not yet reached nationwide coverage. Social services projects specifically for the communities of the urban poor have also been started in Korea, Malaysia, Pakistan, and Nigeria, but it remains to be seen whether sufficient support will be forthcoming to expand them to large-scale programs.

INTERAGENCY COORDINATION AND LINKS WITH THE POOR

Programs to serve the urban poor generally face two difficult administrative problems: coordinating multiple agencies and developing effective links with poor communities. Although the structure of administration necessarily varies from one project to another, these two problems are common to all. Therefore, the analysis of the administrative structures in the cases particularly focuses on these two issues.

The Nadi program in Kuala Lumpur is a particularly ambitious effort to coordinate the work of twenty different agencies providing services to the urban poor.<10> The program was linked to the establishment of a unique Ministry of Federal Territory (MOFT), a national-level ministry with overall responsibility for the Kuala Lumpur metropolitan region. Under MOFT a consultative committee was set up for Nadi with a new Social Development Division to be the secretariat. However, execution of all projects, except income-generating projects for women, will remain under the various agencies or the city hall. Action committees were set up in each of five districts and in each poor neighborhood to channel community requests and participation. The director of each district office was designated as a Nadi Coordinator, but these were city hall staff. Neighborhood offices were never established because of budget cutbacks. Several problems emerged with the system. Coordination below the MOFT/consultative committee level was weak because district offices were responsible to city hall, not to the committee. Coordination in planning was not necessarily translated into coordinated implementation for similar reasons. Community requests were channeled through political parties rather than neighborhood action committees. In spite of the well-defined structure, both interagency coordination and linkages with poor communities remain weak.

The Urban Community Development (UCD) Project in Hyderabad started in December 1967 with establishment of a UCD Department in the Municipal Corporation. The project was designed to function as a "link between the people and the Municipal Corporation." The project staff sought to develop close working relationships with the other departments of the Municipal Corporation from the outset, particularly the Engineering Department, which was to carry out physical improvements in the project site. However, the main emphasis was on working with community residents to identify problems and develop local organizations, particularly the basti welfare committee and mahila mandals. After the project had been expanded to several other slum areas in 1976, the UCD department was given the responsibility of coordinating the major programs in slums--slum improvement or clearance, health and family planning, and nutrition. Subsequently it was also given the responsibility of supporting the rehousing of slum dwellers. The initial staff of eight community organizers was expanded by the addition of eight volunteer social workers when the project was expanded to two additional communities, and an engineering and planning wing was added to UCD when it was given the responsibility for rehousing. Besides engineers and architects this wing had a cadre of slum helpers to assist families during the house reconstruction process. The housing also made it necessary for UCD to develop a close working relationship with the National Urban Development Cooperation and eight commercial banks that were providing the housing finances. The original staff of trained community organizers could not be expanded as the project grew so there is increasing reliance on volunteer social workers and teachers. Both interagency coordination and linkages with the community seem to be very effective in the Hyderabad UCD Project.

In Indonesia, the Department of Public Works played a leading role in the Kampung Improvement Programme (KIP) at the national level.<11> However, with the introduction of social services and economic activities, a large number of national-level departments became involved. The government already has established a three-tiered structure of planning boards (Bappedas) for overall planning coordination, at the national, provincial, and district levels. However, since the social programs related to KIP required coordinated implementation and were limited to urban kampungs, special coordinating structures were created: at the national level, an interdepartmental technical committee; at the city level, a designated coordinator and a team of directors of concerned offices; and, to coordinate between levels, an annual sectoral consultation of city government officials with national counterparts. The involvement of communities in most sectoral programs is limited to the selection and training of volunteers or cadres. The block grant projects analyzed in the case study, however, were selected, approved, and managed by the community with technical assistance from the sectoral departments of the city. As a result, the block grant projects became an important link with and support for community organizations.

The two projects studied in Pakistan were intended to have quite different administrative structures.<12> The Lahore Development Authority (LDA) was responsible for physical infrastructure upgrading in both cases. Although an Interagency Coordinating Committee was proposed, the LDA, through which World Bank loans and project funds flowed, took on the role of a general contractor and called on other agencies to provide services as needed. The physical upgrading of both katchi abadis and the walled city became almost exclusively identified as LDA projects. However, the katchi abadi social services project required the cooperation of a number of additional agencies to provide health, education, and social welfare services. The Planning and Development Department (PDD) of Punjab was responsible for project coordination. However, with most project funds flowing through the PDD, it became an implementor rather than merely a coordinator, and the roles of the other agencies were reduced. The community development committees set up in katchi abadis were used for project implementation and have become effective links between the government and the communities.

The local government in Korea routinely provides rice, manual jobs, and free medical services to the urban poor under the Livelihood Protection Programme (LPP). The Integrated Urban Services Projects in Seoul, which is supported by UNICEF and administered by the Kwanak District Office,<13> provides primary health care, family counseling, technical support for preschool education, income-generating projects for women, and community development through several agencies. A series of coordinating meetings and seminars was sponsored by UNICEF, but no special coordinating structure has been set up. The community development committee, which was organized under the project, has helped link the community to government and NGO activities, but it remains weak.

The Chaani Project in Mombasa and the Dandora Community Development Project in Nairobi were primarily financed by a World Bank (IDA) loan. The Chaani project was implemented through the Housing Development Department (HDD) of Mombasa Municipal Council.<14> Although it involved four national ministries and the National Housing Corporation, funds and authority rested entirely with HDD so coordination was not a problem. The Community Development Division of HDD informed and involved residents once the project was under way but not in planning. No community organization was established until the project was already being implemented, but the community did communicate through political leaders. The Dandora project in Nairobi, the model for the Mombasa project, was also implemented by a Housing Development Department, which was specifically established for this project. In the Dandora project, the community was more actively involved in all stages of project implementation.

The upgrading project in Olaleye-Iponri in Lagos was spearheaded by the Urban Renewal Committee of the Urban and Regional Planning Division of Lagos State and UNDP/UNCHS consultants working on the master plan.<15> Lagos state ministries, specialized agencies, and UNICEF also joined in the effort. The Division of Urban and Regional Planning is the lead agency and coordinates the work of the other government agencies, NGOs, and international agencies involved. Funding comes from at least five different agencies. The representatives of the existing community organizations are active in attending coordinating meetings and raising issues and requests. These effective links with the community also help in interagency coordination.

The project for Environmental Health and Community Development in the Slums and Shanties of Colombo was implemented through the existing agencies of the municipal and national governments, particularly the Municipal Health Department (MHD), Common Amenities Board (CAB), and the Urban Development Authority (UDA).<16> The lack of a clear coordinating structure resulted in many instances of uncoordinated activities early in the project. However, by 1982 most interagency coordination problems were resolved by establishment of a coordinating committee under the mayor. A special unit was set up in the CAB along with improved procedures for UDA approvals. Construction of facilities by community organizations rather than contractors was introduced. A major factor facilitating these improvements was the establishment of community development councils (CDC) in each community. The health wardens of the MHD also acted as community development workers to help establish CDCs in some 279 communities. After the CDCs were developed, they were organized into district development councils, and finally these joined the City Development Council in 1983, which had already been formed to coordinate among government agencies. This structure provided both horizontal interagency coordination and direct links with community organizations. Although the immediate impact of the project on health and environment is important, the creation of these administrative and community development structures may be even more significant in the long-term development of these communities.

The examination of the administrative aspects of the case studies indicates that the appropriate organizational structure for physical upgrading may be quite different from the structure for social services projects. Both interagency coordination and linkages with community residents seem to be much less important in purely physical upgrading projects.

Although several case studies identified multiple-agency involvement in physical upgrading (Lahore walled city, the projects in Kenya, and the KIP in Indonesia), in final analysis funding and authority for implementation were supplied through a single agency. The case studies show that implementation by a single agency for physical upgrading and sites and services projects is effective. When a single agency is responsible and other related agencies are clearly subordinate, coordination is not a problem. The use of community relations or community development officers, with or without community organizations, was usually limited to obtaining cooperation of residents in allowing physical upgrading by outside contractors.

Multisectoral social services projects, however, required some type of coordinating structure and coordination activities at one or more levels. In most cases, the local government coordinated through a committee or council, but in some cases coordination with and among national- and/or provincial-level agencies was also necessary. Thus, a structure and/or mechanism for multilevel as well as multisectoral coordination evolved. The strong support and involvement of local governments are the most common elements in all these projects.

More active participation of residents also required better links with the community, including the establishment and/or strengthening of community organizations. In diverse situations (India, Korea, Nigeria, Pakistan, and Sri Lanka), the formation of community development committees or councils (CDCs) was deemed necessary. Apparently, the existing community organizations in the urban areas of most countries are too politicized or not development oriented. However, such organizations are more effective when they link with or incorporate existing community organizations and have the support of government and outside agencies. When community participation was well organized, it also helped in coordination among the implementing agencies.

In two social services projects in which external support was an important factor (Kuala Lumpur and Lahore), administrative structures were developed that are difficult to sustain without continuing outside support. Similarly, the project in Seoul has not yet developed a formal government coordinating mechanism. In the long run, out-

side assistance cannot be a substitute for strong government commitment, especially in multisectoral service projects in which effective government coordination is
needed. Although external support can be used to start
projects and provide initial coordination activities,
government support, both in policy and administrative
authority, must eventually be increased to ensure coordination and continuity.

COMMUNITY PARTICIPATION

     The nature of community organizational structure and
the leadership in poor urban communities are important
factors in determining how government agencies relate to
them and how participation and mobilization of the people
will occur. Often existing community organizations and
the leadership structure are controlled by a few wealthier
members of the community. This circumstance may limit and
distort participation in planning, project selection, and
access to services.
     Various methods can be used to mobilize community
participation and to ensure that weaker members of the
community have access to services. The effectiveness of
participation and access is a major determinant of the
success or failure of projects for the poor. The mere
availability of services has little impact if there is no
involvement and utilization by the community. Mobilization
implies a purposeful and directed participation to achieve
some improvement in the provision, distribution, and utilization of services.
     Most kampongs or squatter settlements in Kuala Lumpur
are monoethnic: 33 percent are Malay, 43 percent are Chinese, 8 percent are Indian, and only 16 percent are mixed.
Ethnicity is extremely important because political and
cultural groupings are based on it.[17] Considerable differences are evident in the style of leadership and organization in different ethnic communities. The two leading
political parties are particularly effective in mobilizing
support among Malay and Chinese communities and act as
channels for them to express their demands to the government. Neighborhood action councils were set up under the
Nadi program to provide a constructive channel for people
to express their wishes, but the corresponding government
structure, the neighborhood office for Nadi, was not set
up as planned because of budget cutbacks. The local leaders continued to go through their party channels to make

demands on the government rather than through the new
action councils. Implementation of the Sang Kancil projects, which primarily dealt with women and children, have
resulted in the organization and mobilization of women.
Traditionally, kampong leadership has been dominated by
men, and this mobilization of women has had a significant
impact in kampongs, particularly in situations in which
women's income-generating activities have been introduced.

The fist site selected for the Hyderabad UCD project
was a mostly Muslim community with numerous mosques and
strong religious organizations. Work within these communities was carried out by pairs of community organizers
(COs) with a female organizer working with the women, many
of whom observed purdah. "To build up strong communities
meant understanding the local system and the nature of
local conflicts and factions COs had to bring differing
groups together to resolve conflicts and prevent communal
feeling (ethnic-religious rivalry) because the project
could only work effectively if all the people were
united." One important feature of the program was that
the better-off lower-middle-class areas adjacent to slums
provided support in the form of volunteers and resources
from voluntary organizations. This type of cross subsidy
not only provided resources but also increased contacts
and mutual understanding among communities of different
classes. Several new community organizations were formed
in the project since most existing organizations were not
primarily developmental and rarely had broad enough membership to include all elements in the community. The
principal organization created was the Bustee Welfare
Development Committee, complemented by a variety of existing or new special-purpose organizations such as balwadis
(preschools) and mahila mandals. These new broad-based
organizations helped to diversify community leadership and
bring together the various factions and ethnic groups.
Local community leadership also had continuing support of
COs, volunteer social workers, volunteer teachers, and
slum helpers from the UCD project.

Community organization in Indonesia is uniformly
defined down to the level of the village as part of the
government structure. At this level and below several
people's organizations are officially recognized: the
Village Social Development Council, the Women's Family
Welfare Organization, the Neighbourhood Association; the
Lane or Block Organization, and a variety of special organizations for youth, sports, welfare, and so on, which may
vary from community to community.<18> Leaders are elected

by the members through informal concensus to these voluntary, unpaid positions. The village chief is appointed by
the government as are the leaders of all higher levels--
subdistrict, district, and province. The women's organization has become the most active community organization
in the areas of social services and welfare. The community
is usually organized and mobilized through these established channels, and, therefore, the linkage with government programs is ensured. However, a low level of community participation occurs in some programs, which may be
related to this highly regulated structure, and government
programs are difficult to adapt to specific community
situations. The block grant projects, which allow local
flexibility in programming, are specifically intended to
overcome these problems and seem to have been quite effective.

The two projects studied in Pakistan had distinct
differences in beneficiary participation.[19] The walled
city project, which is concerned primarily with physical
improvement, had no specific mechanism to mobilize participation. On the other hand, the community development
orientation of the katchi abadi project gave great importance to beneficiary participation. In the walled city
area existing family and caste organizations were used to
achieve the limited resident participation needed. However, the katchi abadi projects were initiated with the
formation of a community development committee and the
training of its members. Subsequently, all project activities were coordinated with or carried out through the
CDC. This system of organization seems to be quite effective in mobilizing participation in planning, implementation, and long-term management of the community services.

All communities in Korea are organized through village, neighborhood, and block associations.[20] For each
neighborhood there is, in addition to the chief, a male
and female Saemaul Undong leader. However, this formal
leadership structure and delineation of neighborhoods do
not necessarily mean that all communities are highly
organized, especially in urban squatter settlements. In
fact, only one-fourth of the residents expressed the feeling that there was community solidarity in the case study
site. The existing organizations are mainly a channel for
information from the government and not a means to organize and initiate community projects. Therefore, a community development committee (CDC) was organized at the
village level. Although the same people are involved, the
CDC is intended to be a broader and independent organiza-

tion. Although the CDC has carried out several projects, it has difficulty getting the trust and full participation of residents. However, participation in some specific purpose organizations, such as the housemaids' club, has been quite high.

In the Chaani and Dandora projects in Kenya, community organizations were created as part of the project. Few community organizations existed previously except some limited political organizing for elections. The beneficiaries were expected to participate in the construction of their own homes but were not involved in planning. The project planning and construction of the infrastructure and services were done by the relevant agencies and contractors before the creation of community organizations. The level of community participation has been greater in Dandora than in Chaani.<21> How this will affect long-term management, maintenance, and repayments by residents remains to be seen.

Before the onset of the project in Olaleye, Nigeria, two organizations were prominent—the Council of Elders and the community development committee. The CDC was enlarged to include members of the elder's council, women's, youth, religious, and market organizations at the suggestion of the project planners.<22> It became the main consultative forum for the project. Members of the CDC are involved in the task forces taking care of various aspects of the project. Decisions on location of facilities, obtaining land for services through relocation, and mobilizing residents for project activities are made through the CDC. The high level of community participation in all stages and aspects of the project is a significant departure from past projects for slum clearance and rehousing.

Prior to the organization of the CDCs the slums and shanties in Colombo had few community organizations. The project health wardens helped initiate CDCs in some 279 communities. However, some facilities and services were provided before the CDCs could be organized in several communities. Furthermore, not all CDCs became fully active, and 58 became or remained inactive. A random-sample survey of communities was stratified to cover 10 active, 5 less-active, and 1 control community outside the project area. The communities with active CDCs were smaller and homogeneous and had a tradition of working together. Inactive CDCs were in communities that were too large, covered more than one slum, or had distinctly different social groups. Leadership in inactive CDCs often represented only one group in the community. There was a consistent, direct, and significant relationship between active community participation and health and environment conditions. In active, less-active, and control communities, the infant mortality rates were 41, 48, and 65 per thousand, respectively; child death rates were 7, 20, and 25 per thousand, respectively; and incidence of diarrhea among reported illnesses was 11, 21, and 24 percent, respectively.<23>

Participation of beneficiaries seems to be much more important when several types of social services improvements are involved. Physical improvements were usually carried out with a minimum of participation. Although the contractor system of construction is more costly, it is easier to administer and allows more direct quality control and enforcement of uniform standards. However, community participation in construction was found to improve future maintenance of the improved facilities.

For most social services projects, some type of new organizations were developed (for example, the CDCs in Korea, Sri Lanka, and Pakistan), or some adaptation or strengthening of existing organizations was included in the project. Community organizations and leadership seemed most effective when based on some existing arrangements and when found in small and homogeneous communities. Somewhat broader representation was introduced through the organizational adaptations in several cities. Misuse or inequitable distribution of project benefits by a few elite community leaders was apparently rare and did not seem to be as serious a problem as in more conventional projects that are planned and managed without specific efforts to enhance community participation.

Only the Colombo project clearly measures the impacts and directly relates them to the level of community participation. However, the consistency and significance of this relationship in that project are compelling arguments for systematically enhancing community participation in planning, providing, and managing urban services.

ACHIEVEMENTS: RESULTS AND IMPACT

Programs and projects to provide services to the urban poor are often complex and difficult to implement. Furthermore, shifting and conflicting interests and forces are active within communities and the bureaucracy at the policy level. Therefore, the results seldom conform exactly to the plans. Often unexpected results are achieved, and often a variety of side effects are unanticipated. These case studies provide several examples of both the planned and the unplanned effects upon the beneficiaries.

Some case studies illustrate the effects that service projects have on policymakers and project implementors. In pilot projects such as these, the effects on policymakers determine the long-term support and replicability of such projects. Therefore, the perception of impacts by policymakers may be more important than the real impact on the affected communities. Thorough evaluation of this type of project is needed so that the real impacts on the situation of the urban poor can be more accurately conveyed to policymakers. Most of these case studies have not adequately documented project impacts either because projects are still under way or because the time and resources needed for a full evaluation were not available.

The services provided under the umbrella of the Nadi program in Kuala Lumpur, as listed in the budget, are parasite control, Sang Kancil (maternal and child health, preschool center, and women's income-generating activities), electricity supply, general development, water supply through public standpipes, community center buildings, ICE (information, communication, and education), training, and evaluation. Of these activities, only the Sang Kancil and electricity supply are being implemented at higher levels than planned. Provision of public standpipes and parasite control is about on schedule in expenditures, but all the other elements have been significantly cut back or eliminated through budget reductions. Only the Sang Kancil project has been evaluated, but that evaluation indicated a high degree of awareness and satisfaction among beneficiaries. The most strongly expressed needs—for water supply and drainage for flood control—are only partially being met. However, there is also a "perceived instrumental value of the basic services package to legalize their ownership of the land they are squatting on."<24> The elements not being implemented are those that support organizing, training, and mobilizing the communities and the field-level staff of the service agencies. Thus far, the Nadi program has not achieved the desired extent of institutional restructuring, nor has it generated the political, bureaucratic, and financial support to sustain long-term growth and extension of services on a large scale in the kampongs.

The UCD program now covers most of the slums of Hyderabad. Over 13,000 houses have been built by self-help and financed by the banks and the National Urban Development Corporation as a result of organizing and supporting communities by UCD. Numerous nursery schools were set up, and training in handicrafts and vocational skills were provided to women. Commercial banks have been induced to provide loans routinely to bustee dwellers, and credit and production cooperatives have been established. Nutrition training and improved health services have also been provided, but the main demand has been for physical improvements and economic development activities. Perhaps the most important impact has been in the educational effect on city planners, managers, and policymakers. The right of the poor to live in the city and not be subjected to clearance and resettlement schemes has been firmly established along with the need for broad public participation in slum improvement. Specifically the project demonstrates that (1) the community development approach can work in providing social services in urban slums; (2) despite poverty, there are economic resources in slums that can be mobilized; (3) one key to community development is the careful selection and training of the project staff; (4) effective coordination with government agencies and private and voluntary organizations is essential to mobilize resources; and (5) there should be systematic linking among physical, social, and economic improvement in urban community development.

In the case study in Indonesia, the block grant projects in Surabaya are assessed primarily on the basis of their direct benefits for the communities. The impact of sanitation-related projects seems to have been significant. Initial results indicate that garbage carts and sanitation facilities built through these projects are better maintained that those provided as part of the normal government programs. Community centers and kindergartens have generally been well used and maintained. Some income-generating projects, although creating difficulties in management, have been effective, especially when the modest income generated is used to support nutrition or other community welfare activities. However, difficulties arose in the effective use and maintenance of several smaller block grant projects such as libraries, sports, and musical equipment. The benefits of the projects in terms of increasing participation and organizational capacities of communities and strengthening city government capacity for intersectoral programming and management

are stated but not explicitly assessed.<25> The projects
have also improved the links between national-level staff
and the cities and made them more responsive to the problems of the urban poor.

The walled city and katchi abadi projects in Pakistan
have only recently been completed in the first pilot
areas, and, therefore, a full assessment of results is not
possible, particularly in terms of long-term impact. However, initial reactions to the newly installed water
mains, piped sewage system, street repaving, and street
lighting in the walled city are quite positive.<26> Property values have risen, and some housing improvement has
started. Residents in the affected katchi abadis were
asked to evaluate the project results: Ninety-five percent were positive and only 5 percent had complaints
related to displacement or damage to their houses during
physical infrastructure improvements. Highest satisfaction was noted for drainage improvement, provision of
drinking water, and the maternal and child health center.
The other services (including midwife training, skills
training, income-generating projects, improvement of education facilities, and management training for community
leaders) were perceived to be beneficial for only some of
the residents. The effect of these projects on policymakers is not explicitly noted, but the continuation of further phases of both projects is expected.

The results of the Integrated Social Service Project
in Seoul are assessed from three perspectives: supplying
relief services, fostering self-reliance, and encouraging
community participation.<27> The regular public assistance program (LPP) supports over 1,300 households in the
project community and 19,000 worker-days of public works
jobs were provided. The community development committee
was assisted under the project to improve roofs of twenty-
seven shanties and convert heating systems in sixty-seven
of the poorest houses. Greater self-reliance was encouraged by technical training for 37 persons, job placement
for 313 persons, and construction of a community workshop
by the subdistrict office. The maids' training and organizing resulted in improved job skills and higher-income
employment for over 200 women. Longer-term improvement in
human resources was supported by improved health care and
health knowledge brought about by the primary health care
project. Community participation in these projects and
other community initiatives were encouraged through leadership training and organization of the community development committee. The effects of the project on city gov-

ernment officials and policymakers are not explicitly
stated. The project's impact has not yet been formally
evaluated.

The results of the Chaani project in Kenya are
reviewed in terms of physical, sociopolitical, and economic impacts. The housing project is still under construction, and therefore only tentative conclusions are
possible. The new layout and road network are considered
to be a considerable improvement. But the water, drainage, and sewerage systems have already begun to have problems. Standards were lowered to make the services affordable by residents, but maintenance problems and improper
use are already occurring. Social services facilities
such as schools, health centers, a market, and a community
center are physical improvements, but whether the services
they house will be more effective remains to be seen.
Garbage collection and disposal have not yet been
improved. Somewhat more active community organizations and
political participation have been observed to alleviate
some of these problems in the Dandora Community Development Project. One unanticipated effect is the displacement of some households to make way for infrastructure
development and/or because of their inability to pay for
the services and construction of permanent houses.<28>

In the upgrading project in Olaleye-Iponri slum in
Lagos, Nigeria, significant sanitation improvements have
been made by the installation of public latrines near the
market, introduction of improved private latrines, which
are being spontaneously replicated, and dredging of a
major drainage canal, which has stopped flooding in the
area. These improvements not only improved the physical
environment and health conditions but have created positive community attitudes resulting in mobilization of
"community resources that are usually outside the reach of
established government agencies." Community organization
has also been strengthened as is shown by "vigilante
groups who mount night-watch to ensure that residents do
not dump refuse in the drain." Some landlords have also
begun improving their housing. Perhaps most important are
the effects on public opinion and policymakers: "The
political, economic, and social gains accruing to the
government and the residents weigh heavily in favour of
slum upgrading instead of total slum clearance and redevelopment."<29>

By 1984 the Environmental Health and Community Development Project in Colombo had already covered about 300
slums and shanties containing a population of 70,000

people.<30> About 90 percent of the communities had received assistance for upgrading common amenities such as toilets, bathrooms, and standpipes. Immunization programs had been implemented in 88 percent of the communities. One hundred and twenty-three health wardens had been recruited and trained; two hundred and seventy-nine CDCs had been established. Some shanty communities have still not received adequate amenities because the focus of project activities has been mainly on slums. The facilities' standards are still below the project targets, but population coverage has been larger than planned. The amenities were provided in an ad hoc manner in the early stages of the project, and the poorest households are not sharply focused on. Nevertheless, substantial reductions in infant and child mortality and in the incidence of malnutrition and water-borne diseases have been recorded.

The case studies clearly illustrate that improvement of both physical infrastructure and social services in settlements of the urban poor significantly changes not only the environment and quality of life but also the attitudes and behavior of community residents. Such improvements are valued not only for their direct benefits but also because they help legitimize the community concerned. Physical improvements, particularly, are perceived to be an assurance of tenure security in illegal settlements and hence often trigger substantial investments in housing improvement and increases in land values and rents.

Physical improvement projects bring about dramatic visual change, which makes them popular with planners, politicians, and the general public. However, such visual improvements may obscure the fact that social and economic conditions may remain the same unless specific social services improvements and broader community development are also introduced. One consequence of such an unbalanced emphasis on physical improvement is the displacement of poor residents who are then forced into other slums and squatter settlements. As noted in Kenya and Pakistan, such displacement can be direct, as a result of housing being removed to make way for public services, or indirect as a result of higher land values, higher rents, fees, or loan repayment. Displacement, both direct and indirect, is much less common when standards for services and infrastructure improvement are kept low and affordable.

Although infrastructure improvement such as water supply, drainage, and electricity is the most frequently expressed need, the benefits of less frequently expressed needs such as maternal and child health care and day-care/preschool centers are clearly appreciated once they are available. Except for the Sri Lanka case study, the cases reviewed have not yet been able to quantify the impact of many social services, and this area should give rise to subsequent research and thorough evaluations by project implementors. In the Colombo case study project areas, infant and child mortality and the incidence of water-borne diseases were reduced by over 30 percent and malnutrition was virtually eliminated.

Both the perceived and the actual impacts of services improvement are much greater in projects in which the level of community participation is high. This is noted particularly in the cases from Indonesia, Nigeria, Sri Lanka, the katchi abadi project in Pakistan, and the Sang Kancil project in Malaysia. Community organization and participation are particularly important in adapting planned improvements to resident needs, affordability, and other local conditions; mobilizing community resources; integrating the various services at the community level; and assuring long-term maintenance and further development of project components.

FUNDING, COSTS, AND REPLICABILITY

The large and increasing size of the poor population in most Asian and African cities makes project cost, funding, and replicability a vital issue. Although loans are available for physical slum improvement and sites and services, funding for social services is generally quite limited. Loans from international agencies such as the World Bank often do not adequately cover social aspects of projects. Replicability, therefore, depends on keeping costs down and mobilizing support from many sources such as national government agencies, the local government, nongovernment organizations, and the poor communities themselves.

The initial generous government funding for the Nadi Program in Malaysia was sharply reduced in 1983, from 10 million Malaysian dollars (M$) to M$5.5 million for the 1981-1985 period. Simultaneously, UNICEF's social planning adviser was reassigned. To compensate for the declining governmental budget, a nongovernment organization called the Sang Kancil Organization for Social Services has been formed for fund raising. The Sang Kancil project and electricity supply received a M$3.4 million budget by the end of 1983, and less than M$1 million remained for the final two years. It remains to be seen whether the new organization can raise sufficient private funds to offset the declining government support for the Nadi program. The necessary funding for continuing at the current modest level is in doubt, and expansion of the program to a level commensurate with the proportion of the population living in squatter settlements would take a major shift in policy and budget allocations. Although the government continues to spend very large amounts on clearing and rehousing squatter settlement residents, the problems of the urban poor have not been resolved. A strong commitment to the policy shifts embodied in the Nadi program is needed, but such a commitment has not yet been made.

The direct cost of the Hyderabad UCD Project works out to about 5 rupees per capita for the population served. Most of this goes for staff salaries for the community organizers and the various volunteer workers. Although there is not direct cost recovery for this service, it has an enormous effect in terms of increasing the effectiveness and coverage of other programs and reducing their cost. For example, self-help housing can be built at a fraction of the cost of publicly provided housing, and this saving alone would more than recover the cost of the UCD project. Similarly, nursery schools greatly improve subsequent performance and participation in school, and nutrition and health education reduce dependence on curative services. Because of the effectiveness and very low cost of the UCD, this program is now operating in forty cities, and the government of India and UNICEF have recently agreed to extend coverage to 200 cities in the next five years. Some components such as housing reconstruction may eventually be limited by financial resource constraints, but most social service and training components can be financed from local budgets and contributions of private and voluntary agencies. No major source of international financing is required.

Replicability of the physical Kampung Improvement Programme (KIP) in Indonesia is no longer an issue. With loans from the World Bank and Asian Development Bank and grants from a number of other donors, as well as strong budgetary support from both the central and local governments, the physical sector of KIP has been started in all cities and has achieved nearly full coverage in most large cities. The social service programs, although expanding at a slower rate, also have continuing strong support

through the development budgets of the departments of
health, education, and home affairs. The cost per capita
for both the KIP physical improvements and social services
is quite low (approximately US$50 and US$10, respectively), and, therefore, full coverage is affordable, both
by the government and the communities concerned. The
block grant projects, the specific focus of this case
study, are still mainly funded by UNICEF and the communities themselves; the national government and city governments have not yet made significant budget allocations to
support these projects. However, these grants are for a
limited period (two to three years) in each kampung and
cost an average of only $1 per capita.

The physical improvement of one-third of the 150
recognized slums and katchi abadis in Lahore has already
been completed. However, the remaining slums are mostly
on private land or in the walled city. The walled city
project, financed by the World Bank, ensures that most of
that area will be upgraded, but upgrading the other slum
areas may be deferred primarily for legal reasons rather
than lack of funding support. The upgrading has been
relatively high standard and high cost in Lahore, but the
strong political commitment and large budgets provided to
the Lahore Development Authority have made it possible to
extend the program widely. The social services program,
although much less expensive, also has less government
support. The case study noted that 77 percent of the
project funds came from UNICEF. Furthermore, some 30 percent of project funds were used for personnel and overhead
costs of government agencies. Therefore, the replication
of the social service projects depends upon a significant
increase in government support and continuing UNICEF and
NGO support.

Government welfare-oriented public assistance to the
urban poor in Korea is well established. However, few
government programs have a developmental or services
orientation in slum and squatter areas. The emphasis of
the case study project is the development of the capacity
among the poor (including skills training, community organization, and health and education) for long-term human-
resource development. So far these kinds of projects are
mostly funded by NGOs and external agencies such as UNI-
CEF. Fortunately, a wide variety of NGOs continue to
support these projects. However, until there is a significant shift in government policy toward support for developmental social services and legitimization and upgrading
settlements of the poor, the cost of relief programs will

continue to be a burden on government budgets. The problem in Korea is not funding but policy orientation.

The Chaani project in Mombasa provides slum inhabitants with a range of serviced lots with options from a slab to a complete house. Even assuming that 25 percent of a household's income is available for housing, the lowest-cost lots are beyond the reach of two-thirds of the residents of Chaani. Although there is a provision for house owners to develop rental accommodations, both to supplement income and provide housing to lower-income households, standards and costs are still too high for the poor majority. Plot sizes of 250 to 350 square meters, road standards and right of ways, water and sewerage standards, and so on all indicate that this project is not a sufficiently radical departure from traditional urban services standards. Although the World Bank has financed 72 percent of the project, the delays in implementation and questions raised regarding affordability indicate such projects are not likely to be replicated or extended fast enough or at low enough cost to serve the poor majority. In spite of strong external financial support, further substantial lowering of costs and hence standards will be required.

The improvements made so far in the Olaleye-Iponri project in Lagos, Nigeria, have been relatively low in cost and have mobilized support from the community, international agencies, and the government. "The provision and rehabilitation of roads and the construction of community facilities such as clinic and market is expected to cost . . . a small fraction of the cost of providing low income and middle income housing units that would be built under a total redevelopment scheme." In spite of the apparent financial and political advantages of this type of upgrading scheme, the long-term commitment of the government, community, and international agencies cannot be taken for granted. This project is a first attempt at upgrading in Lagos, and the formal structure for long-term financial, technical, and managerial support needed for a larger program of upgrading has not yet been developed.

The direct cost of the Colombo project over a four-year period was about US$1.3 million. This charge works out to a cost of less than US$20 per capita for the 70,000 people benefiting from the project. Although UNICEF provided about two-thirds of the direct project funds, the overhead costs were covered in routine government budgets, and community participation was voluntary. Because it has been fully integrated into the existing government oper-

ations and because of its low cost, this type of slum and
shanty improvement is being continued in Colombo and used
in other cities in Sri Lanka. Some interest has been
expressed in adding further housing and physical improvements, which would be more costly and require substantially more financial support, but the basic environmental
sanitation, health, and community development components
can be continued without further increases in the level of
external support.

The cost of physical upgrading and sites and services
projects varies substantially from a low of about US$50
per capita in Indonesia to several hundred dollars per
capita in Pakistan, Kenya, or other countries in which
piped sewage, individual water connections, and direct
road access are provided. However, even with very high
standards, the cost of slum upgrading is substantially
less than the cost of clearance and rehousing schemes. The
cost of basic social services and community development
programs has varied depending on the number and type of
services but has averaged from US$10 to US$20 per capita
for the population served. Thus, the marginal cost of
adding social service and community development components
is small.

Although most of the projects studied represent a
significant shift toward adapting services to the needs of
the poor, the long-term funding and administrative and
policy support needed for large-scale replication are
still not ensured. In some cases, the technical standards
and hence costs are still too high, both in terms of beneficiary affordability and/or the government subsidy
required. Ideally, standards and costs should be at a
level that can be extended to the entire population.
International loans are available for sites and services
and slum-upgrading projects from such agencies as the
World Bank, the Regional Development Banks, the UN Centre
for Human Settlements, USAID, and other bilateral
agencies. The support of social services improvement in
slum and squatter settlements, however, has been mainly
provided by NGOs and local governments with some support
from UNICEF. Although construction of schools and health
centers is included in some physical upgrading projects,
the social services themselves usually are not given special support.

If governments accept appropriate, low-cost standards
for physical improvement of slums and squatter settlements
and mobilize available financing, programs for improvement
can be implemented on a scale adequate to cover most set-

tlements of the poor in the foreseeable future. Similarly, social services can be provided to all the urban poor at a basic level, if governments are committed to a basic services approach that encourages and mobilizes community participation. The problem of replicability seems to rest on policy orientation, legal issues, and administrative arrangements rather than on financial constraints.

CONCLUSIONS AND IMPLICATIONS

Four major conclusions can be reached based on the experiences examined in these case studies.

1. It now seems feasible to extend basic services on a scale adequate to cover most settlements of the urban poor in the developing countries.
2. The main development that makes massive coverage possible is a dramatic reduction in costs for both urban infrastructure and social services through the application of lower standards for urban infrastructure in sites and services and slum-upgrading projects and through a basic services strategy for social services.
3. The socioeconomic impact of physical improvement is greatly enhanced by community participation and the development of basic social services.
4. Community participation is the main factor that enables the provision and management of low-cost basic social services and the maintenance of lower standard urban infrastructure.

A number of policy assumptions are behind these conclusions. First, governments should accept and extend some type of tenure security to settlements of the urban poor. Second, they should develop and accept appropriately lower standards for urban infrastructure in the existing and planned settlements of the urban poor. Third, they should adopt a basic services approach to social services, which implies a high degree of organization and participation among community residents. If these policy conditions are met, they will provide a solid base for extending basic urban services to most of the urban poor. However, such policies also imply a number of adaptations in the structure and functions of government.

Complementary physical upgrading and social services improvement imply an effective intersectoral coordinating structure to guide planning, budgeting, and implementation. To the extent that local urban services require central government support, this also implies a coordination mechanism between the central and local levels and intersectoral coordination at both levels.

Achieving a high degree of community organization and participation also implies that government structures, regulations, procedures, and attitudes will encourage community participation. This usually requires a decentralization of authority to local officials who deal directly with communities, flexibility to support community initiatives, the involvement of community residents in planning and implementation, and the existence of some type of community development workers to motivate residents to organize and participate in development activities.

If these policy and administrative reforms can be made, the financial resources, either from internal reallocations or external sources, can be made available at an adequate level to extend basic services to all the urban poor.

NOTES

1. UNICEF has assisted many of these urban basic services projects, which have the following common elements: (1) the mobilization of community participation through trained community volunteers linked to government social service systems; (2) the use of low-cost and replicable methods and technologies; (3) the mobilization and channeling of resources to benefit the poorest people in the community, particularly children and mothers; and (4) the coordination of sectoral services delivery and community-based services and activities. This experience with projects in over forty developing countries has been distilled into UNICEF's urban basic services strategy.

2. Lim Hong Hai, "NADI Integrated Service Project," paper presented to the International Seminar on Managing Urban Development, Seoul, Korea, 20-23 November 1984, pp. 5-12.

3. S. Tarigan, Dr. Soedarjo, and Saukat Sacheh, "Delivery of Basic Services for the Urban Poor: A Case Study of Block Grant Projects in Surabaya," paper presented to the International Seminar on Managing Urban Development, Seoul, Korea, 20-23 November 1984, pp. 4-6.

4. H. R. Goel, "Indian Experience in Managing Services for the Urban Poor--Urban Slum," paper presented to the International Seminar on Managing Urban Development, Seoul, Korea, 20-23 November 1984, p. 6.

5. Feroza Ahsan, "Provision of Services to Urban Poor--A Case Study of Lahore Katchi Abadis and Slums," paper presented to the International Seminar on Managing Urban Development, Seoul, Korea, 20-23 November 1984, pp. 41-45.

6. Whang In-Joung, "Management of Integrated Social Services for the Urban Poor in Korea--The Case of Bong-chundong, Seoul," paper presented to the International Seminar on Managing Urban Development, Seoul, Korea, 20-23 November, 1984, pp. 1-3.

7. James O. Kayila, "Chaani Upgrading and Sites and Service Project--Mombasa, Kenya," paper presented to the International Seminar on Managing Urban Development, Seoul, Korea, 20-23 November 1984, p. 7.

8. Paulina Makinwa-Adebusoye, "Improving Urban Services to the Poor in Nigeria: Upgrading Olaleye-Iponri Slum in Lagos Metropolitan Area," paper presented to the International Seminar on Managing Urban Development, Seoul, Korea, 20-23 November 1984, pp. 5-7.

9. S. Tilakaratna, S. Hettige, and W. Karunaratna, "Environmental Health and Community Development Project: A Case Study in the Slums and Shanties of Colombo" (Colombo: UNICEF, 1984), unpublished manuscript.

10. Lim, op. cit.

11. Tarigan et al., op. cit.

12. Ahsan, op. cit., and Vigar Ahmad, "Case Study on Lahore Walled City Upgradation Project," paper presented to the International Seminar on Managing Urban Development, Seoul, Korea, 20-23 November 1984.

13. Whang, op. cit.

14. Kayila, op. cit.

15. Makinwa-Adebusoye, op. cit.

16. Tilakaratna et al., op. cit.

17. Lim, op. cit.

18. Tarigan et al., op. cit.

19. Ahsan, op. cit.

20. Whang, op. cit.

21. Kayila, op. cit.

22. Makinwa-Adebusoye, op. cit.

23. Tilakaratna et al., op. cit.

24. Lim, op. cit.

25. Tarigan et al., op. cit.

26. Ahsan, op. cit., and Ahmad, op. cit.

236

27. Whang, op. cit.
28. Kayila, op. cit.
29. Makinwa-Adebusoye, op. cit., p. 31.
30. Tilakaratna et al., op. cit.

About the Contributors

Vigar Ahmed

Director of Studies,
Pakistan Administrative
Staff College, Lahore,
Pakistan

Feroza Ahsan

Senior Research Associate,
Pakistan Administrative
Staff College, Lahore,
Pakistan

G. Shabbir Cheema

Development Administration
Planner, United Nations
Centre for Regional
Development, Nagoya, Japan

William J. Cousins

Senior Adviser on Urban
Affairs, UNICEF, New York

Catherine Goyder

Staff of the Joint Centre
for Urban Design, Oxford
Polytechnic, United
Kingdom

S. Hettige

Professor, Department of
Sociology, University of
Sri Jayawardenepura, Sri
Lanka

Wilfred Karunaratna

Research Officer,
Participatory Institute of
Development Alternatives
(PIDA), Colombo, Sri Lanka

237

James O. Kayila — Head of Department of Regional and Urban Studies, Kenya Institute of Administration, Nairobi, Kenya

Lim Hong Hai — Assistant Professor, School of Social Sciences, University of Science, Penang, Malaysia

Paulina Makinwa-Adebusoye — Professor and Director, Centre for Social, Cultural and Environmental Research, University of Benin, Benin City, Nigeria

Saukat Sacheh — Urban Programme Officer, UNICEF, Jakarta, Indonesia

Clarence Shubert — Regional Adviser, Urban Development, UNICEF/EAPRO, Bangkok, Thailand

Soedarjo — Head of Surabaya Municipality Health Services, Surabaya, Indonesia

S. Tarigan — Chief, Division of Urban and Environmental Services, Directorate of Urban Development, Jakarta, Indonesia

S. Tilakaratna — Professor of Economics, University of Sri Jayawardenapura, Sri Lanka

Whang In-Joung — Director, International Development Exchange Program, Korea Development Institute, Seoul, Korea

Index

244